# THE PSYCHOLOGY OF LANGUAGE

# THE PSYCHOLOGY OF LANGUAGE

BY

WALTER B. PILLSBURY, Ph.D.
PROFESSOR OF PSYCHOLOGY IN THE
UNIVERSITY OF MICHIGAN

AND

CLARENCE L. MEADER, Ph.D.
PROFESSOR OF LINGUISTICS IN THE
UNIVERSITY OF MICHIGAN

P
105
P64P

C78911

*McGrath Publishing Company*
College Park, Maryland

*1970*

ST. PAUL PUBLIC LIBRARY

Copyright, 1928, by
D. APPLETON AND COMPANY

Reprinted by
McGrath Publishing Co., 1970

ISBN: 0-8434-0102-8
LC # 76-119313

Reprinted from the copy at the
University of Virginia Library

Manufactured in the United States of America
by Arno Press Inc., New York

# PREFACE

This book attempts to give a full discussion of those phases of psychology which have a bearing upon the general phenomena of language and to treat the accepted laws of language from a psychological point of view. It is hoped that the coöperation of men interested in the two fields will have the advantage of coördinated treatment and possibly provide some new points of approach. The book is designed to give a general survey of the facts of language and a psychological interpretation of those facts which shall meet the needs of students of language and of students of psychology. The first of the authors is responsible for Chapters II and IV-X; the second for Chapters I, III, XI, and XII.

Throughout the volume language is treated from the point of view of current psychological theory. From the days of the ancient Greeks, language has been studied in the West from the points of view successively of metaphysics, of formal logic, of scholasticism, and (particularly during the last century) of psychology in the various stages of its development, including the recent phase of physiological psychology. This last stage paved the way for the biological study of language. Few linguists, however, have broken away from the traditional views and awakened to a realization of the importance of applying the data of the biological sciences to the interpretation of language phenomena. To realize what a flood of light can be thrown upon the language processes by this means one has only to reflect that there are really no speech organs in the strict sense of the word, but that all the organs used for speech were originally developed in connection with the more directly life-serving processes. The parts of the body most directly employed in speech, namely, the nose, mouth, pharynx, larynx, trachea and lungs, as well as the accessory organs such as the contents and walls of the abdomen and the pelvis, had as their original functions the processes of respiration, mastication, deglutition and excretion, and only at a later stage came to be employed for communicative purposes. This being true, it follows that the articulatory movements are the outgrowth of the movements attending these fundamental biological processes. They still bear many of the earmarks of their origin. To illustrate, the vocal folds (lips, cords or ledges) originally served as a valve to the lungs and were originally used (and are still used) in connection with all physiological processes that involve a stoppage of the lung chambers, such as mastication, deglutition, coughing, micturition, lifting, bracing, striking heavy blows, and indeed wherever a relatively rigid state of the chest is required. Such closures involve more or less compression of the air and consequently frictional and explosive sounds when the air is released. Such were unquestionably the most primitive sounds of the speech organs and presumably were associated with such mental states (*e.g.*, tension, strain, hunger, pleasure, relaxation, comfort, indifference, etc.) as attended the performance of the various functions. In this sense they were expressive, and like the famous "Song of the Volga Boatmen" followed the rhythms of the respiratory processes. Contrary to the current view (*cf.* page 118), the complex articulate movements of human speech are modifications and extensions of such primitive movements of the vegetative organs and should be studied as such. Linguists have given but slight attention to this point of view, but considerable material may be found in medical literature and some in biological literature.

As for the other side of language, the processes of sensation and feeling, that is, meaning, the view is certainly gaining ground that all mental processes, including even those complex states of mind which we call human character, are the products or outgrowths of the ceaselessly operating vital processes which constitute and control the growth and maintenance of the organism as a whole—the so-called vegetative processes. In these processes the endocrine glands play a dominating or even controlling part as the regulators of the organic feelings and sensations, out of which all other sensations and feelings eventually developed. From this point of view our thoughts and emotions are the concomitants of those same physiological processes that have resulted in speech sounds. The junior author has in preparation a handbook of biolinguistics, in which these questions will be taken into account as far as the present state of our knowledge permits.

The authors desire to thank the various publishers and authors for permission to reproduce illustrations for the book, and Mr. John H. Muyskens for the use of certain speech records.

W. B. P.
C. L. M.

## CONTENTS

| | | PAGE |
|---|---|---|
| PREFACE | | V |

| CHAPTER | | |
|---|---|---|
| I. | THE SCOPE OF LANGUAGE STUDY | 1 |
| II. | THE NERVOUS MECHANISMS OF SPEECH | 20 |
| III. | THE SPEECH ORGANS | 43 |
| IV. | THE SENSES INVOLVED IN SPEECH | 67 |
| V. | MENTAL PROCESSES IN SPEECH | 91 |
| VI. | MOTOR PROCESSES IN SPEECH | 105 |
| VII. | THE ORIGIN OF LANGUAGES | 112 |
| VIII. | LANGUAGE RECEPTORS: READING AND LISTENING | 129 |
| IX. | THOUGHT AND LANGUAGE: WORDS AND THEIR MEANINGS | 152 |
| X. | THE MENTAL ANTECEDENTS OF SPEECH | 187 |
| XI. | SOUND CHANGES IN LANGUAGE | 209 |
| XII. | SYNTAX | 248 |
| INDEX | | 293 |

# ILLUSTRATIONS

| FIGURE | | PAGE |
|---|---|---|
| 1. | Schematic representation of the speech processes . | 16 |
| 2. | Various types of neurone or nerve-cell found in the brain, spinal cord, and nerves . . . . . | 22 |
| 3. | Illustrating the afferent pathways extending by way of the spinal cord from receptors in the skin to cerebral cortex . . . . . . . . . . | 27 |
| 4. | Functional areas, sensory and motor, laid out upon the left side of the cerebral cortex . . . . . | 31 |
| 5. | Sagittal section of the head and chest . *facing* | 44 |
| 6. | Sagittal section of the nose, mouth, and throat . | 47 |
| 7. | Frontal sectional view and sagittal sectional view of the larynx . . . . . . . *facing* | 48 |
| 8. | The cartilages of the larynx . . . . . *facing* | 48 |
| 9. | Semidiagrammatic section through the right ear . | 70 |
| 10. | Cross-section of the organ of Corti, showing nerve endings in the cochlea . . . . . . . | 72 |
| 11. | Pictures of vowel sounds . . . . . . . | 78 |
| 12. | Transverse section through equator of left eye seen from above . . . . . . . . . . | 81 |
| 13. | Schematic representation of the human retina . . | 83 |
| 14. | The kymograph with accessory phonetic recording apparatus . . . . . . . . *facing* | 216 |

# THE PSYCHOLOGY OF LANGUAGE

## CHAPTER I

### THE SCOPE OF LANGUAGE STUDY

The great complexity of the language processes and the manifold applications of language to life make it inevitable that different persons should approach language study from different points of view, conditioned by their various aims and interests. For example, the technical expert of a telephone company will be interested in such facts as the degree of distinctness with which similar speech sounds can be distinguished by the ear. Over the telephone *nine* and *five* sound alike. The company would like to obviate this difficulty. The student of logic of other days might be interested to discover how far the mental processes involved in language run in harmony with the rules of formal logic. The public speaker will be interested in the emotional effect of intonation and in the relationship between gesture language and speech. One who is acquiring a knowledge of the language for some practical end, as for the purpose of foreign travel, will seek merely to acquire the correct pronunciations and to associate the correct ideas with the muscular movements of the speech organs, with the sounds, and with the forms of the printed or written words. All these persons and others are interested in language from the point of view of applying their knowledge to specific ends.

### FIELDS OF LANGUAGE STUDY

The term *language study* or *science of language* as the broadest of all expressions is used to include any or all types and fields of language study. The specific fields are designated by various special terms. *General linguistics* [1] is the designation applied to the investigation of the nature of the language processes as such. It is the broadest of all the fields of language study. While the general linguist makes his own vernacular the basis of his work, he utilizes the whole range of human speech as far as possible, examining the character of widely divergent types of languages, both of savage tribes and of the highly civilized nations. He will also call into requisition the gesture languages and the language of animals as the precursors of human speech. Nor can he afford to overlook the simplest biological processes, such as the flow of tears, saliva, and other secretions that are indicative of states of mind.

Other students, however, limit their field to some special group of genetically related languages, that is, languages that have descended through centuries or millenniums from a common ancestor. This is the province of *comparative philology*. The aim of the comparative philologist is to determine the relationships between the various languages of the group and the manner and extent to which each has changed from the parent language. Clearly there will be as many special fields of comparative philology as there are related groups available for investigation. Examples are the comparative philologies of the Indo-European languages (formerly called Aryan and also now frequently called Indo-Germanic), of the Ural-Altaic languages, of the Semitic

---

[1] The French call it *la linguistique,* the Germans *allgemein-Sprachwissenschaft,* the Russians *obshchoe iazykoznanie.*

## THE SCOPE OF LANGUAGE STUDY

languages, of the Bantu languages, and of several others. Incidentally, the comparative philologist may be interested in reconstructing the primitive sounds and meanings out of which later ones developed. In this work he is aided by the anthropologist and the geologist. This last mentioned avocation has been designated *linguistic paleontology*.

Lastly one may confine one's self to the study of some particular language. This one may investigate with a view to determining what its structure is at some particular stage in its development. This is the business of *systematic grammar*. Or one may trace its development over longer or shorter periods of time—*historical grammar*.

General linguistics comprises two branches: *phonetics*, or the study of the speech sounds, their method of production, and their changes; and *semantics*, or the study of meanings, including syntax. The corresponding fields of special grammar are *phonology* and *semasiology*.[2] The psychology of language is a special aspect of general linguistics, in which stress is laid principally on the mental processes involved in speech. The term phonetics is now very widely used not to designate a field of language study as defined above, but to designate the art of teaching the pronunciation of particular languages on the basis of the muscular movements involved.[3]

All the above designated fields are interrelated. The student of general linguistics accepts the data accumulated by the student of comparative philology and special grammar and seeks to interpret them as biological processes.

---

[2] The term semasiology is at present more commonly employed as strictly synonymous with semantics.

[3] The term philology is used in so many senses that it is often very misleading. It would probably be better to avoid the use of the word entirely except in such combinations as comparative philology, and classical philology, in which its meaning is clear and specific.

The student of historical grammar or of comparative philology draws from general linguistics information concerning the growth of language and applies it to the solution of his specific problems. The subject matter of all the fields is essentially the same, but is applied to different ends and in different ways.

### LANGUAGE AND THE COMMUNICATION OF THOUGHT

It seems best not to offer at this point a concise definition of language, but rather to give a brief description of language which will set into relief all of its important processes. We may begin with the statement that language is a means or instrument for the communication of thought, including ideas and emotions. Thus at the very outset we mark off thought and language as different processes, though they are very intimately related, are to a large degree interdependent, and are in part identical in a certain sense. The popular belief that there can be no thought without language is incorrect. It is true, as all psychologists recognize, that thought tends to pass over instantly into movement; yet it is possible to think, for example, in concrete pictures instead of words. Although in the thought processes our ideas are usually, perhaps nearly always, represented by words, still elaborate and complicated thought processes may take place without the use of language. On the other hand, thought is greatly facilitated and its possibilities greatly extended by the use of language.

As an instrument for the expression (and communication) of thought, language is in the main [4] muscular movement,[5]

---

[4] Secretions, as we shall see later on, also serve as language.

[5] By the active (physiologically conditioned) movement of muscles other tissues, such as bone, cartilage, connective tissue, tendons, etc.,

either voluntary or involuntary, organically determined by changes in the nervous system of the communicator, and capable of being appreciated as significant by another individual.[6] Before an infant has learned to speak, it expresses its mental states in ways that are obvious to the observant parents. When a pleasant food particle is taken into its mouth, there are changes in the facial expression indicative of pleasure, the color is heightened (due to the relaxation of the muscles in the walls of the capillaries), the eyes are bright from the secretion of tears and the enlargement of the pupil, the mouth waters from the excess flow of saliva, etc. If delicate physiological instruments are applied to the child, it will be found that many vital processes are changed. The rate of the heartbeat is altered, breathing may be slowed down, the digestive secretions are increased. All these organic processes are expressive of the mental, or at any rate the nervous, condition.

In a similar manner, a blush and the rapid blinking of the eyes are involuntary expressive movements common in adults. When one is seized by sudden terror, the eyelids move wide apart, the mouth opens, and the face assumes the familiar expression indicative of the emotion. Likewise, on the appearance of some threatening object, the hand of the person threatened may be raised as if to ward off a blow, even though the object may be so remote that the movement is quite useless. In a case like this, the movements may be even more complex than those just described. For example, in addition to the opening of the mouth, there

---

are passively (mechanically) moved. Though the movement of non-muscular tissue may constitute important or even essential elements of language, yet we must ever remember that the physiologically active muscle cells provide the driving force for the whole group of movements.

[6] It follows from this that the psychology of language may be regarded as one portion of the broader field of the psychology of movement.

may also occur a tensing of the vocal cords [7] and a partial rounding of the lips. When these movements are attended by a marked contraction of the abdominal muscles, a stream of air may be sent through the larynx and mouth, causing the vocal cords to vibrate. In this case the muscular movement through the mediation of air waves will reach the consciousness as a groan or grunt or perhaps as the exclamation *oh*. Other complex involuntary movements similar to these result in other brief utterances, for example, a sigh, expressive either of ideas or of the intensity and quality of the emotion experienced at the time.

Passing on to the sphere of voluntary movements, we find that for our purposes they may be classified into two groups: those designed to be communicative and those not so intended. A rapid walk or run, to take an illustration of the latter group, is always indicative of some mental state and sometimes, when understood in its proper setting, conveys information of the greatest moment. A witness in court by a very slight movement has often unintentionally revealed the truth in a far more unambiguous and vivid manner than spoken words could have done it. Movements designed to be communicative constitute not only the greater bulk of ordinary spoken and written language but also all gesture languages, such as those of the North American Indians, the Neapolitans and the Cistercian monks, and in part the languages of the deaf and dumb.

In the involuntary emotional cries described above, we find all the essential elements of language. They differ from ordinary spoken language only in that they are (1) wholly involuntary, (2) expressive mainly of emotion, and (3) less complex. These three distinctions, however, are

---

[7] The concomitant closure, partial or complete, of the laryngeal passage and the consequent compression of the air in the lungs render the body more rigid, as if to resist attack.

not of fundamental importance. All human speech and perhaps all language of animals involve emotional elements in a greater or less degree. All normal speech involves numerous automatic, involuntary elements, in as much as only the initial impulse is ordinarily voluntary, the detailed movements which follow proceeding quite automatically. The more complex character of ordinary speech arises from the predominance of ideational elements in thought, and even ordinary speech is relatively simple. All these differences are differences of degree and not of kind.

"Language" in its broadest sense includes all expressive movements of all muscles and all expressive secretions. But it is often popularly used in the sense of "speech." In this book it is used only in the broader sense, and the word "speech" is restricted to such movements of the muscles of the abdomen, chest, larynx, and of the mouth and nose as result in vocal sounds. "Language" is thus the broader term and includes "speech."

### LANGUAGE MOVEMENTS AND PROCESSES

Between the thought processes, which are communicated by language, and the muscular movements there intervene other complex nervous processes which mediate between the thought and movement, which serve as a bridge, so to speak, between the two. Of these the best understood are the motor processes, which are discussed in detail in Chapter VI. The motor processes are preceded by others involving the Wernicke and Broca centers (described in Chapter II) and other parts of the cerebral cortex.

The language movements are attended by, or result in, certain other secondary, but essential, movements and nervous processes. These are (1) sensations of movement, strain, touch, and pressure resulting from the stimulation of sense organs located in the moving tissues of the communicator (kinæsthetic sensations); (2) air vibrations resulting chiefly from the movements of the vocal organs; (3) modification of ether vibrations brought about by the movements of the visible parts of the communicating individuals; (4) auditory, visual, and tactual sensations in both communicator and communicatee. The visual sensations of the communicatee are the reflex of facial movements and gestures of the communicator, which awaken in his mind thoughts and feelings similar to those of the communicator. The visual images of the latter are stimulated by his own movements as far as he can see them, and another very important group of movements, namely, those of the listener, which reveal his reaction to the ideas he has just received and which exercise a continuous control over the language movements of the communicator. Finally, all these elements are bound together by an intricate and interlocking web of associative processes.

### THE DEVELOPMENT OF WRITTEN LANGUAGE

Picture writing (ideographs) is generally regarded as the earliest form of written language. It is of later origin than gestures and sound languages and consequently has been greatly influenced by them. Ideographic symbols that represent concrete objects differ from plastic gestures mainly in their possibilities of greater precision and detail and in permanence. In so far as they stand in immediate and direct association with their meanings, they may be regarded as secondary language. By the normal working of the mental processes they came secondarily to represent also the abstract ideas of time, space, and inner relationship that inhere in man's conceptions of the objects themselves.

## THE SCOPE OF LANGUAGE STUDY

It was inevitable that they should also become associated with the sounds of the spoken language representing the same ideas, and thus gradually pass over to the state of alphabetic, or at any rate phonetic, symbols. This resulted in early Semitic in the acceptance of the symbol of the object as the symbol of the initial consonant of the spoken word plus a variable vowel—a condition naturally resulting from the fact that in the Semitic languages inflectional forms are characterized chiefly by vowel variation, the consonants remaining unchanged or only slightly changed. Thus a combination of two or more pictures, in simplified form, came to represent a succession of sounds constituting the word for the object that had formerly been represented by a single symbol. Having lost (through the process of simplification characteristic of all expressive movements) all resemblance to the objects they formerly represented, they became arbitrary symbols of sounds and thus forfeited their immediate kinship to gesture language. But the function of suggesting the meaning *through the sound image* characterized this later complex symbol as it had characterized the earlier concrete one. Out of these early Semitic signs there developed through the Greek and Latin alphabets all the modern alphabetic systems of Europe and several Asiatic systems. In as much as in reading we do not give attention to the individual letters but only to certain essential characteristics of the entire group of letters forming a word or phrase, the symbol suggests directly the whole mass of sounds that constitute the word or phrase, not sound by sound, but as a unified group. Thus our abominable system of writing English, being unphonetic, is really on about a par with the Chinese system of ideographs which we are wont to regard as so inferior to our own. Alphabetic systems of writing must be carefully distinguished from spoken and written language, since they

10   THE PSYCHOLOGY OF LANGUAGE

are only conventional symbols either of sounds[8] (and through them of ideas) or directly of ideas. They persist with only trifling changes, excepting those made by the conscious efforts of reformers, from generation to generation, while speech movements are subject to continual and unconscious flux and variation in accordance with the laws of protoplasmic change.

### STIMULUS AND RESPONSE IN COMMUNICATIVE PROCESSES

As a rule, the series of communicative processes enumerated above, which begin either directly or indirectly with the stimulation of some external or internal sense organ or some physiological state within the body, such as thirst, is therefore to be considered biologically as a form of response to environment or behavior. The stimulus may be the words of another person; it may be light waves from some object that reminds us of a forgotten duty; it may be the odor of burning steak, which the cook is neglecting. In any case it awakens a realization of some action to be performed, some duty to be accomplished, or some other end to be attained, for the achievement of which, however, we need or desire the coöperation or at least the companionship or sympathy of some other person or persons. Thus the goal to be attained (the purpose to be accomplished) is steadily before our mind, and under its control we rapidly (though sometimes very slowly and deliberately) and commonly quite automatically formulate the statement, query, or command we wish to make, selecting appropriate words, arrangement, intonation of voice, gestures, etc. This

---

[8] In the case of the congenitally deaf, auditory sensations cannot serve as associatory links between the visual image of the symbol and its meaning, and so the visual word picture cannot be the conventional sign of a sound group but must pass over directly into meaning.

# THE SCOPE OF LANGUAGE STUDY

preliminary thought process may be extremely brief. In fact, it may be entirely absent, in which case the whole response process takes on the form of an automatic reflex, such as the batting of the eye or the pressing of the button that toots your automobile horn. Or the preparation for movement may be more delayed and even extended over the act of uttering the sentence. Again it may be clearly formulated in advance and then modified during the process of utterance under the influence of the listener's attitude toward us. The nervous activity (chemical processes in the nerve cells) that constitutes this preliminary state of mind arouses to similar activity other nerve cells located in the appropriate parts of the motor area of the cortex of the brain, or, as the case may be, in those areas which control the action of the glands or, as is usual, of both.

All of these nervous processes beginning with the stimulation of the sense organs and terminating with the activity of the motor area involve chemical activity (metabolism) in the protoplasm of the nerve cells. The physiological disturbances, initiated by some form of energy in our environment (applied to the sense organs), are propagated along the sensory nerves to the sensory areas of our brain, thence along association nerves to the various areas of the cortex in which the thought processes occur, and so on through the Wernicke and Broca areas (in the case of speech) to the motor areas and finally out through the motor neurones to the surface of the muscle fibers (or to the glandular areas and out along efferent neurones to the glands). It must be remembered that *all* nerves which conduct impulses outward from the brain lead directly or by relays either to muscles or to glands, and hence, so far at least as our knowledge goes at present, there is no way in which central nervous activity can manifest itself in the body other than by movement and secretion. In other words these are the only forms of language possible. The nervous impulse on reaching the surface of the muscle fibers initiates chemical changes in the protoplasm of the muscle cell, which in turn bring about the contraction, that is, the shortening and thickening of the muscle fiber. The contracting muscles drag with themselves the bones, cartilages, and other attached tissues. These may be external parts of the body, in which case their movement will occasion changes in the distribution of the light waves impinging on the retinas of the eyes of the observer and will, therefore, be appreciated by him through his visual sensations. Again they may be such movements of tissue, whether external or internal, as may result in various forms of air vibrations, for example, the rustling of garments, panting, the sounds of the human or animal voice, as may be appreciable through the auditory sensations. Most speech movements are appreciable, in part at least, through both the eyes and the ears and on occasion through the sense of touch. This fact greatly enhances their value as communicative movements. These visual, auditory, and other sensations of the communicatee pass over at once through habitual association lines into ideas similar to those in the mind of the communicator.

The communicative process is often popularly assumed to have been completed at this point. "I've told him what I wanted to." We must not forget, however, that the purpose which prompted the communication is still in the communicator's mind and that he will remain in suspense until he receives from the person to whom he is appealing some sign, by movement or secretion, of the latter's reaction to his idea. Thus the communicative process is normally a complete circle, setting out from one individual and returning to him after passing through another's mind and body. The response may be long delayed, as in the case of a letter sent to Australia, or in the case of a proposition taken under advisement, or it may never be given in full, as in the case of a man who writes a book and never hears from a large percentage of his readers.

### NON-COMMUNICATIVE LANGUAGE PROCESSES

The language processes are not always employed for the purpose of communication. As will be seen later on, there are no organs of the body that were developed originally for communicative purposes. All communicative movements are indirectly life serving and are carried on by organs that were developed in the first instance through the performance of direct life-serving activities, such as breathing and eating. Communicative movements were thus modifications of direct life-serving movements, and they still retain numerous traces of their original character. Just as the human embryo in the early period of its growth passes through many stages of development corresponding to the various strata of the lower animals through which he has evolved in ages past, so man still retains the capacity to perform separately with different parts of his body all the elementary processes which are now coördinated in the highly elaborated processes of human speech. "Speech," therefore, occurs in a variety of more or less abbreviated and incomplete forms. It may be used in silent thinking, in which case the thought processes are attended by abortive speech movements. Possibly all thought is attended by such movements. At any rate, psychologists are generally agreed that every central activity of the nervous system tends to pass over immediately into action. One may talk aloud to one's self, in which case the factor of communication is absent, unless one imagines one's self to be "communicating with one's self." Many other "abbreviated" forms of communication occur.

## THE PROBLEMS OF GENERAL LINGUISTICS

The problems of general linguistics fall into two groups: (1) those which center about the act of expressing one's self, and (2) those which have to do with the processes of interpretation. The foremost problem in the first group is that of the relation of thought to language. This involves, incidentally, a consideration of all the thought processes and of the general relation between psychical and physical activities. The special problems of the origin of language and the genesis of speech [9] as heretofore prosecuted have been concerned largely with the question of the manner in which particular ideas came to be connected with particular sounds. It should be modified and extended so as to include the development of muscle tissue and its functions in relation to the development of nervous tissue and neuromuscular activities. In this connection arise also the questions of the degree of completeness and accuracy with which language expresses thoughts, of the extent to which the forms and content of thought are determined by the mechanism of language, and vice versa, of the extent to which the thought processes determine the forms of language. Of special importance is the inquiry into the nature of abstract thought and the part played by concepts in the development of language, and also the manner and extent to which words take the place of ideas in consciousness.

Another question arises as to the effect of our immediate social environment on our speech (form of thought, selection of words, tone of voice, etc.). This social environment, taking the word in its widest sense, is very complex. One of its most important elements is our purpose in speaking. The immediate purpose of speech is, of course, the con-

---

[9] F. N. Scott first made this useful distinction in *Publications of the Modern Language Society of America*, Vol. XXIII, p. 4.

veyance of intelligence to our fellow men. However, we seldom speak merely for this purpose, our ultimate end being to direct the conduct of someone or at least shape his views and policies in such a way as to bring some advantage or disadvantage to ourselves, to him, or to society or social groups. A second element of our environment is made up of our knowledge of the listener's character and habits and also of his attitude toward ourselves and toward the purpose we wish to accomplish. A third element is made up of the immediate situation, for example, the place, time, and surroundings, and even so seemingly unimportant a factor as our distance in feet or yards from the person addressed. A failure to give due heed to the effect of social surroundings on discourse has in the past often led distinguished philologists into error; and the young student cannot be too frequently admonished of the importance of these elements.

Passing over to the muscular movements and related phenomena, we find the following problems of expression presenting themselves: (1) those concerned with the anatomy and physiology of nerve and muscle and the localization of brain functions; and (2) those embracing all questions of the control of muscular movements in respect to range and rapidity of individual movements and also the coördination of simultaneous and successive movements —all of them being questions which involve a consideration of the part played by the sensations in the control of movement.

The student of general linguistics is directly interested in the physical problems of sound, especially if he be concerned with phonetics. The more important problems in this field have to do (1) with the recording and analyzing of speech sounds in order to determine the exact nature of the air vibrations that constitute them; and (2) with

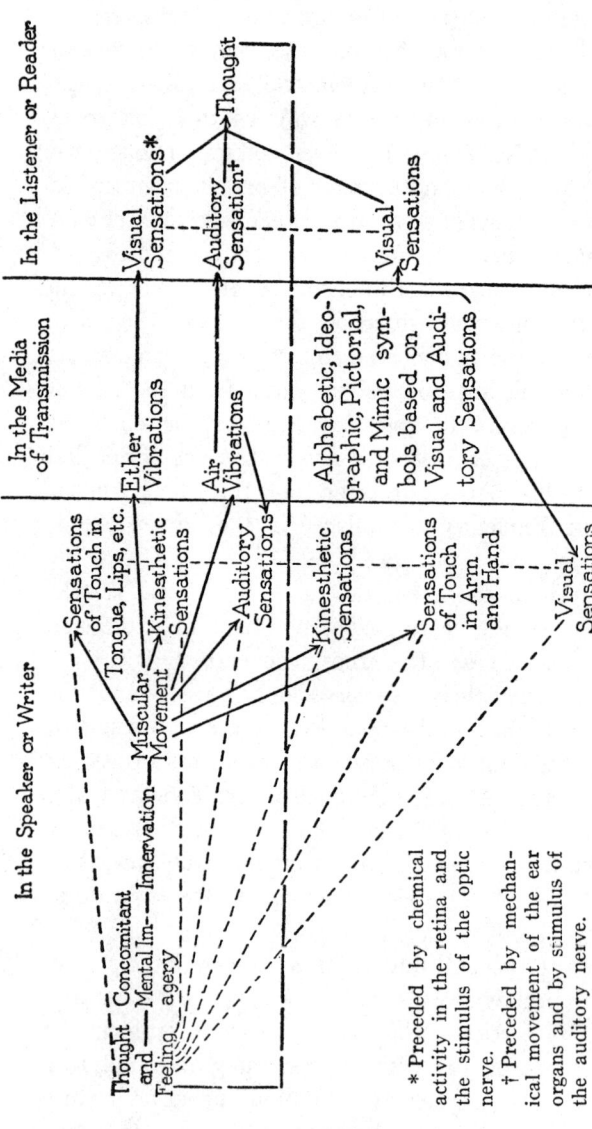

FIG. 1.—SCHEMATIC REPRESENTATION OF THE SPEECH PROCESSES.

The arrows indicate the directions of the developing processes. The lines of short dashes indicate associative connections. The long dashes indicate the reaction of the listener as appreciated by the speaker. All the processes above the line of long dashes are those of oral communication; those below the line occur in gesture language, writing, reading, etc.

## THE SCOPE OF LANGUAGE STUDY

the identification of the particular movements of the speech organs to which particular sound waves are due.

The problems of interpretation fall into two classes: (1) the problems of sensation; and (2) the problems of understanding. Sensations of touch are involved not only in the reading of the embossed letters of the alphabets of the blind but also in the contacts of the tongue, palate, and lips, and, in the case of gesture languages, in the contacts of the hand with various parts of the body. Sensations of sight are involved not only in ordinary reading, in lip reading, and in the appreciation of gestures and gesture languages, but are also important accessories. Some persons appreciate orchestral music better if they watch the players; others, if they close their eyes. There's a difference. The problems of understanding are of equal importance with those of sensation. The chief question which arises here concerns the degree of accuracy with which sensations correspond to stimuli, or, to put it differently, the extent to which the state of mind is determined by other factors than the stimuli. Connected with this is the special study of mishearings, misreadings, and consequent misunderstandings. Of equal importance is the determination of the relations between sensations and ideas. The part played by the social environment in the processes of understanding is as important as the part it plays in determining the form and content of discourse as it is shaped in the mind of the speaker. Some of these problems have been solved in part; others await solution.

### GENERAL LINGUISTICS AND PSYCHOLOGY

The science of language, like that of law, history, economics, etc., is assigned to the field of the humanistic, or, as they are sometimes called, the sociological sciences.

Accordingly, its subject matter is, in a sense, the creation of the human mind The muscular movements which constitute language are the result of nervous activity and are largely controlled by or through it. In consequence of this intimate relationship, it becomes necessary for him who would study the nature of language to master first the essentials of psychology. One may, of course, attain a perfect mastery over one's own vernacular and may even learn any number of foreign languages without giving a single thought to psychology; but when any question is raised concerning the origin of language, the growth of language, the interrelations of kindred languages, or even the methods of teaching languages, in a word, concerning the nature of language, he who would answer the question must turn perforce to the laws in accordance with which all mental activities take place and endeavor to explain the phenomena of language on this basis. In a sense, therefore, general linguistics may be called applied psychology.

Mention should be made in this connection, however, of another group of facts, the importance of which should not be underestimated. There is already securely established and widely recognized a field of physiological psychology. Furthermore, the parallelism between the states of mind on the one hand and the physiological processes on the other —a parallelism extending sometimes even into minute details—is so intimate, and our psychical life is so inseparably bound up with the chemical processes taking place in the protoplasm of our bodies, that one is strongly tempted to believe that the mental states are the result of the physicochemical changes of protoplasm. Should this assumption prove true, the science of language would become a natural science in the fullest sense of the word, and the term biolinguistics might with complete justification be applied to it.

# THE SCOPE OF LANGUAGE STUDY

## REFERENCES

BLOOMFIELD, LEONARD.—*Introduction to the Study of Language* (New York, Holt, 1914).

BRUGMANN, K.—*Vergleichended Grammatik der Indogermanischen Sprachen* (1st and 2d ed., Strassburg, Trübner, 1897-1900), Vols. 1-4.

DELBRUECK, B.—*Introduction to the Study of Language*, Trans. by Jevons (London, C. Griffin & Co., 1882; 6th German ed., revised and enlarged, Leipzig, Breitkopf & Haertel, 1919).

GILES, PETER.—*A Short Manual of Comparative Philology* (2d ed., London and New York, Macmillan, 1901).

OERTEL, HANS.—*Lectures on the Study of Language* (New York, Scribner's, 1901).

PAUL, HERMANN.—*Principien der Sprachgeschichte* (5th ed., Halle, Niemeyer, 1920; Eng. trans. by Strong, New York, Macmillan, 1889).

ROUSSELOT, J. L'ABBÉ.—*Principes de la phonétique expérimentale* (Paris).

SCRIPTURE, E. W.—*Elements of Experimental Phonetics* (New York, Scribner's, 1902).

———, *Researches in Experimental Phonetics* (Washington, Carnegie Institute, 1906).

TUCKER, T. G.—*Introduction to the Natural History of Language* (London, Blackie & Son, 1908).

WUNDT, WILHELM.—*Voelkerpsychologie* (3d ed., Leipzig, Koener & Englemann, 1911), Vols. 1 and 2 Die Sprache.

# CHAPTER II

## THE NERVOUS MECHANISMS OF SPEECH

### GENERAL PRINCIPLES OF NERVOUS ACTIVITY

LANGUAGE like all mental processes depends fundamentally upon the action of the physical organism. The sounds presuppose sounding bodies for their production, and these in turn must be controlled by muscles and nerves. The same must be said of the hand movements in writing. Hearing and reading involve the ear and the eye, and the central nervous system is necessary to connect sense organ with muscle and is also involved in all of the thought processes that precede speech. Before one can go very far in the discussion of language, it is necessary to know something of these bodily mechanisms. We may begin in this chapter with the central processes and leave the discussion of the more peripheral mechanisms to later chapters. There are involved in speech all the general principles of nervous activity, and we may begin with them in preparation for the discussion of our particular problem.

All activity of a higher organism depends upon the nervous system, and the nervous system in turn may be regarded as a means of transforming sensory excitation into muscular contraction; it is a means by which movements may be adjusted to external conditions. In the very lowest forms of animals the adjustment of response to excitation is possible without a nervous system. It may be made by the tissue that is common to all parts of the animal. In these organisms which have but one cell, that cell suffices *cell body* and two extensions or prolongations, the *dendrites* and the *axones*. The dendrites are ordinarily short and receive impressions from the more external parts and from the axones of another neurone. The sense organs are modified dendrites. The axones are usually longer and transmit

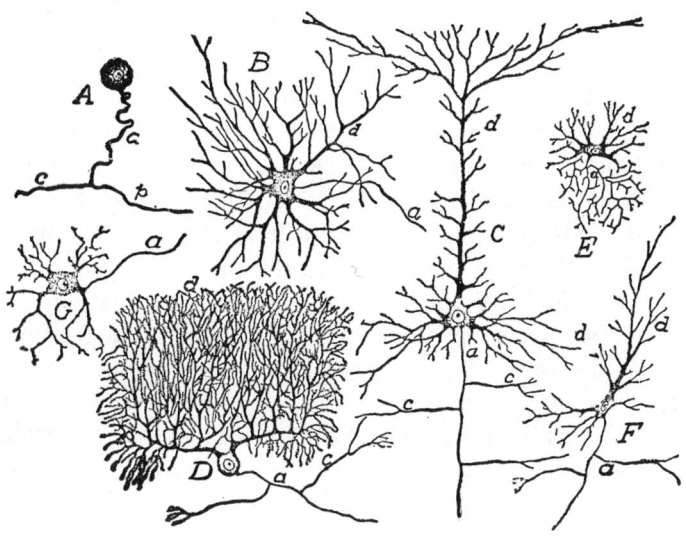

FIG. 2.—VARIOUS TYPES OF NEURONE OR NERVE-CELL FOUND IN THE BRAIN, SPINAL CORD, AND NERVES.

*A,* from spinal ganglion; *B,* from ventral horn of spinal cord; *C,* from cerebral cortex; *D,* from cerebellar cortex; *E,* from spinal cord; *F,* from cerebral cortex; *G,* sympathetic ganglion cell: *a,* axone; *d,* dendrites; *p,* teledendrion; *c,* central branch. From C. M. Jackson, *Morris' Human Anatomy* (P. Blakiston & Co., 1923).

impressions to the next unit on the way to the muscle. The cell body is the more massive body from which these fibers project. The cell bodies are of various sizes from 1/10-1/140 millimeter (1/250-1/3500 inch). The axones also vary much in length from a fraction of a millimeter to half the length of the human body. The dendrites are much for all functions, although these require a vast number of different sorts of structures in the higher forms. When a paramecium swims into an alkali solution its ciliæ at once begin to beat backward, and the movement takes it away from the injurious stimulation. When an amœba is stimulated by contact it quickly draws itself up into a ball. Both animals are unicellular, and the tissues that perform the movement are the same as those that receive the stimulus.

The higher animals may be regarded as made up of a number of similar simple cells which have been differentiated in function and structure. There are different cells for carrying out the action from those that receive the impulse, and these are all different from those that transfer the impulse from place to place in the body, and again all are different from the digestive and secretory cells or from the supporting cells. Of all the cells which together constitute the body, the nerve cells are probably, next to the blood corpuscles that are still free swimming organisms, those which most resemble the original unicellular animals. If we think of the higher animals as colonies of cells in which each has a different work to do, the function of the nervous tissues is to receive excitations from the outside world and transform them into muscular actions. Aside from this, it has the task of keeping the other tissues working together, of coördinating their activities so that there shall be no lack of harmony between them. To understand the action of the nervous system we may begin with a discussion of the separate elements and then proceed to the explanation of their interaction.

#### THE STRUCTURE OF THE NERVOUS SYSTEM

The elements of the nervous system are called the *neurones*. Each neurone is composed of three parts, the

## THE NERVOUS MECHANISMS OF SPEECH 23

shorter, unless the fibers that extend from the skin to the spinal cord are called dendrites. There is some difference of opinion about this, as they have the appearance and structure of axones, although they have the function of dendrites. Whether structure or function shall determine the classification is not as yet a matter of agreement. The cell body develops first and the processes are outgrowths from it. They have been actually seen to grow in the frog, and studies of human embryonic tissue make it certain that the same rule holds in man. In the full-grown neurone, the processes are dependent upon the cell for nourishment. This is shown by the fact that, when an axone or dendrite is cut, the end away from the cell degenerates. The axones are covered by a sheath in places and, outside of the central nervous system, by two coats of sheaths. All of the nervous system is made up of neurones.

There are two sorts of nervous tissue ordinarily distinguished, *white matter* and *gray matter*. In terms of their composition, white matter is composed of axones and dendrites, the gray matter of cell bodies. The gray matter is found for the most part in the central part of the cord and brain stem and on the outside of the cortex. White matter constitutes the peripheral nerve fibers, the nerves that connect sense organs with the central nervous system and that system with the muscles. White matter is also found on the outside of the cord and brain stem and scattered here and there through the cerebrum and inner part of the brain stem.

Viewed in this larger way, we may regard the central nervous system as divided into three parts: (1) the *spinal cord*, which is in the upper two-thirds of the spinal column; (2) above this the *brain stem*, composed of *medulla* and *mid-brain*, with the *cerebellum*, as a growth between the medulla and mid-brain; and (3) above all the *cerebrum* which, in man, is the largest portion and fills the upper part of the skull.

We can perhaps best understand the arrangement of the parts of the central nervous system, if we consider the nervous system of some lower form, such as the earthworm. In this animal it is composed of a separate pair of ganglia for each of the segments into which the body is divided, and in addition are fibers that connect the different segments. The impulses received from the sense organs of that segment come through a nerve cell directly to the muscle tissue of the same segment and produce its contractions. The ganglia on each side are connected by fibers, and the ganglia of each segment are connected by a relatively small number of fibers. These cross connections serve to keep the different segments working in harmony with each other. In the head segment there is found a pair of ganglia which are larger than the others and which probably serve for more general coördinations. They are accordingly the analogue of the brain in man, but they do not have the disproportionate size relative to the other ganglia that the brain of man has to the rest of his nervous system. They can be seen to be distinct from the ganglia of other segments and from each other.

In man it is possible to see this segmental arrangement, but the different pairs of ganglia are united by fibers and cells, so that the ganglia no longer stand out as distinct structures. The lower part of the nervous system or cord is now a cylinder with enlargements where the nerves from legs and arms enter, but otherwise of approximately uniform diameter. The main indication of the early segmental arrangement is the fact that pairs of nerves are given off here and there that correspond somewhat roughly to the original segments. The ganglia that were in the head segment have been enormously enlarged. With this greater connection of the segments has gone a tendency for the neurones of one segment to be less and less independent. The earthworm continues to act almost normally after he has been cut in two. A higher animal that continues to live after the cord has been severed, performs relatively few of his usual acts. The severed part loses much of its former function. A few rudimentary reflexes are still executed, but the animal is unable to walk or make other movements that require the coöperation of other parts of the nervous system. The higher one goes in the animal series, the more each part of the nervous system depends upon the action of all of the other parts.

### NERVOUS ACTION

One principle, however, holds throughout all nervous activity. This is that every movement arises from the stimulation of some sense organ or from the excitation of some sensory neurone. Nervous action always originates in some sense organ and is transferred by a longer or shorter path to some muscle or group of muscles. The simplest act may involve only two neurones, a neurone connected with the sense organ, the sensory neurone; and a neurone connected with the muscle, a motor neurone. The impulse spreads from the axone or end brush of one to the dendrite of the other. In the cord, where these simplest reflexes occur, the cell body of the sensory neurone is in a swelling of the spinal nerve known as the *spinal ganglion*, while the motor neurone is on the opposite, the anterior, side of the cord. The impulse through the neurone is probably some sort of chemical action; just what is not at present known. The impulse travels at the rate of about 120 meters a second through the neurone itself. Even less well understood is the way in which the impulse passes from one neurone to the other, from the end brush of one to the dendrite of the other, across what has recently been called the *synapse*. That there is some peculiar obstacle to its passage at this point is indicated by the fact that it requires much more time for the passage of this slight gap than for all the rest of the path. What offers the resistance is not known. It has been assumed at different times to be some sort of open space and recently to be some sort of semipermeable membrane. Whatever it is, it is found to offer less and less resistance as the impulses pass over it. More evidence for this will be found when we come to consider the action of the nervous system. This, in a large part, depends upon the openness of the synapse.

The structure of the cord is represented in the accompanying diagram. One can see that the butterfly-shaped mass of gray matter in the center is made up of nerve cells, while the outer layer of white matter is composed of axones. In addition to the neurones that are involved in the simplest reflexes from the sense organ on one side of the body to the muscles of the same side, there are other paths that carry the impulse across to the muscles of the opposite side of the body, represented in the cord by motor cells of the opposite side of the gray matter. Aside from this there are fibers that run up and down the cord to connect other cells at different levels.

The action of the cord and of reflexes in general will be clearer if one considers the movements that can be made by a frog whose cord has been severed in some way from the rest of its nervous system so that it alone can control movements. If, after this operation, the frog is suspended by his head and any strong stimulus is applied to the skin of one of its legs, that leg will be drawn up. The stimulus will be conducted from the sense ending to the cells in the spinal ganglion, and from there over the axone of that

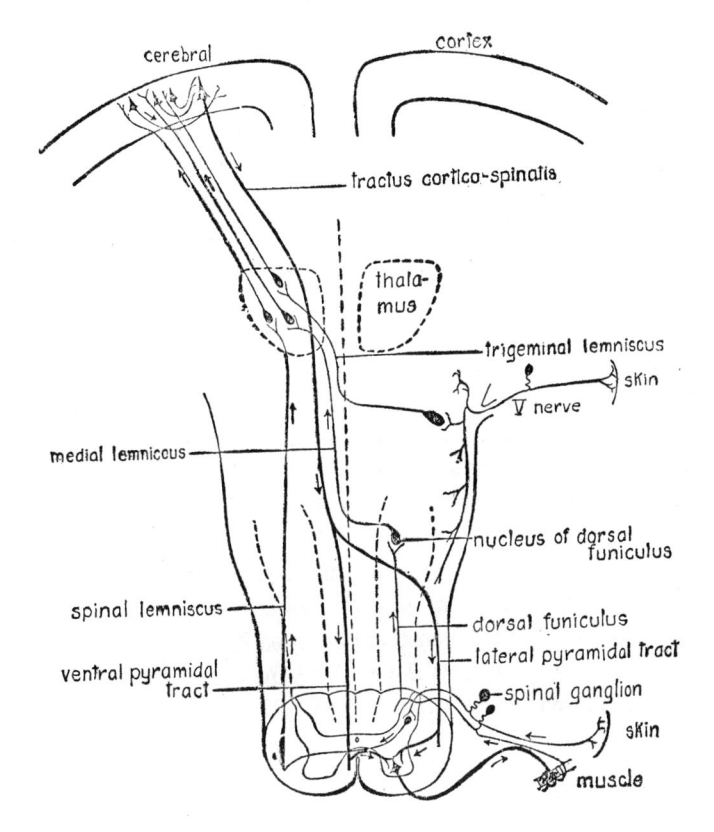

FIG. 3.—ILLUSTRATING THE AFFERENT PATHWAYS EXTENDING BY WAY OF THE SPINAL CORD FROM RECEPTORS IN THE SKIN TO THE CEREBRAL CORTEX.

The motor pathway running from the cortex to a muscle is also shown. (From C. J. Herrick, *An Introduction to Neurology* (W. B. Saunders Co., 1916).

neurone to the motor neurone in the anterior part of the cord; and the impulse from that would be conveyed to the muscle and produce a contraction. If now the leg stimulated be held, the other leg will be brought across and will attempt to wipe away the stimulation. The reason for the stimulus taking the more usual path first and the less usual one later is that the first is easier; the synapses offer less resistance, probably. When, however, action induced over that path is not sufficient to remove the stimulus, the impulse increases by summation until it is sufficient to cross the more difficult synapses. If this movement proves ineffectual, the nervous impulse will travel up the cord to other motor neurones at other levels, and movements of muscles of the forelegs and of the trunk will be evoked. The synapses that lead to these muscles may be regarded as more difficult to open and in consequence to require a stronger stimulus to open them or to pass over them. Which movements are made is determined by the degree of openness of the synapses, although the action seems to be intelligent.

In addition to these reflex paths, there are fibers in the posterior columns of the cord that lead up to the higher centers and paths, and in the lateral and anterior columns that lead from the brain and higher centers down to the motor cells and so to the muscles. It is along these paths that man becomes aware of the sensations from the skin and muscles of the trunk and limbs and that voluntary impulses are sent down to the muscles. In the cord, then, are found the paths that make possible reflexes of all degrees of complexity, and the paths that conduct sensory impressions to the brain and higher centers and that send motor impulses down from the higher centers to the muscles. It is not within our province to trace the paths that may be followed by different impulses, and it must be con-

# THE NERVOUS MECHANISMS OF SPEECH

fessed that many of them are not as yet altogether clearly determined. This action of the neurones in the cord is typical of all nervous action. Other structures differ from it only in having a larger number of stimuli coöperating in the control of movement and in having a larger number of movements to control. They still constitute reflex paths by which impressions may be carried from sense organ to muscle, and the contraction of the muscle depends upon the stimuli that are received and transmitted to it. In the regions above the cord and below the brain, we find evidence of the segmental arrangement of the lower animals and of reflexes similar to those in the cord. Thus in the medulla, which lies just above the cord, one finds the center for respiration, from which the impulses go out to the respiratory organs. This is also involved in the voluntary movements required for speech. Above in the mid-brain and other masses below the cerebrum are centers for the reception of impulses from the ear, eye and tongue, and from the skin and mucous membranes of the head, and also the motor centers from which impulses are sent to the muscles of the head and neck. Many of these are involved in speech. The adjustments of the larynx, the tongue, the lips, the soft palate, etc., are directly affected through these centers. Certain wider coördinations are carried out through these structures.

## THE CEREBELLUM

The cerebellum is the center for the coördination of all the movements of locomotion, and it is probable that other centers, the *corpora quadrigemina* and the *thalamus*, also act as centers for the coördination and distribution of impulses that lead to movements involving different parts of the body. The general function of these regions may be indicated by the fact that a frog deprived of his cerebrum but with the lower centers intact will carry on many of the activities of the uninjured frog. It will move as the normal frog does when stimulated and will avoid obstacles; it swims; it takes food when it is near and there is no obstacle. It will croak when its back is stroked. The main difference from the normal frog is in the loss of initiative, the necessity for stronger stimulation to call out the movement, and the failure to be controlled by any but the immediately present stimuli. These intermediate parts of the brain are still the seat of reflex paths; but, in addition to caring for the reflexes of the same segments and serving as transmitting paths from the cortex, they also serve to coördinate movements of different parts of the body and to receive and transmit sensations from widely separate sense organs to muscles all over the body.

### THE CEREBRUM

In the cerebrum we have the most highly complicated part of the nervous system, but in essentials it obeys the same laws as the lower portions. The gray masses of the cerebrum are on the outer portions, the cortex. Inside are scattered masses of gray, or cell bodies, and the remainder is made up of fibers of white matter. The inner fiber coats serve to connect the different regions of the cortex with the lower parts of the nervous system and with each other. The cortex is much furrowed or fissured. It is assumed that the folds serve to increase the area of the cortex, and hence bear some relation to intelligence. Superficially, certain large fissures serve to divide the cortex into regions that may serve a useful purpose in description and reference. The most prominent of these is the median fissure that divides the cerebrum into

# THE NERVOUS MECHANISMS OF SPEECH

two hemispheres. This is very deep at the back, extending clear through to the bottom. The sides of this fissure are known as the median surfaces. One can understand the character of the fissure by reference to the way the hemispheres develop in the individual. In the prenatal development they grow out from near the forward end of the original neural tube, then grow up and back until they

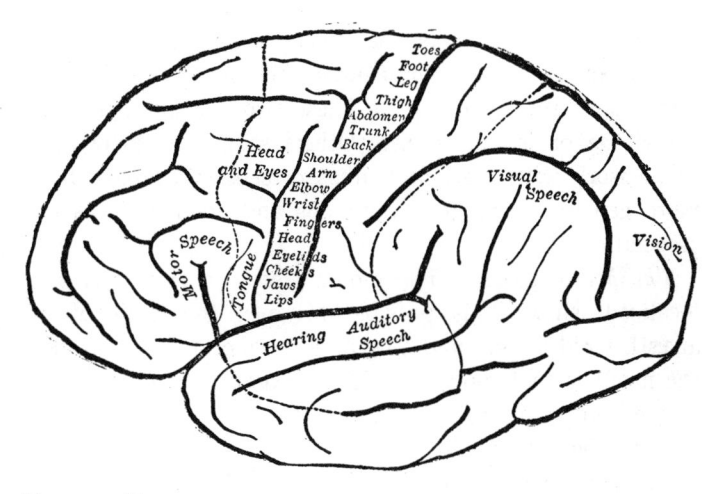

FIG. 4.—FUNCTIONAL AREAS, SENSORY AND MOTOR, LAID OUT UPON THE LEFT SIDE OF THE CEREBRAL CORTEX.
From C. J. Herrick, *An Introduction to Neurology* (W. B. Saunders Co., 1916).

meet. On each hemisphere there is a lateral fissure, the *fissure of Sylvius,* which is also very deep. It runs forward and down from a point more than halfway back on the cerebrum. It can be made out easily on the diagram. Much less prominent is the central fissure that runs up from near the upper end of the Sylvian fissure to the top of the cerebrum and may be traced on the median surface. The area below the fissure of Sylvius is known as the *temporal lobe;* that above the Sylvian fissure and in front of the central fissure is the *frontal lobe;* back of the central fissure is the *parietal lobe;* while the back of the cerebrum is known as the *occipital region.* This is separated from the parietal lobe by the parieto-occipital fissure, which is by no means easy to make out. The walls of the fissure of Sylvius constitute the *island of Reil.*

The areas of the cortex are said to have three different functions. Certain areas, the sensory areas, receive impressions from the sense organs; others, the motor regions, send impressions to the muscles. These two together are often called the projection areas. Others still serve to connect the sensory with the motor areas or sensory areas or have more general associatory functions and are known as the association areas.

*The Motor Areas.*—The motor areas are most certainly localized, since it is possible to open the skull of an anæsthetized animal and stimulate the motor area and note the member that moves and also to destroy different parts of the brain and note the paralysis that results. The motor area has been found to be above the fissure of Sylvius and in front of the fissure of Rolando or the central fissure. Within this area it is also possible to assign different parts to separate regions of the body. The muscles of the face, used in speech, are in the lower part of this region, of the arms above, while the trunk and legs are controlled by the upper portion and the upper part of the median surface. The surgeon has this region sufficiently accurately mapped to be able to open the skull in a very limited area and remove a growth that may be causing paralysis or other motor disturbances.

*The Auditory Area.*—The sensory areas are more scattered. Hearing is less specifically located than the others. It is agreed that it is connected with the upper part of the

## THE NERVOUS MECHANISMS OF SPEECH 33

temporal lobe, below the central fissure. It is probable that each ear is connected with both temporal lobes, so that complete deafness in either ear could be produced by brain injury only if both temporal lobes were affected simultaneously. This could happen only rarely, unless the brain were so generally injured that the hearing defect would be obscured by other more complete mental deteriorations. Sufficient evidence from deterioration of hearing and the interpretation of words heard has accumulated to make it clear that the temporal lobe is fundamental for the reception and interpretation of tones.

*The Visual Area.*—Studies of war cases have made possible a very definite localization of the visual functions. These are found mainly on the median surface of the occipital lobe on both sides of the calcarine fissure, as indicated in the diagram. The right half of each retina is projected upon the right cortex, the left half of each retina upon the left cortex. The upper halves of the retinas are represented on the upper edge of the calcarine fissure and the lower halves upon the lower edge of that fissure. Localized injuries of the visual area produce local blindness in accordance with this general law. In addition, the fovea, the central depression in the retina, is projected upon the posterior tip of the occipital lobe, on the median and lateral surface. One may lose vision for the periphery of the retina and still retain foveal vision. It seems very probable that the specific verbal-visual associates are intimately connected with the lateral area about where the fissure of Sylvius ends, the so-called *angular gyrus;* but not all accept this fact or interpret it in the same way.

*The Kinæsthetic or Touch Area.*—The sensory impressions from the skin and muscles are also definitely localized in the region back of the central fissure. As in the case of motor areas, the fibers cross, so that the left half of the body sends its sensations to the right cortex and vice versa. In general, also, the lower parts of the body are represented high up on the cortex, and the higher portions lower down.

In connection with all statements of localization it should be emphasized that opinion divides into two sharply opposed schools. One holds that the cortex has very indefinitely localized functions, that any part can take the place of almost any other part. This school supports its conclusions by evidence that removal of the brain of a rat has relatively little influence upon the activity of the rat. It seems to learn almost as well after the loss of the cortex as before. Even in injuries to human brains, there is ultimate recovery of a large part or all of the functions that are disturbed. In the extreme form, this school almost goes to the extreme of asserting that the brain acts as a whole. The other school insists that there is a definite localization of sensory and motor functions. These functions are much more differentiated in man than in the rat, but even for the rat they will not grant that the experiments of the other men are conclusive. They admit the possibility of recovery and explain by a substitution of function. The patient does, within limits, replace the injured part by another. The main difference is that one school denies the specific limitations of one part of the cortex to one function alone, while the other insists that movement is closely connected with one part, a single sensation with another, originally. They grant, however, that when one of these parts is injured, its functions may in some degree be taken over by other areas.

*The Association Areas.*—All parts of the cortex that are not projection areas are assumed to be association areas. These, it will be seen from the diagram, form the larger part of the cortex. The association areas, according to Flechsig, who was a pioneer in the use of one method for

## THE NERVOUS MECHANISMS OF SPEECH 35

tracing the paths in the brain, are to be divided into two classes. First, near each projection area there is a small region supplied with short association fibers that lead to the corresponding projection areas. These areas are supposed to care for the elaboration of various associations of the sensory processes connected with that sense. They have been made much of at different times in the theories of word associations, as will be seen when we come to the discussion of theories of aphasia. The other association areas connect different projection, or different association areas with each other, or connect association with projection areas, and seem to have a more general function. The greater part of the frontal lobes, the large area between the sensory part of the parietal lobe and the hindermost part of the occipital region, and most of the temporal lobe would thus constitute the association regions. The island of Reil, or the walls and bottom of the fissure of Sylvius, constitutes another association area that is apparently very important in speech, since it serves to connect the auditory area with the motor center for speech.

### ACTION OF THE BRAIN IN SPEECH

The functions of the brain as a whole may be best illustrated if we turn at once to a study of the parts that are to interest us most and discuss the action of the brain in speech. The speech centers were among the first to be localized and the speech functions are as well understood as any. We may state, first, the view held by those who localize specifically. Any talking is said to require at least five regions of the brain for its proper execution. There must be (1) a receptive organ for the sensory impulse; (2) an area in which the mere sensations are organized into true word images; (3) an associatory or connection region that shall transfer this impression to the regions that are involved in expression; (4) a place in which the word is definitely coördinated and prepared for expression; and finally, (5) the immediate motor area from which the motor impulses emanate, which receives its impulses from the motor center mentioned above. Of these, the immediate sensory or receiving centers require no discussion. If one is reading from a book the printed words must obviously arouse impulses in the visual region before any other activity is possible. But as these impressions come to the brain they are not words but mere combinations of visual sensations without unity and without meaning. To become real words, they must be connected and coördinated. As a result of a study of clinical cases and of the structure of the cortex in these regions, the coördination is assumed to take place in areas closely adjoining the corresponding sensory area. The center for visual words is assigned to the angular gyrus or to regions nearer the restricted sensory visual center. This is not so generally recognized as distinct as is the corresponding auditory word center, the Wernicke center. The auditory center was localized by Wernicke, in the early days of cerebral localization, in the back portion of the first frontal convolution. It, too, is immediately contiguous to the sensory auditory area. Both of these organizing centers are indicated by cases in which words are confused or not understood while the sounds are heard and retained perfectly.

The associatory tracts are perhaps less definitely established in detail, but it is obvious that these impulses must be transferred to the motor areas if speech is to result. The island of Reil, the bottom and sides of the Sylvian fissure, is said to be where the connections between the auditory and motor areas are made. In fact, much of the region on both sides of the Sylvian fissure has been given

# THE NERVOUS MECHANISMS OF SPEECH

this function by certain authors. The connections between the optical word center and the motor areas are less definitely known but must on theory exist, and associatory fibers and areas can be traced. It should be said that the greater number of German authorities who do not believe in the visual word center would ascribe the associatory function for the optic motor functions to connections between the sensory visual center and the Wernicke auditory word center and thence through the island to the motor regions. That these associations do take place and may be interfered with by disease is indicated by the existence of cases in which the victim can think the word as he would hear or see it but cannot pronounce it, although his other speech functions may be intact.

The existence of the motor coördinating center or motor speech center was the first to be definitely made out. It was described by Broca in 1863 and is perhaps the most generally accepted of any of the centers. When the center is injured, there results inability properly to pronounce words, but with no paralysis of the vocal organs. These organs may be used for other purposes, but it is not possible to formulate words. It is assumed that this region has a function analogous in some respects to the sensory speech areas. Various incentives to speech are combined into a unitary process which serves as the immediate incentive to the action of the motor center for the vocal organs. The exact function of the area is not easy to picture, but it seems to serve as the motor analogue of the sensory correlating centers discussed above. The last set of neurones involved is that which has immediate control of the muscles of speech. Even these so-called immediate motor centers probably involve a considerable amount of correlation that is cared for by the lower centers. It is seldom that a single muscle can be excited from the cortex. One always by

## 38    THE PSYCHOLOGY OF LANGUAGE

electrical stimulation arouses a group of muscles that have been used together. The difference, then, between the correlation that is effective in the speech center of Broca in the third frontal convolution and the motor center for speech just back of it in the anterior central convolution is one of degree. The coördination in the speech center permits words or other sounds to be spoken as units, and perhaps permits of the union of different words into phrases, while the motor center gives rise to the combinations that constitute single sounds or other single groupings of the complex of the movements involved in speech. How much of this coördination is made possible by each element is not certainly determined, but in general it is safe to assume that there is a lower form that may be referred to the immediate motor speech area and the lower connections, and a higher form that must be ascribed to the center of Broca.

If, then, we take this simple and fairly generally accepted picture of the cortical regions that are involved in speech, we may say that when one repeats words that are spoken before one, the sound wave falls first upon one's ear and affects the nerve of hearing. The impulse is transmitted to the temporal lobes in the median portion of the first temporal convolution. If one may distinguish mental operations for the different stages of the hearing process, there would correspond to this a bare auditory sensation that is not understood, that has no meaning. From this region the sounds would take shape as a word; they would be in some degree, understood. This understanding is a process of connecting with other images and acts. From this region it would be transferred through association fibers to association regions in the island where probably new connections are made that add to the understanding and at least serve to transmit the excitation to the motor areas. In the Broca region the coördinated word finds a unitary or at least co-

# THE NERVOUS MECHANISMS OF SPEECH

ordinated group of neurones that by their excitation may add a new conscious element, the active feeling, kinæsthetic images perhaps, to the word idea and transmit the impulse to the different elements that serve to excite the widely spread motor centers in the mid-brain, medulla, and cord that leads to the regulated and ordered contraction of the muscles involved in speech. As will be seen in the later chapters, talking requires working together of the muscles in the chest, the abdomen, the throat, and the mouth cavity, if the simplest word is pronounced. This coöperation is made possible by the connections of the motor cortical area for speech and the various subordinate centers scattered over much of the central nervous system.

### RECENT STUDIES OF LOCALIZATION OF FUNCTION

If we may regard the statement we have given as the approximately accepted formulation until Marie wrote in 1906, we should add that since then, and particularly since the study of the effects of wounds inflicted on the brain during the War, there has been a tendency to make all less definite. Two studies, one by Piéron, the other by Head, appeared in 1926 which summed up these results, although coming to slightly different conclusions.[1] Both are alike in emphasizing the associative functions of speech rather than the separate sensory and motor elements. Piéron recognises the Broca center or its equivalent as a place where motor impulses are coördinated, as we have done above. This would be disturbed in motor aphasia. He has similar regions for coördination and association of sensory processes that provide the region where meaning is ascribed to the mere sounds and visual impressions. The auditory word

---

[1] Piéron, *Thought and the Brain* (New York, Harcourt, Brace, 1927); Head, Henry, *Aphasia* (Cambridge University Press, 1896).

center he would put in the temporal lobe and assign it about the function of Wernicke's word center. It differs from Wernicke's notion in that, instead of regarding a mere auditory image as effective in initiating the speech movements, he would make the incentive an entire group of associates that irradiate from that area. The region is a place from which nerve impulses go out to the related cortical speech areas and to which impulses come from them. A group of nerve units makes possible understanding and prepares for expression. He would place a similar coördinating mechanism for vision in the angular gyrus. There, seen words might be said to be understood. He would also grant that these regions are not independent but interact mutually in all speech operations.

Head would go farther in that he makes the cortex in general a region for coördination and would place little emphasis upon the specific localization even of separate sensations and movements. The different types of aphasia would be distinguished as due to interference with different forms of thought activities. He names four of these and assigns each to a different part of the cortex. (1) Verbal aphasia is marked by inability to express one's self in words, although ability to think is retained. This he associates with injury of the left cortex in front of and behind the central fissure. (2) Syntactical aphasia is marked by defective rhythm of speech and lack of ability to put sentences together. This is associated with injury to the temporal lobe. (3) Nominal aphasia is characterized by inability to find words or to recognize objects. It is an accompaniment of injury to the angular gyrus and the neighboring parietal and occipital regions. (4) Semantic aphasia is a condition in which the patient does not recognize the ultimate meaning of a logical and consecutive statement and cannot keep in mind the intention of an act that is originated spontaneously or at command. This is found in connection with injury to the *supramarginal gyrus,* which lies roughly at the end of the Sylvian fissure and above the *angular gyrus.* If one tries to harmonize the two classifications, it will be seen that they agree only roughly. The disturbance of the motor functions is recognized by both, although Head puts its seat in the regions directly involved in movement and in appreciation of one's own movement, while Piéron places his motor aphasia or aphemia a little below the Broca center in the upper wall of the island of Reil, although he does not limit it so closely as was the Broca center. He assigns a function of verbal thought to the temporal lobe, including the Wernicke center and the region just back of it. This is in general the region of Head's syntactical asphasia. A similar region for visual coördination (a region associated by Head with lack of recognition) he would assign to the occipital lobe, roughly in and about the *angular gyrus.*

The differences are perhaps more marked than the resemblances, yet both can be seen to give some definite localization, while both emphasize the dependence of each fact of speech upon widely extended regions of the cortex. Piéron inclines more to a localization in terms of the sensory and motor components of speech, while Head makes all division on the basis of more general functions. Both agree that injury of the left cortex in any part of relatively wide areas will produce speech disturbances, that each region gives a disturbance of roughly the same function. That they differ so widely is to be assigned to the varying emphasis that they put upon the complicated phenomena that are presented by each case. One emphasizes the sensory and motor similarities in symptoms that are produced by similar brain injuries, the other the differences in these symptoms and the similarities in the disturbances of understanding and the thought processes.

It should be insisted that there is always great complexity in the problem. No two injuries are exactly alike. In practically every case, not only the regions that are ascribed to speech are injured, but considerable other tissue. The interpretation must make allowance for the symptoms that are to be regarded as indifferent to the speech functions and try to see the essential elements of the injury in their proper relations. It is here that the differences of interpretation arise. The problem is complicated, too, by the fact that with time the functions are recovered and the speech disturbances more and more disappear. On the whole it is probably more to be marveled at that the harmony in interpretation is so great rather than that the differences are great.

## REFERENCES

HERRICK, C. J.—*Introduction to Neurology* (Philadelphia, Saunders, 1922).
PILLSBURY, W. B.—*Fundamentals of Psychology* (New York, Macmillan, 1922), Chaps. II and III.
VILLIGER, EMIL.—*Brain and Spinal Cord* (Philadelphia, Lippincott, 1918).

# CHAPTER III

## THE SPEECH ORGANS

### ANATOMY AND PHYSIOLOGY

THE speech organs in the broader sense of the word are as follows: (1) the lungs with the trachea and the bronchial tubes, the diaphragm, and other muscles employed in breathing; (2) the larynx; (3) the pharynx, with the mouth and nose cavities, the lips, and other structures contained within the mouth. It is probable that the frontal and sphenoidal cavities of the skull play some part in speech. During the act of speaking the organs of the first group are continuously active, speech being a modification of the act of breathing. The larynx, or more properly the vocal ledges, act intermittently, being employed for the production of some sounds but not for others. The mouth acts continuously, either as a sound-producing apparatus or as a resonance chamber; the nose serves almost wholly as a resonance chamber and is frequently not employed.

*The Lungs, the Trachea, and the Bronchial Tubes.*—The lungs consist of two elastic and porous lobes each of which occupies one half of the chest cavity. They are roughly wedge-shaped and rest with their partly concave lower surface in contact with the floor of the chest cavities and with their convex outer surfaces adjacent to the side walls of the lung cavities. The central cavity of the chest between the two lung cavities is occupied by the heart, the arteries, the veins, the esophagus, and other structures. The *trachea*, or windpipe, passes downward behind the breastbone (sternum), where it bifurcates, thus forming two smaller tubes on each side, of which one again bifurcates. Each one of these five smaller tubes enters a lobe of the lungs. After entering the lungs each of these tubes bifurcates again and again until they terminate in the minute *bronchioli respiratorii*. These are small sacks about $\frac{1}{10}$ inch in diameter and about $\frac{1}{35}$ inch in length, through the walls of which the process of respiration takes place. The entire volume of air that these passages are capable of containing is about 4,000 cubic centimeters, or 240 cubic inches. This capacity varies with the size of the individual, with the posture of the body (being greatest in a standing position and least in the prone position), and with other factors. However, the lungs are never completely emptied of air, there remaining after the deepest expiration about 700 cubic centimeters of residual air. After ordinary quiet expiration there remain about 1,600 cubic centimeters more than this amount. This is called *reserve* air and can be called into requisition for speech purposes. Each normal inspiration adds to this about 450 cubic centimeters, called *respiratory air*. To this total of about 2,800 cubic centimeters a very deep inspiration can add about 1,600 cubic centimeters, making a total of approximately 4,400 cubic centimeters, of which all except the residual air is available for purposes of speech. Ordinary conversation probably employs little more air per minute than ordinary breathing.

The tubes of the lungs branch from the trachea downward in such a way that, while each of the two successive branches is smaller than the bifurcating tube from which they spring, still the sum of the areas of the two cross sections of the two branches is greater than that of the parent tube. Consequently, as the outflowing breath passes upward toward the trachea, it is moving continually into a steadily narrowing space. This has the effect of pro-

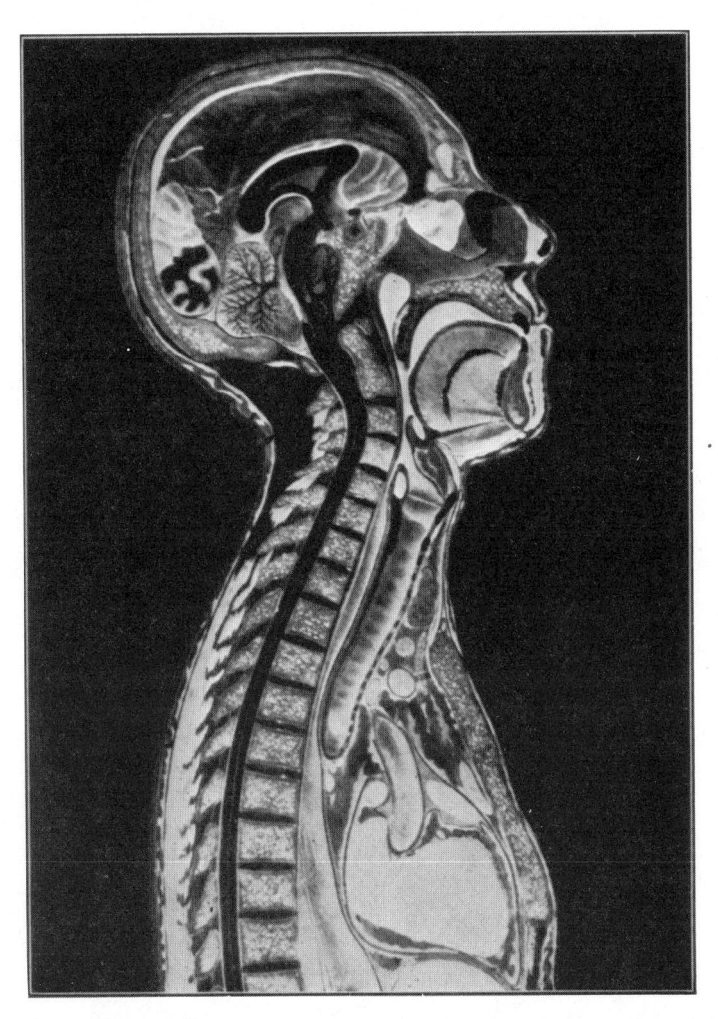

FIG. 5.—SAGITTAL SECTION OF THE HEAD AND CHEST.

## THE SPEECH ORGANS

ducing a swifter movement of air through the trachea than through any other part of the air passages. Thus a generous supply of air is continually brought into a container of relatively small volume, and a very slight relaxation of the rather clumsily working diaphragm and abdominal muscles can greatly accelerate the speed of the flow of the outgoing column of air. The larynx and mouth are further provided with devices for exercising a delicate control over the pressure and flow of this column of air for the purposes of speech.

The adjustable supporting framework of the chest cavity is formed by the ribs, the sternum, the spine, and the tissues that connect them. The chest cavity is divided into three compartments, the pulmonary or lung cavities and that in which the heart and certain other organs are located. The floor of the chest cavities is formed by the diaphragm, a thin partition of muscle and tendinous tissue, which rises dome-shaped above the stomach and liver. The central tendinous part of the dome lies directly below the heart, while the arching, muscular sides, radiating backward, forward, and sidewise from the central tendinous portion, dip slightly downward, their upper surfaces on each side adjacent to the lower medial surface of the lungs. As the muscle fibers approach the periphery of the body, where they are attached to the lower ribs, they bend more sharply or steeply downward. The diaphragm receives its nerve supply from the phrenic nerve.

*The Larynx.*—At the upper end of the trachea and anatomically continuous with it, is situated the larynx (Figs. 5, 6, 7 and 8). It is a small box of irregular shape. Its walls are supported by four cartilages. The lowest one, the *cricoid cartilage,* lying parallel with the upper ring of the trachea and often grown together with it, has roughly the shape of a signet ring with a large gem; this lends to the lower part of the larynx a circular form. Above it is the *thyroid cartilage*. This cartilage has the shape of a triangular trough set on end, which gives to the upper part of the larynx a horizontal cross section of triangular form with its apex directed forward—the "Adam's apple." The back wall of this triangular passage, parallel with a line joining the two shoulders, is supported by two small cartilages—the *arytenoid cartilages*—which are articulated on the broad upper back of the cricoid. From the interior surface of each of the other walls, about at the midpoint of their height, projects a ledge like a plate rail. These two ledges start in front from a point just behind the Adam's apple and proceed backward to the arytenoid cartilages to the vocal process of one of which each ledge is attached. These ledges or lips are popularly known as the *vocal cords*. When the arytenoid cartilages are brought together, the proximal edges of the two ledges are brought into contact, thereby dividing the laryngeal passage into two chambers. The lower surfaces of the vocal ledges form the rather steep dome of the lower chamber, while their flat upper surfaces form the floor of the upper chamber, which has two cavernous extensions, one on each side, called the *ventricles of Morgagni*. Two overhanging folds of tissue —the false vocal cords—form the roofs of these ventricles. A cross section through the vocal ledges parallel with the face shows them to have the following chief elements of construction: Their core is formed by two small muscles, the *musculi vocales* or vocal muscles, approximately triangular in frontal cross section. Their upper and median faces are covered with a layer of tough connective tissue, in which are embedded many elastic fibers parallel with the edge of the ledges, and large numbers of mucous glands, which lubricate the inner surface of the larynx. It also contains isolated muscle fibers or scattered small bundles of

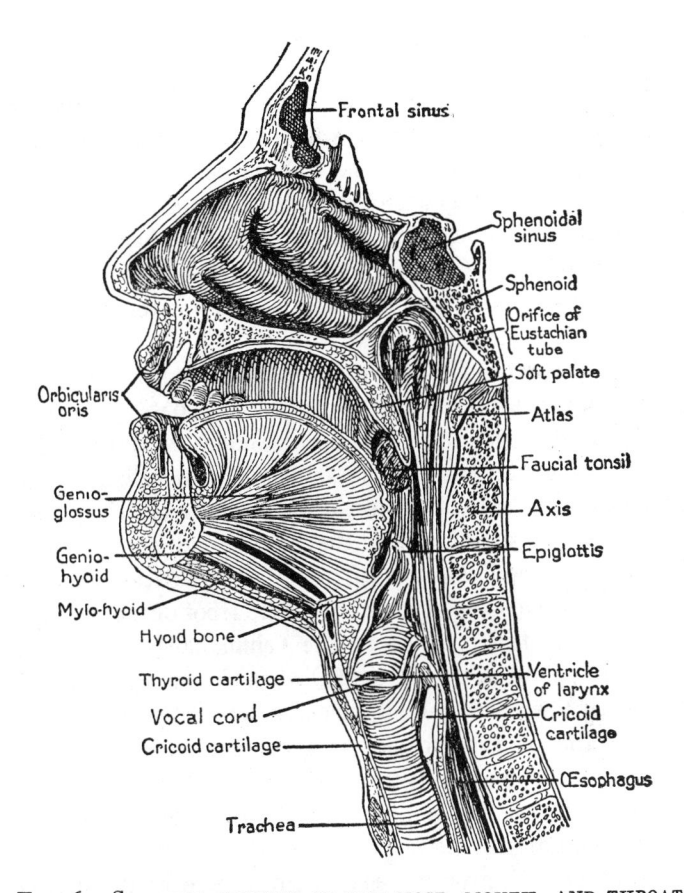

Fig. 6.—Sagittal section of the nose, mouth, and throat.
After Luschka, *Der Kehlkopf des Menschen.*

muscle fibers. The entire inner surface of the larynx is lined with mucous membrane, which is continuous with that of the pharynx above and the trachea below. The larynx is held in place by its attachment to the trachea below and to the pharynx behind, the front wall of the pharynx being the rear wall of the larynx; and also by a group of muscles that join the thyroid cartilage with the *hyoid* (tongue) bone above and the sternum below.

*The Pharynx.*—The laryngeal passage opens into the pharynx above. The pharynx is a long passage, rather flattened from front to rear and extending vertically from the larynx to the base of the skull. The mouth and nose chambers are forward projecting extensions of this chamber. The division between the mouth and nose cavities is formed by the *Velum palati*, a muscular partition forming a backward extension of the hard palate (roof of the mouth). From the posterior fringe of the velum hangs the *uvula*. The soft palate with the uvula, when drawn upward and backward toward the simultaneously forward moving back wall of the pharynx, comes into contact with the latter and closes the opening between the oral and nasal portions of the pharyngeal chamber, thus entirely separating the mouth and nose cavities.

No special description need be given here of the mouth and its contents, since the student should familiarize himself with its shape and with the movements of the jaws, the tongue, and the soft palate by direct observation of himself and others. The rather intricate structure of the tongue should be studied with the aid of an anatomical atlas.

*The Nerve Supply of the Larynx.*—The nerve supply of the larynx is derived from the right and left vagi or tenth cranial nerves, which also send fibers to the pharynx, trachea, and lungs. The fibers are derived from two pairs

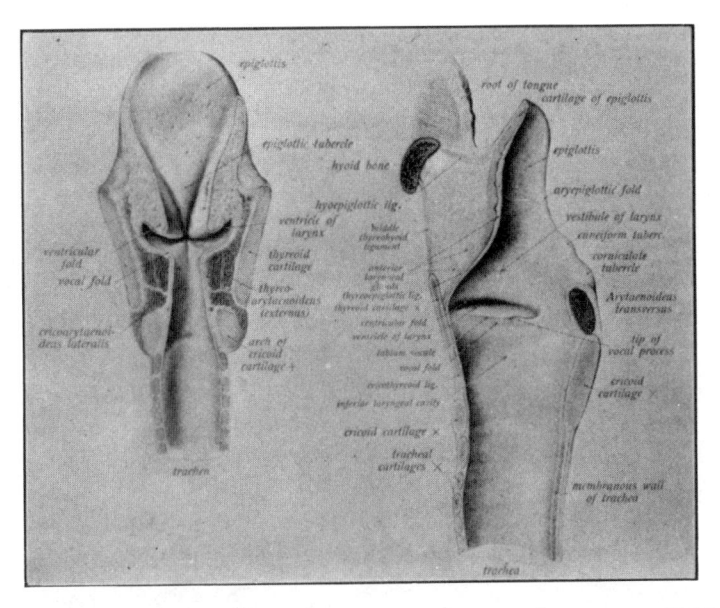

FIG. 7.—FRONTAL SECTIONAL VIEW (AT LEFT) AND SAGITTAL SECTIONAL VIEW (RIGHT) OF THE LARYNX.

From Sobotta and McMurrich, *Atlas of Human Anatomy* (W. B. Saunders Co., 1913-1921).

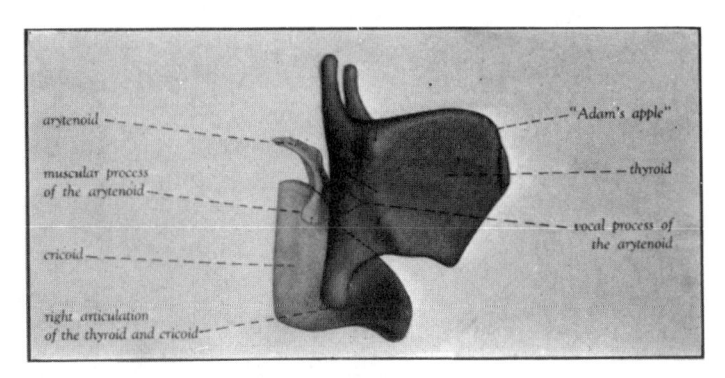

FIG. 8.—THE CARTILAGES OF THE LARYNX.

From Figures 426, 428, 431, Sobotta and McMurrich, *Atlas of Human Anatomy* (W. B. Saunders Co., 1913-1921).

## THE SPEECH ORGANS

of branches: (1) the two superior laryngeal nerves, which branch off from the vagi at about the level of the base of the tongue, and (2) the right and left *nervi recurrentes,* or inferior laryngeal nerves, which arise about the level of the collar bone. The inferior nerves at first descend, looping around the subclavian artery and the aorta respectively, then ascend, giving off fibers to the esophagus and the trachea, to the level of the cricoid cartilage. Thence they send motor fibers to all the muscles of the larynx except the cricothyroid. They also contain some sensory fibers, while other anastomosing fibers from it unite with descending fibers from the superior laryngeal nerves. Each superior nerve bifurcates soon after leaving the vagus. The smaller branch proceeds downward and forward outside of the larynx and pharynx and supplies the cricothyroid muscle. The other branch penetrates the outer wall of the larynx just below the hyoid bone and distributes sensory fibers to the larynx.

### THE NATURE OF MUSCULAR ACTIVITY

The nature of muscular activity is not as yet fully understood, but many features of it have been made plain by the researches of physiologists. As a rule, each efferent motor nerve fiber, proceeding either directly or by relays from the motor center, terminates at the surface of a muscle fiber. These terminations, which are usually located near the center of the length of the muscle fibers, have a distinct anatomical structure, the nerve fiber branching out like antlers. They form a very close physical union with the muscle fiber and thus combine the nerve and muscle into one functioning system. Consistent with this anatomical union normal muscular activity takes place only in connection with coördinated nervous activity, that is, the stimulation of the nerve fiber is followed by the contraction of the muscle fiber. However, muscle tissue is capable of activity independent of the corresponding nerve fiber, as is shown by the fact that by means of artificial stimulation (electrical, mechanical, or other) it can be made to contract, although the corresponding nerve endings have been completely destroyed.

Muscular activity involves a chemical process within the protoplasm of the muscle fiber marked by the liberation of considerable quantities of carbon dioxide, by the formation of nitrogenous waste products (chief among them being creatin), by the decrease or even the exhaustion of the store of glycogen in the muscle, by a large increase in the lactic acid contained in the muscle, and by other chemical changes less fully understood. The chemical process is attended by electrical phenomena and by the development of considerable quantities of heat. Various theories have been advanced to explain how this chemical process brings about the contraction of the muscle.[1]

### MOVEMENTS OF THE SPEECH ORGANS

*The Lungs.*—In ordinary, quiet breathing inspiration is an active process, while expiration is generally believed to be passive. In the former case the diaphragm contracts. As its central, tendinous part can descend but little and its circular line of attachment to the lower edge of chest framework rising very slightly expands somewhat in diameter, the effect of the contraction is to slightly flatten the dome-shaped diaphragm, so that it becomes more cone shaped. As the diaphragm is the floor of the two lung

---

[1] See W. A. Nagel, *Handbuck der Physiologie* (Baumschweig, Wieweg, 1909), Vol. 4, p. 541; W. H. Howell, *A Text-Book of Physiology* (10th ed., Philadelphia, Saunders, 1927), p. 71.

## THE SPEECH ORGANS 51

chambers, its descent on contraction has the effect of increasing their vertical diameters. Simultaneously, the external intercostal muscles and the others that control the ribs and sternum contract, raising the entire framework of the chest. Owing to the peculiar form and placement of the ribs and sternum, this contraction has the effect of expanding the lung cavities in all horizontal directions and also slightly raising their roofs. The increase in volume of the chest cavity by these acts tends to create a partial vacuum. The air outside the body rushes in to fill this vacancy and inflates the lungs, which are thereby expanded against the contractile force of their tissue. In forced inspiration the muscles contract more vigorously. As this more vigorous contraction of the diaphragm tends materially to restrict the horizontal expansion of the chest by exerting an inward pull upon the ribs, in this case the chest expansion takes place more in a vertical than a horizontal direction. The act of quiet expiration, as usually understood, consists in the passive resumption by the lungs and chest walls of the position occupied by them at the beginning of quiet inspiration. The muscles that have been in a state of contraction during inspiration relax; the highly elastic lung tissue which was distended during inspiration instantly shrinks, forcing the air out. The collapse of the chest walls is facilitated by the force of gravity, which, whatever the momentary posture of the body, draws the chest walls downward toward the feet and inward toward the heart; and also by the elastic reaction of the intercostal tissues, the cartilages of the chest framework, and the walls of the abdomen, all of which are compressed, twisted, or stretched by the act of inspiration, and which mechanically resume their more normal position on the withdrawal of the disturbing forces.

For speech purposes we employ almost exclusively the

outflowing stream of air, although occasionally the inflowing current is used. An instance of the latter is the familiar cluck used by a driver to urge on his horse. Numerous suctional clicks occur in languages little known to Europeans and Americans. The ordinary passive act of expiration is subject to much variation during speech. All are familiar with the fact that public speakers and singers undergo extensive training in breath control. On the whole the amount of air required for the utterance of a sentence of the length of those used in ordinary conversation is surprisingly small. A clinical case is reported of a person with a diaphragm of the larynx which completely closed the passage below the vocal lips except for a small aperture about a millimeter in diameter. Yet this small opening allowed the passage of sufficient air to enable the patient to speak in a normal and even in a loud voice. The rate of breathing is about seventeen expirations per second. In the ordinary conversation of daily life, sentences do not in all probability exceed as an average two or three seconds in length. The majority of them would not, therefore, fall within the limits of a single expiration, which occupies somewhat less time than a single inspiration. During phonation, that is, during the pronunciation of the vowels and the voiced consonants, the rate of output is considerably less than that of normal expiration, since the vocal lips are brought into contact or nearly so and at best leave only a narrow chink for the passage of the air. The closures of the oral passage during the pronunciation of the stop consonants ($p$, $b$, $t$, $d$, $k$, $g$, and hard $c$) entirely shut off the air current. It is evident, therefore, that the elastic contraction of the lungs must be checked at frequent intervals during speech, and the act of expiration correspondingly prolonged. Another element in speech that necessarily modifies the expiratory act is the "stress" or dynamic (expiratory) accent. As this accent

## THE SPEECH ORGANS

consists in a continuous variation in the force of utterance,[2] there must be a continuous active control over the pressure of the air in the lungs. This pressure is probably regulated both by the innervation of the muscles active in forced expiration and by the control over the area of the openings in the laryngeal and oral passages. During reading aloud and during public speaking as well as on other occasions, the volume of air required for a sentence may exceed that of normal expiration. In this case one may call into requisition the supply of reserve air, and if one anticipates an unusual output, one may call also upon the volume of complementary air (1,600 cubic centimeters) available through forced inspiration. These are the more evident modifications of breathing during speech.

*The Larynx.*—The chief function of the larynx is to produce, by means of rapid and regular mechanical vibrations of the vocal lips, a succession of equally rapid and regular condensation and rarefactions in the column of air passing through it. These air waves, appreciated by the ear as musical tones, enter into all the vowels and about half the consonants of ordinary speech. In whispering the situation is, of course, different. The character of these vibrations is determined by the shape, the length, the mode of attachment, and the tension of the vocal lips. The variation in shape, length, and tension of the vocal lips is effected by the following muscles: (1) the *thyro-arytenoid muscles* (also called the *musculi vocales*), a pair which make up the main body (core) of the vocal lips themselves and which on contraction would, if acting alone, tense and shorten them and cause them to bulge in the center; (2) the *transverse arytenoidal muscles*, a triune group which on contraction bring the arytenoid cartilages together and thereby cause

---

[2] Popularly spoken of as a variation in the loudness of successive "syllables."

the vocal cords to approach each other along the median line; (3) the *posterior cricoarytenoids,* a pair, each of which spreads fan-shaped downward from the muscular process of each arytenoid cartilage to its line of attachment along the lower portion of the broad back of the cricoid cartilage, and the contraction of which, if acting alone, would cause the anterior (vocal) processes of the arytenoids to move upward, outward, and backward, thus lengthening the vocal lips and at the same time raising and separating their posterior ends; (4) the *lateral cricoarytenoids,* a pair partly antagonistic to the last mentioned pair, the contraction of which tends to raise, and bring together the posterior ends of the vocal lips; and (5) the *cricothyroid,* on the contraction of which, if acting alone, the distance from the inner angle of the thyroid cartilage and the dorsal crown of the cricoid would be increased, thus lengthening and, presumably, tensing the vocal lips. However, the elongation effected by these groups of muscles is not great, amounting to only a fraction of the total length of the vocal lips, and is insufficient to bring about of itself a sufficient variation in the length of the vocal lips to account for the wide range of variation in rate of vibration of which they are capable. It seems certain, therefore, that the range of variation in rate of vibration is effected more by the variation in tension than by the variation in length.

Although study has been made of the effect of the contraction of each one of these muscles acting alone, nevertheless it is difficult, if not impossible, to determine just what part each particular pair contributes to the total effect produced by their synergic contraction. Neither is the exact nature of the action of the vocal lips fully understood, notwithstanding the extensive and painstaking study that has been made of the subject. It is plain that they are capable of vibrating at rates varying from as low as 41 times per

## THE SPEECH ORGANS

second to as high as around 2,000 per second, although these extremes are found only in very few individuals. In ordinary conversation the rate usually runs in American English from 80 to 150 vibrations per second. The accuracy with which the vibrations can be controlled is truly marvelous. For example, an amateur singer of the writer's acquaintance on a test maintained the note G[1] for from 10 to 15 seconds at varying loudnesses at a rate of vibration frequency not exceeding 440 nor falling below 439. Doubtless a skilled singer could surpass this record of accuracy, but this example gives a fair idea of the extraordinary delicacy of control exercised over the muscles involved in phonation.

It has been held that in the falsetto voice the lips do not come into contact along the median line during vibration, but that they leave a small chink, whereas in the chest register they do come into contact. Later photographs show no such approximation of the lips. Very likely there are individual variations in this particular. In the case of the chest notes, assuming the correctness of the older view, it would seem that the mechanics of vibration is as follows: The cords are brought into contact along the median line, thus causing a complete closure of the glottis. The air pressure in the lungs and trachea is increased until it becomes sufficient to force the lips apart.[3] Through the chink thus formed (the glottis) the air immediately escapes, reducing the air pressure below and allowing the lips by virtue of their elasticity to regain the contact position. The process is then repeated. In the case of the falsetto register, and also of the chest register, provided the lips do *not* come

---

[3] Whether the breaking of the contact is due wholly to the air pressure or whether, as in the case of the breaking of closure characterizing the stop consonants, the initial break is effected by the aid of the laryngeal muscles, has never been investigated.

into contact, the mechanics of vibration is similar, the variation in intrapulmonary air pressure being effected by the varying in width of the glottis instead of by the alternate presence and absence of a glottal chink. It is also certain that a greater mass of the vocal lips is in vibration in the production of notes of the lower registers than in that of the higher registers. The main direction of the vibration is along a curve upward and outward. Owing to the technical conditions under which laryngoscopic observations have to be made, it is very difficult to determine the amplitude of the vibrations in a vertical direction, although it is certain that the popular notion that the vibrations are chiefly up and down is false. By means of a stroboscope the vibrations of the vocal lips can be observed and photographed, but the work requires an extraordinary degree of care and great patience on the part of both the observer and the subject.

It has been suggested that the increased tension of the vocal muscle at the times when it is at or near the extremes of its excursions to either side of its center of oscillation may occasion rhythmic stimuli to the sensory nerves of the muscles and that these, resulting in nervous impulses, thus may cause corresponding rhythmic contractions of the muscles. Thus a physiological element would be added to the otherwise purely mechanical process. For various reasons, however, the existence of such a physiological factor appears to be extremely doubtful.

The rate of vibration (corresponding to musical pitch) depends upon three factors: (1) the lengthening and shortening of the lips, yielding lower and higher notes respectively. If, as is said, the lips do not vary more than about a millimeter in length, this factor must play a relatively unimportant part in tone variation, except in so far as the lengthening of the lips may incidentally involve an increase

## THE SPEECH ORGANS 57

in the tension of the lips. (2) Variation in tension of the lips is clearly the chief factor in tone variation. It is effected by the contraction of *musculi vocales* and their antagonists. The muscles do a work analogous to that of a piano tuner. (3) The contraction of the vocal muscles causes them to bulge in the center. Since their two ends are attached to the thyroid and the arytenoid cartilages respectively and consequently vibrate but little, the greatest amplitude of vibration is found in the particles of tissue midway between the two ends. When by the contraction of the muscles a larger mass of tissue is accumulated in this bulging central part, the rate of vibration of the lips is thereby decreased and the note correspondingly lowered.

The loudness of the tones depends in general on the amplitude of the vibrations and to some extent also upon the form of the vibrations. The subjective element of attention (on the part of the listener) also conditions to a large extent the loudness of the sound. Thus far no method has been discovered for measuring this element with exactness, although the amplitude and rate of vibration of the resulting air waves can be determined with great exactness.

The vocal lips are employed not only to produce the musical tones above mentioned, but two other kinds of sound as well. (1) The whisper voice is produced by the friction of the air as it passes between the slightly separated median surfaces of the arytenoid cartilages. The lips themselves are generally supposed to be in a position of median contact during whispering. It is quite conceivable, however, that this contact in individual cases might be imperfect or even absent and yet not materially modify the quality of the whisper. Some laryngoscopic investigations appear to confirm the existence of this last-mentioned type of whisper. (2) The second kind of noise produced by the vocal lips is a brief single explosion caused by bringing the lips and arytenoid cartilages into median contact, increasing the air pressure in the chest cavity and then suddenly snapping the contact surfaces apart, thereby allowing a puff of air to escape. This sound is called the *glottal stop*. Though said to be uncommon in English, it occurs frequently in German and Arabic and is identical with the smooth breathing in ancient Greek. The term noise, in distinction from musical tones, is for convenience applied to these two varieties of sound. An accurate scientific distinction between musical tones and noise has not yet been discovered and so the sounds are judged mainly by their appeal to the ear.

In addition to these delicate adjustments of the vocal lips, the larynx is also capable of movement as a whole. On account of its firm attachment to the trachea, it is drawn down along with the trachea when the latter, in company with the lungs, descends slightly during the act of inspiration. Furthermore, the muscular and ligamentous attachments of the larynx to the hyoid bone, which is embedded in the root of the tongue, cause it to rise and fall with the rise and fall of the base of the tongue. These movements are important elements in the speech process not only by reason of the kinæsthetic sensations they generate, but also because they bring about changes in the shape of the resonance chambers and consequently change the form of the air waves. One of the first lessons that a student of singing is required to learn is to depress the larynx during phonation. The effect of this is to straighten and lengthen the throat passage from the larynx to the soft palate and thus allow direct, free, and untrammeled passage of the air as far as the palate, reflected from which vibrations issue from the mouth as clear, ringing notes.

*The Throat and Mouth.*—These are used both as resonance chambers and as noise-producing instruments. In

## THE SPEECH ORGANS 59

addition to the explosive sounds and whispering produced by the larynx, the mouth organs produce a louder whisper or hiss and the so-called trills.[4] The *affricates* consist of a stop followed by a *spirant*. Under this last term are included all the *fricatives* (frictional sounds), that is, breathings, murmurs, and hisses (also called *sibilants*). Just as the glottal stop is produced by springing the contact between the two vocal lips, so the mouth stops are made by contacts (1) between the two lips; (2) between one lip and the teeth; (3) between the tip, blade, or back of the tongue and the teeth, gums, palate (front, mid, or back), or back of the pharynx; (4) between the soft palate (velum) and the back wall of the pharynx; and (5) between the epiglottis and the back wall of the pharynx. If, instead of making a close contact, the two organs concerned approach each other only so close as to leave a narrow chink between them, the breath, forced rapidly through the opening, will produce a frictional sound which will be louder in proportion to any increase of the breath pressure and any narrowing of the opening, both of which cause a more rapid flow of the air. The murmur is a faint sigh-like sound produced by the slower flow of the air through a larger opening. It occurs as a concomitant of the *r* and *l* sounds, and in fact constitutes voiceless *l* and *r*. If the passage be still wider open, no audible frictional sound will occur and the mouth will serve merely as a resonance chamber.

In connection with all these sounds,[5] the vocal lips may either vibrate or remain at rest. In the former case we have *voiced consonants* (also called *sonants*), in the latter *voiceless* (*surds*). In most of them the lips may assume a more

---

[4] Of course, these last two kinds of sound can also be produced by the vocal lips, but this is done so rarely in speech that it seems better to describe them in connection with the mouth and nose sounds.

[5] Except, of course, the glottal stop.

or less puckered or rounded form which gives the air waves a special character.

The following are the principal sounds that result from the above movements:[6]

### A. Lip Sounds (Bilabials)

1. *Explosives:* *p*ut (voiceless),[7] *b*ut (voiced).
2. *Trills:* b*rrrr* (voiced exclamation). In Russian this means "whoa."
3. *Spirants:* *w*itch (pronounced either voiced or voiceless). The voiced form is only a faint b*oo*t attended by a faint hiss.
4. *Affricates:* *pfff* (voiceless; exclamation of contempt). The voiced affricate is easily made but does not occur in English, except when a final *b* is immediately followed by an initial *v*.

### B. Lip-Tooth Sounds (Labiodentals)

1. *Explosives:* none in English.
2. *Trills:* The apertures between the teeth make the trill difficult or impossible.
3. *Spirants:* *f*ull (voiceless), *v*oice (voiced).
4. *Affricates:* none in English.

### C. Tongue-Tip–Tooth Sounds

#### I. INTERDENTALS

The tongue extends between the two rows of teeth.

1. *Explosives:* *t*ick (voiceless), *d*ig (voiced), *t* and *d* made

---

[6] The student should not only read the following tabulation, but should repeatedly make each movement, giving attention to the kinæsthetic auditory, and tactual sensations and also noting in a concave mirror which will illuminate the mouth cavity, the character of the movements.

[7] Read: "voiceless *p*, as in *put*." The sound illustrated is italicized. The explosives are also called *plosives* and the voiceless sounds are also called *breathed*.

# THE SPEECH ORGANS

in this way occur frequently in the speech of Americans even though not of foreign extraction.
2. *Trills:* difficult or impossible.
3. *Spirants:* *th*ick (voiceless), *th*ose (voiced).
4. *Affricates:* grea*t th*ing (voiceless), le*d th*em (voiced).

### II. POSTDENTALS

The tip of the tongue touches the back surfaces of the teeth.

1. *Explosives:* *t*ick (voiceless), *d*ig (voiced), so pronounced by many Americans.
2. *Trills:* voiced and voiceless trilled *r* can be made by this contact, but it is difficult for most Americans and requires practice.
3. *Spirants:* *th*ick (voiceless), *th*ose (voiced). A common way of making these sounds in American English.
4. *Affricates:* grea*t th*ing (voiceless), le*d .th*em (voiced). More frequently Americans make these two sounds as a combination of (II) and (I), causing the tongue to slide forward and downward for the utterance of *th*.

### III. DENTAL-ALVEOLAR AND ALVEOLAR

In this case the tip of the tongue comes into contact or approximates both the backs of the teeth and the gums. This is the most common way in America of making *t*ick, *d*ig, *s*ing, be*ts*, and a*dz*e (or adds), although often in pronouncing these sounds the tongue touches or approximates only the gums, thus yielding Group IV.

### IV. ALVEOLARS [8]

These are represented by all the sounds mentioned under III.

1. *Trills:* trilled *r* is almost always made as an alveolar.

---

[8] Sometimes called *teethridge,* or less accurately, *postdentals.*

2. *Fricatives:* *l*, on the other hand, is more usually dental-alveolar; *s*in (voiceless), *z*ink (voiced).
3. *Affricates: ch*urch (voiceless), *j*udge (voiced).

### D. Tongue-Blade Sounds

As a considerable area of the upper surface of the tongue just behind the tip comes into contact in making these sounds, they mostly correspond to Group III above. The Russian "soft" *t*, *d*, and *s* are made in this way (explosives) as are usually English *th*ick and *th*ose. In *sh*all and a*z*ure the tongue moves through a range a little farther back, so that these sounds might in some cases be aptly called tongue-blade–alveolar–palatal.

The tip of the tongue may also be brought into contact or approximated to the front, mid, and back palate, although in this last case it is somewhat awkward to curl it back so far. The front and mid palatals resemble *t* in sound, while in the back palatals some resemblance to *k* and *g* may be detected. These palatal contacts are, of course, made more naturally with the top of the tongue, yielding Group E.

### E. Tongue-Top–Pre-, Mid-, and Back-Palatal Sounds

1. *Explosives:* These are our various *k* an*d* *g* sounds, ranging in the voiceless series from *k*eep to *c*argo and in the voiced group from *g*eese to G*h*andi.
2. *Trills:* none.
3. *Spirants:* The German *ch* sounds from i*ch* to au*ch* and the corresponding *g* sounds.
4. *Affricates:* These can be easily made but seldom occur in the modern European languages, except between adjacent words.

### F. Tongue-Back (Base)–Velar-Pharyngeal and Epiglottal-Pharyngeal Sounds

The explosives, spirants, affricates, and perhaps trills, voiced and voiceless, can be made in these regions of the mouth as in

## THE SPEECH ORGANS

the front part. It is unnecessary to describe them in detail. Some of them are of frequent occurrence in Arabic.

### G. Velar-Pharyngeal and Uvular Sounds

The word palate is used above as synonymous with hard palate. The velum is the soft palate. Velar-pharyngeal explosives, spirants, affricates, and even trills, voiced and voiceless, can be made by anyone with some practice. The exclamation *humph*, expressive of contempt, consists of this voiceless spirant followed instantly by the voiced one. The grunt which follows a heavy strain with the lips compressed also concludes with this spirant, but the explosion that precedes it is glottal. Uvular trilled *r* is the most widespread uvular sound. It is produced by laying the rear surface of the uvula along the median line of the top of the tongue and executing a rapid succession of explosions by causing it to flutter. This *r* is common in some parts of France.

With reference to the vowel sounds, most of the very recent serious study that has been devoted to them has been directed to the determination of the exact physical character of the air waves. Considerable progress has been made in this particular. Without doubt they are complex musical tones, composed of fundamental and overtones. As many as thirty of the latter have been calculated for individual tones. Most of them are very faint and not distinguishable to the ear as individual tones. One or two [9] of them in the case of each vowel has considerably greater amplitude than the others and consequently plays a larger part than the others in determining the tone quality of the whole. These tones are quite properly called the characteristic tones. There is a close correspondence between the frequency of vibration of these characteristic tones and the movements of the tongue and jaw during their pronuncia-

---

[9] One for each low vowel and two for each high vowel.

tion. The following table shows the vertical distances between the upper and lower left incisors of a woman pronouncing the following vowels:

| Vowel | Distance | Difference between Successive Distances |
|---|---|---|
|  | Inches | Inches |
| mach*i*ne | .100 |  |
| p*i*n | .125 | .025 |
| b*a*ke | .155 | .030 |
| b*e*t | .222 | .067 |
| f*a*t | .375 | .155 |
| r*o*te | .500 | .125 |
| c*o*rd | .650 | .150 |
| f*a*ther | .750 | .100 |

The third column gives the differences between the successive distances. They may be interpreted as confirming the resonance theory of vowels, in as much as they correspond to the variations in size of resonance chambers necessary for the reënforcement of tones of different frequency. The apparent discrepancies in the last four vowels are explained by the fact that the vertical distances give no indication of the increase in size of the mouth chamber brought about by the widening of the mouth chamber as in the pronunciation of *father*.[10] The action of the vocal lips in producing certain tones of definite frequencies is not necessary to the pronouncing of the vowels, as is proved by the existence of whispered vowels; but they do make possible a much louder and more distinct pronunciation.

The number of different consonant sounds mentioned and implied in the above enumeration is large, amounting to considerably more than a hundred. If we add to these the nasals and the variations caused by rounding, the total

---

[10] A complete table of the vowels would still further confirm this view.

THE SPEECH ORGANS 65

is still further augmented. The vowel sounds with their grosser variations add at least half a hundred more. However, if we enumerate the distinctly different sounds used in any one language, we shall find that they seldom exceed forty or fifty and are usually fewer than that. At least that is all the grammarians enumerate, and in this particular their judgment corresponds to that of the naïve man. That is as many as the naïve man is conscious of hearing. What are the reasons? In the first place, there is no need of more. The number of combinations and permutations of forty-five sounds taken by twos, threes, etc., up to twelve, even with the limitations imposed by anatomical and physiological conditions, runs into the millions, and no community has need of anything like so many words. In the second place, the attention of both speaker and listener is centered upon the thought that is being conveyed. He gives no special heed to the sounds as such, and he necessarily fails to hear or appreciate the great bulk of minor variations, such as that between dental, alveolar, and prepalatal *t*. Again, the front half of the tongue, because of its form and attachment, is capable of much greater ease and freedom of motion than the rear half and for purely biological reasons has become more highly differentiated both as a motor and sensory organ. Hence the fact that the back half of the tongue is much less frequently used as a noise-producing instrument. The part it plays in molding the shape of the mouth for resonance effects also is largely conditioned by the movements of the front half. Limitation of the number of vowels results from the peculiarity of the auditory apparatus, by virtue of which musical tones, the frequency of the vibrations of which are exact integral multiples of some lower tone, bear a striking resemblance to that lower tone. In other words, middle C hears a striking resemblance to the

C's above and below it. This very materially reduces the number of vowels easily distinguishable as sounds. Further detailed discussion of speech sounds is reserved for Chapter IX.

## REFERENCES

BETHE, A., and others.—*Handbuch der Normalen und Pathologischen Physiologie* (Berlin, Springer), Vol. 1 (sense organs, 1926), Vol. 2 (breathing, 1927), Vol. 8 (muscles, 1925), Vol. 10 (central nervous system, 1927).

GRAY, HENRY.—*Anatomy* (21st ed., Philadelphia, Lea & Febiger, 1924).

HERMANN, L.—*Handbuch der Physiologie* (Leipzig, Vogel, 1879-1881). This book contains an exceptionally full discussion of the physiology of speech.

LUCIANI, LUIGI.—*Human Physiology*, Trans. by Welby (London, Macmillan & Co., 1913-1921).

LUSCHKA, H. VON.—*Der Kehlkopf des Menschen* (Tübingen, Laupp, 1871).

PIERSOL, G. A.—*Human Anatomy* (Philadelphia, Lippincott, 1923).

SOBOTTA, J., and MCMURRICH, J. P.—*Atlas and Textbook of Human Anatomy*, 5 vols. (Philadelphia, Saunders, 1912-1921).

The earlier editions of W. H. Howell's *American Text-Book of Physiology* contain discussion of the physiology of speech, which is omitted from the later editions.

## CHAPTER IV

### THE SENSES INVOLVED IN SPEECH

Not only the muscular mechanisms directly involved in talking and writing must be understood, if we are to have a full knowledge of the physiological mechanisms of speech, but some knowledge of the sensations must also be assumed. Speech depends upon sensory as truly as upon motor organs. Two sorts of dependence may be recognized. Most obviously the function of speech is not accomplished until some one has been made to understand. Listening and reading are as much speech functions as are talking and writing. But even more closely related to speech, if not so obviously, is the control that sensory impressions exert upon each form of expression. Hearing is an important factor in the control of speech, and sight an equally important element in the control of writing. The deaf cannot speak without special training, and the blind can write only after special training and with difficulty. Equally, perhaps even more, important is the influence of sensations from within the body of muscle and tendon. These serve to guide the movements of the vocal organs and the hand in writing and also constitute one means of recalling words. We may now proceed to discuss these various senses in order of their importance for speech.

#### AUDITION

*The Physical Excitation.*—In each sense one can understand the problem if one considers it from three standpoints. Every sensation involves a knowledge of the physical excitation, of the sense organ, and of the sensation proper, the conscious accompaniment. The physical excitation for sound consists of longitudinal vibrations of the air excited by some oscillating body. Each particle of air affected may be pictured as oscillating back and forth in the line of propagation of the sound, receiving an impulse from particles on one side of it and transmitting them to those on the other, but not changing the point about which it oscillates. Vibrations vary in three ways: in rate of vibration, usually stated in number of vibrations per second; in amplitude of vibration, the distance which the particle vibrates from its point of rest; and in wave form or complexity. Upon the first of these characteristics depends the pitch of the sensation, upon the second depends its intensity, and upon the last its timbre or quality. The first difference is represented in speech by the difference between the voices of men and women. Man's voice vibrates ordinarily less rapidly, has a lower pitch than woman's. The second needs no illustration; loudness is familiar to all. The difference in timbre is probably represented by the differences between the sounds of the different vowels. *A* is distinguished from *o* by the differences in the overtones or partial tones that compose it. The piano tone is different from the violin's because of a difference in its composition. To understand how these purely physical differences are translated into the peculiarities of sensation, we turn to the sense organ, the mechanism of the ear.

*The Sense Organ: the Ear.*—The ear is a much more elaborate organ than would appear from the outside. In fact the external is probably of little importance for hearing. The essential parts of the organ are hidden well within the bones of the skull. The *external ear* is constituted by the ear we know and by the tube that leads into the head—the

## THE SENSES INVOLVED IN SPEECH

*external auditory meatus,* as it is known by the anatomist. The tube is closed at the inner end by a thin membrane, the *tympanic membrane.* This has a slightly conical shape with the convex side inward and is drawn diagonally across the tube with the lower side farther within than the upper. This membrane is made of fibers that run in several directions, and is rather loose, so that it has no marked tone of its own and, thus, no tone that might be taken up in preference to the others and be heard more easily or more loudly. The chamber behind the drum is of irregular shape, rather higher than it is long or wide. It is connected with the throat by a tube, the *Eustachian,* that opens when one swallows and thus keeps the pressure inside the middle ear the same as that of the atmosphere on the outside (see Fig. 9).

The portions of the *middle ear* that are directly concerned in hearing are the three small bones that bridge the cavity from the tympanum to the oval window, the entrance to the inner ear. These in order are the *malleus,* the *incus,* and the *stapes.* The hammer is attached by its handle to the membrane of the drum and is suspended by a short ligament attached to its head from the top of the cavity of the middle ear. The head is also closely connected with the incus by a loose joint with ratchet-like teeth on the surfaces of the joint. These teeth are assumed to be so adjusted that the hammer forces the anvil in with it on its inward swing but becomes detached on the outward in such a way that a large outward movement cannot rupture the delicate oval window. The action is very much like the ratchet of a watch in winding. The stirrup is connected by a ligament with the process of the incus, and the oval foot of the stirrup forms part of the oval window. The joint is made watertight by a delicate membrane. The chain of bones acts practically as a single lever. The fulcrum is the ligament attached to the hammer head, the short arm is the handle of the hammer, and the long arm is constituted by the process of the anvil and the stirrup. Both arms are bent downward. The long arm is about one and a half times the length of the short. When an air wave drives the membrane

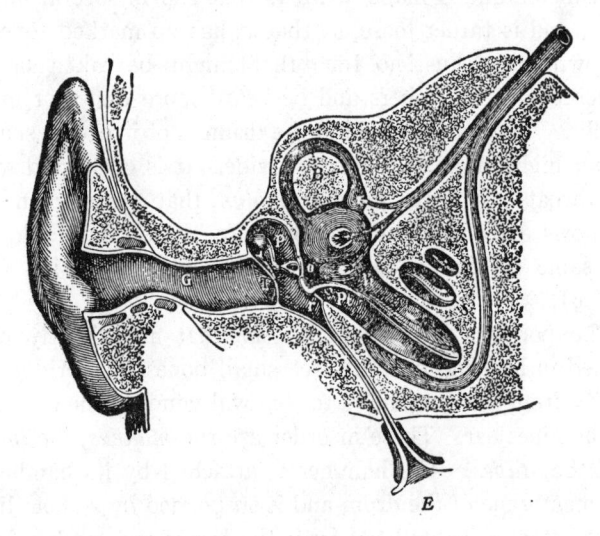

FIG. 9.—SEMIDIAGRAMMATIC SECTION THROUGH THE RIGHT EAR (*Czermak*).

*G*, external auditory meatus; *T*, membrana tympani; *P*, tympanic cavity; *o*, fenestra ovalis; *r*, fenestra rotunda; *B*, semicircular canal; *S*, cochlea; *Vt*, scala vestibuli; *Pt*, scala tympani; *E*, Eustachian tube. From W. H. Howell, *A Text-Book of Physiology* (W. B. Saunders Co., 1905).

of the drum inward, the chain of bones swings on the ligament and presses the stirrup into the middle ear. When there is a rarefaction in the air, the drum head projects and permits the bones to swing back. By virtue of the difference in the length of the arms and the relative size of the two membranes, Helmholtz computed that the movements

## THE SENSES INVOLVED IN SPEECH 71

in the air are reduced in amplitude by ten and multiplied in intensity by ten when they reach the oval window.

The *inner ear* is the region in which the mechanical vibration is transformed into nervous impulse. It, too, is an irregular-shaped hollow in the bone, but filled with lymph instead of air. The auditory part of the inner ear, the *cochlea* is, as its name implies, shaped like a snail shell. It may be best understood if regarded as a tube that has been wound two and a half times upon itself. This tube is divided down the middle by a partition partly made up of a ridge of bone and partly of membrane, the *basilar membrane*. The upper half of the tube that results from this division is connected with the oval window and is known as the *scala vestibuli*. The other, the *scala tympani*, is closed at its lower end by the round window, a membrane that separates the inner ear from the middle ear. As a mechanical system the oval window transmits its vibrations to the fluid of the inner ear. These pass to the top of the scala vestibuli, then down the scala tympani to the round window. The round window has the function of making the vibration possible. Were the cochlea closed at the lower end by bone, the oval window and the liquid of the inner ear could not be made to vibrate. As it is, the liquid moves back and forth very much as would a steel bar freely suspended but restrained at its end by delicate membranes.

*The Sensation.*—But granted that the vibrations of the air are transformed into vibrations of the liquid of the inner ear, there still remains the question of the way in which these waves may affect the nerve of hearing. There is no doubt that the change takes place in the structures that lie upon the basilar membrane. It will be seen from the diagram that the nerve of hearing comes through the ridge of bone and ends in the neighborhood of hair cells on the basilar membrane. Several structures have been suggested as the true organ of hearing. Helmholtz fixed upon the fibers of the basilar membrane. The membrane has a width that varies from .40 millimeter at the upper end to about .176 millimeter at the lower, according to Keith's measurements. It is composed of fibers that stretch across from the bone to the opposite wall of the cochlea, some

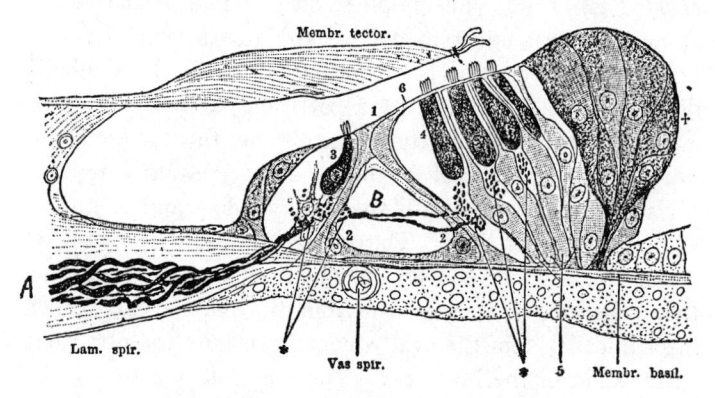

FIG. 10.—CROSS-SECTION OF THE ORGAN OF CORTI, SHOWING NERVE ENDINGS IN THE COCHLEA (MODIFIED FROM MERKEL-HENLE, *Anatomie*).

The fibers (*A*) are seen emerging from the lamina spiralis, some terminating synaptically about the inner hair cells, (3), and the remainder crossing the tunnel of Corti (*B*) to terminate around the outer hair cells (6). The black dots (*) represent cross-sections of the convolutions of the nerve fibers. From Knight Dunlap, *An Outline of Psychobiology* (Johns Hopkins Press, 1914).

15,000 in all. These are interwoven with relatively loose connective tissue to form a continuous membrane. Helmholtz thought that each fiber was tuned to a particular note, the long ones to the bass notes, the shorter to the treble, and that each audible tone had its corresponding fiber. The vibration was communicated by the fibers to the hair cells and from them to the auditory nerve. This theory has recently been severely criticized on the ground

## THE SENSES INVOLVED IN SPEECH 73

that the fibers are too rigidly connected transversely to vibrate singly, if they would vibrate at all to such delicate impulses as those produced by sound waves in the surrounding liquid.

Other structures that have been selected as the receptors of the vibration are the hairs themselves, the rods of Corti, and the tectorial membrane. The hairs need no description. The *rods of Corti* are delicate structures seated on the basilar membrane that unite to constitute the sides of an arch and are jointed at the top. Helmholtz at first thought they might be the organs of hearing, but rejected that assumption on account of their small number, only three thousand as opposed to some eleven thousand distinguishable tones. No particular function is now assigned to them in spite of the perfection of their structure, which a teleologist would insist must have been given for a purpose. Above this whole series of structures is a delicate membrane, called the *tectorial membrane,* that stretches well into the liquid. Hardesty has suggested that this was joined to the walls of the cochlea, was delicate enough to vibrate with the liquid, and may communicate its vibration to the hairs by contact.

At least three groups of theories in addition to the Helmholtz theory are current as to the way hearing may take place. One like Helmholtz's would make the resonance of a suitably tuned organ the basis of the hearing. To each tone would respond some one of these structures. A second, known as the telephone theory, suggested by Wrightson among others, makes some one structure respond to all tones and makes the quality of the tone depend upon the rate of its vibration. The structure that vibrates has been found in the membrane, in the hairs, and in the tectorial membrane. A third group, which is represented by the theory of Ewald, would make the tone depend upon the way in which different parts of the basilar membrane vibrate in relation to each other. Ewald photographed a thin rubber membrane of the shape and size of the membrane when it was affected by sounds and found that each pitch gave a different picture. He assumed from this that the membrane might be similarly affected and the stimulation of the nerves reflect this picture. Max Meyer assumes that the pitch of the tone depends upon the rate of vibration of the membrane but explains different subsidiary phenomena by the distance the vibration extends up the cochlea.

An evaluation of the different theories is at present very difficult. Three facts seem to limit the possibilities of explanation. First, experiments and pathology indicate that different tones have a different position on the cochlea. Thus, destroying the upper end of the cochlea makes a dog deaf in low tones; destroying the lower end makes him deaf to high tones. Occasionally, individuals are found in whom the long and short fibers of the basilar membrane and the long and short elements of the neighboring structures are lacking. Von Bezold has demonstrated in individuals with tone islands, that is, who are deaf to part of the scale, that there are injuries of those areas of the basilar membrane and other structures that would correspond approximately to those portions of the scale, if each part of the cochlea heard a different note. Long-continued stimulation of the ear by a single tone also causes degeneration in a limited region on the cochlea. These observations have been so often confirmed that they may be accepted as assured. On the other hand, however, there seems agreement on the part of those who have made anatomical examination of the basilar membrane, that it is too rigid to vibrate and that certainly the separate fibers are too closely connected to permit them to vibrate singly. The Helmholtz theory cannot, therefore, be accepted as it stands. But against the telephone theory, again, it may be urged that it is hard to conceive on the basis of what we know of the time relations of other nervous activities how one could distinguish a difference of only one vibration in a thousand per second in the oscillation of any structure.

Hartridge, in 1921, and Bannister, in 1926, have discovered new phenomena which cannot be readily explained unless one assumes a resonance hypothesis and have also given new interpretations of the response of the auditory mechanism which remove most of the objections that have been raised to the theory. On the whole, it seems to the writer that the resonance hypothesis offers the most satisfactory explanation that we have at present. Development of new theories is likely to take the form of modifications of that theory. We may, then, tentatively assume the resonance hypothesis as the basis of our discussion, where we need to assume any theory at all.

*Hearing and the Phenomena of Speech.*—On this theory we may correlate the facts of hearing with the structures of the ear and regard their functions as dependent upon the part of the ear that is stimulated—high notes excite the lower part of the cochlea, low notes the upper portion. The range of hearing depends upon the number of different structures present. This range differs for different animals. For man it varies from somewhere in the neighborhood of 16 double vibrations per second to *circa* 25,000. This is of some importance for the understanding of the phenomena of speech, since each of the vowels seems to have certain dominant pitches that are characteristic. When an individual hears certain parts of the scale and not others, he may lack those pitches which are essential to appreciating vocal sounds; he may hear the fundamental tone, but not the higher determinants of vowels and so not be able to understand speech. These characteristic qualities lie mainly between 260 and 4,000 double vibrations. The intensity of the sound depends upon the amplitude of vibration of the structure, upon the energy which is imparted to it and which it in turn imparts to the nerve of hearing. The timbre of the tone again depends upon the number and character of the resonant structures affected. Each fundamental tone affects a different organ as does each overtone. These combine their effects in brain and mind to produce a single note. The fusion is not complete, since by proper attention the elements may be distinguished; but in ordinary listening we are not conscious of anything more than the quality of the note.

Very important for the psychology of language is the influence of these partial tones in giving the peculiar character to the different vowels. All are agreed that the quality of the vowel depends upon the presence of partial tones or added tones. One may speak or sing each of the vowels at the same pitch, say middle C of 256 double vibrations, and give the peculiar quality by adding different tones or increasing the emphasis upon certain of the components. There is a difference of opinion among the authorities as to whether the vowel sound is made in one way or the other.

Helmholtz first propounded the theory that the quality of the vowel was due to the fact that the chamber of the mouth and in minor degree of the nose served as a resonance chamber which could be made to take a size that would respond to different overtones in the sound given off by the vocal cords and so would make that one stronger and more dominant. Hermann immediately suggested that, instead of merely emphasizing through resonance an overtone that was present in the tone from the vocal cord, the chamber of the mouth was made to emit a sound directly by the air that was blown through it. It was made to sound in much the same way that a bottle is made to speak, by blow-ing across its mouth. The tone varies with the size of the bottle. Similarly, the vowel is made by changing the mouth cavity. Hermann called these tones that are produced independently *formants* and the term is still used. Recently three men have conducted experiments on the problem that have led to slightly conflicting, partly harmonious results. The first were obtained by Koehler by listening to pure tones and comparing them with the vowel sounds. He and his observers agreed that each vowel and certain of the consonants had a characteristic tone and the vowels might be arranged in a series an octave apart, beginning with *m* at 130, followed by *u* or the *oo* in English at 260, *o* at 512, *a* (broad as in *father*) at 1,024, *e* (long *a* in English) at 2,080, *i* (English long *e*) at 4,100, and the vowel-like terminations of *s*, *f*, and *ch* at successively higher octaves.

Two more recent workers, Dayton C. Miller [1] in America and Karl Stumpf [2] of Berlin, have repeated experiments on this topic but confirm Koehler's results in part only. Miller photographed the waves of vowels by a special apparatus, while Stumpf elaborated Koehler's method. The results of the methods harmonize pretty closely. Both found that certain vowels had two formants rather than one, and that there was a considerable range of the strongest component of the vowel that varied with different voices. The *oo* sound (German *u*) Miller found to have one formant at 325; Stumpf two, one at 384 ($g^1$), the other at 676 ($f^2$). Long *o* had according to Miller one formant at 461; according to Stumpf, one at 384 ($g^1$). Broad *a* as in *father* was assigned a single formant by both; by Miller from 910 to 1,080, by Stumpf 768 ($g^2$). Both again gave long *a* as

---

[1] Dayton C. Miller, *The Science of Musical Sounds* (New York, Macmillan, 1916), Lecture vii.
[2] Karl Stumpf, *Sprachlaute* (Berlin, Springer, 1926), p. 179, *et passim*.

## 78   THE PSYCHOLOGY OF LANGUAGE

in *fate* (German *e*) two; Miller 498 and 2,461; Stumpf a minor one at 384, a stronger at 2,304 (d⁴). Miller assigned two to *ee* as in *meet* (German *i*), 308 and 3,100; while Stumpf found three for it, subordinate ones at 384 (g¹) and 2,456 (e⁴) and a dominant of 3,840 (b⁴).

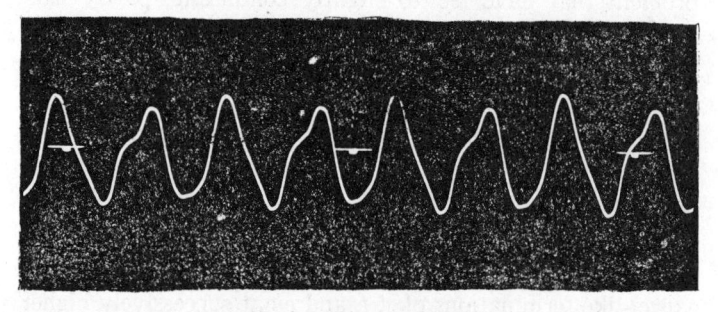

The vowel *oo* as in "room"

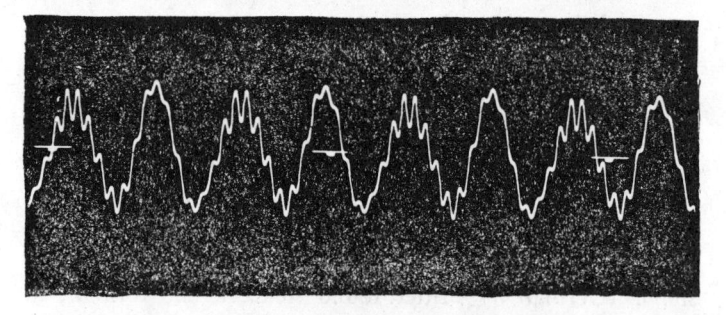

The vowel *ee* as in "bee"

FIG. 11.—PICTURES OF VOWEL SOUNDS.
From R. M. Ogden, *Hearing* (Harcourt, Brace & Co., 1924).

These results are on the whole very similar. The similarity is the more remarkable when we consider that each author states that the formant is a band rather than a single tone and the vibration rate given marks merely

# THE SENSES INVOLVED IN SPEECH

the strongest point in the complex. Where different values are given the bands frequently overlap. Stumpf accepts an intermediate position between Helmholtz and Hermann, in that he points out that the formants all are overtones in the fundamental note, and in consequence are all in harmony with one another, and so unite in consonances. At the same time he believes that the notes are produced in the mouth cavity and are not mere reenforcements of the overtones. For this reason it is possible to produce the vowel sounds in whispering when the vocal cords are not sounding.

### VISION

*The Physical Excitation.*—Vision offers the same three phases that were discussed in hearing. To understand it, we must appreciate how physical excitation, sense organ, and sensation are related. Light is due to vibrations of ether that take place in a line perpendicular to the direction of propagation. These vary, also, in rate, in amplitude, and in the way different rates are compounded. Color corresponds to the rate, brightness to the amplitude, and saturation and some elements of hue to the way in which different vibrations are compounded or superimposed upon each other. White or gray is due to all wave lengths combined in certain proportions; purple to combinations of red and blue; browns and pinks, etc., to compounds of red with other colors of slight amplitude, or with great amplitudes. It is not so easy to state the physical accompaniments of sensation qualities as it is for tones, since most visual sensations may be produced in more than one way. This among other facts indicates that the color depends rather upon the way the retina is stimulated than upon the nature of the external stimulus.

*The Sense Organ: the Eye.*—The eye is a sphere approximately an inch (23 millimeters) in diameter, that is hung loosely in its socket, and turned by three pairs of muscles. The eyeball is kept in place by a membrane behind it, by fatty tissue and by loose connective tissue. The lids in front are joined to its outer surface by the *conjunctiva*, a thin membrane that serves in part to keep foreign bodies out of the socket. The *socket* is a cone-shaped hollow in the skull. The *optic nerve* enters the socket at its apex and extends forward to the eyeball that nearly fills the front portion. The muscles that turn the eye are, with one exception, attached to the apex of the socket about the entrance of the optic nerve and run forward to the eyeball. The muscles are the external and internal, the superior and inferior rectus muscles, and the superior and inferior oblique. Of these, the *recti muscles* turn the eyes directly to the right or left, up or down, in the direction indicated by the name, and run directly to the forward portion of the eyeball. The *oblique muscles* are attached to the eyeball behind the center of rotation and in consequence turn the eye in the direction opposed to that which is indicated by the name. They pull the back portion of the eye up or down, which moves the front portion down or up. The oblique muscles, too, do not pull from the apex of the socket as the others do, but the superior runs forward from the apex to the upper nasal side of the socket and there passes through a loop of cartilage and turns back to its point of attachment to the eyeball. The inferior rectus has its point of attachment on the lower nasal rim of the socket and runs directly back to its point of attachment on the eyeball. It serves to pull the eye up and out. Horizontal motion may be given to the eye by the external and internal recti alone; vertical movement, only by a combination of superior and inferior recti with the oblique muscles. Horizontal movements are

# THE SENSES INVOLVED IN SPEECH

less fatiguing and more accurately estimated than are vertical ones. By means of these muscles the eye is turning constantly from point to point. It is seldom at rest for any long period. It shifts constantly with attention and is continually exploring things in front of it.

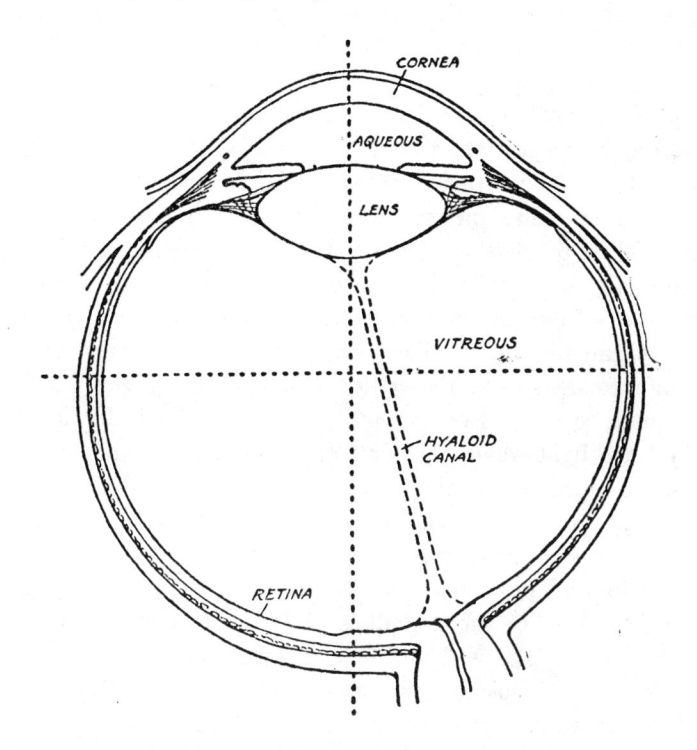

Fig. 12.—Transverse section through equator of left eye seen from above.

From E. H. Starling, *Physiology* (Messrs. J. & A. Churchill, 1920).

The eyeball itself is composed of three coats and a mass of liquids that fill it and keep it distended. The outer of these, the *sclerotic*, is of tough fibrous tissue. In front it bulges somewhat and becomes transparent. This constitutes the *cornea*, through which the rays of light enter. The coat next within, the *choroid*, is largely composed of blood vessels that serve to nourish the eye, although it also contains some muscle tissue and nerves. The interior portion of this coat is not attached to the cornea but draws across the interior chamber to form the *iris*, which gives the characteristic color to the eye with its pigment. The *pupil* is an opening in the iris through which light enters. The innermost coat is the *retina*. This is nervous in structure; there the light waves are transformed into nervous impulses. The retina is composed of three layers of neurones or modified nerve tissue. The outermost of these is the layer of *rods* and *cones*, the actual organs of sight. Next are the so-called bi-polar cells that receive the nervous impulses from the rods and cones and transmit them to the large ganglion cells. The axones of these outermost cells unite to constitute the optic nerve and carry the visual impulse to the central nervous system. It should be noted that the light wave must first pass through the outer coats of the retina before they can excite the rods and start the seeing process. Between the retina and the sclerotic coat is a layer of pigment cells that serves to absorb errant rays of light and probably subserves other functions in seeing.

The center of the eyeball is divided into two chambers, the anterior filled with the aqueous humor and the posterior with the vitreous humor; between is the *crystalline lens*. These together with the cornea constitute the optical system of the eye and serve to bring the image of objects seen to a proper focus upon the retina. The rays of light are refracted three times: at the surface of the cornea, and at the anterior and posterior surfaces of the lens. The total effect is to bring the rays of light to a focus and to reproduce upon the retina an image that would be produced if the rays of light from each point of the object were to cross at

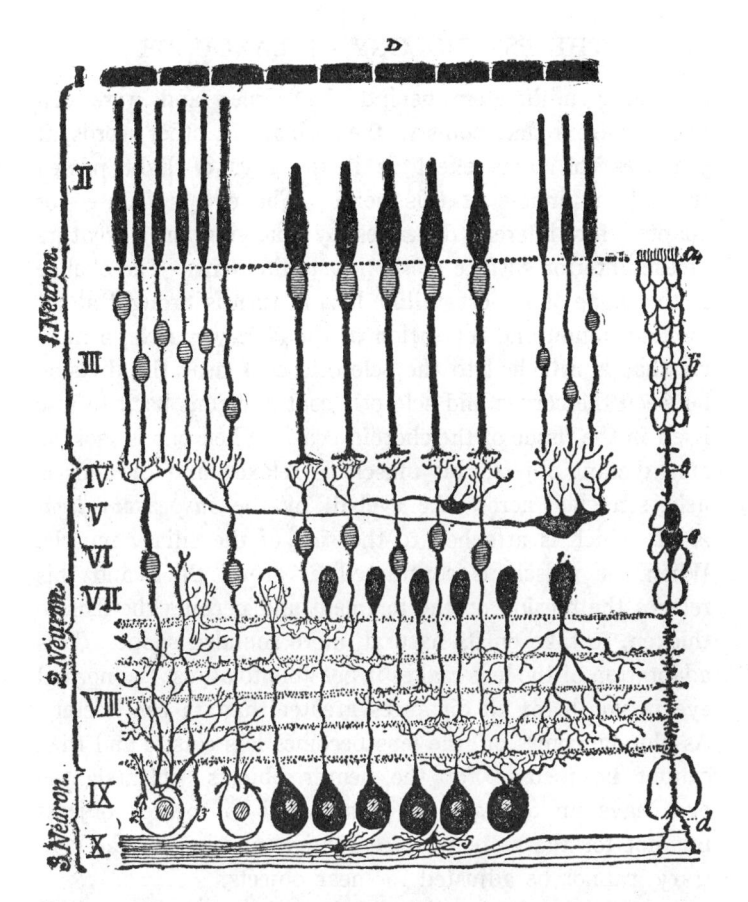

FIG. 13.—SCHEMATIC REPRESENTATION OF THE HUMAN RETINA.

The rods and cones lie in layers II and III. The rods, as are shown on the left, send impulses to the brain through fibers common to several of them. The cones, however, make connection with the brain, each through a separate fiber. From W. H. Howell, *A Text-Book of Physiology* (W. B. Saunders Co., 1921).

a point 7 millimeters behind the cornea and were distributed from that point to the retina. In other words, it produces the same effect as if the rays of light passed through a pinhole at this point. The eye is focused or adapted for different distances by changing the curvature of the anterior surface of the crystalline lens. The change in the shape of the crystalline lens in turn is brought about by contraction and relaxation of the *ciliary muscle,* a muscle that is attached to the sclerotic coat near the division between the cornea and sclerotic coat and runs back to lose itself in the tissue of the choroid coat. When one is looking at a distant object, this muscle is relaxed and the lens is held stretched across the eyeball by the *suspensory ligament,* which is attached to the side of the ciliary muscle. When the muscle is contracted, it grows thick and this relaxes the tension on the ligament and permits the lens to thicken, to take on its natural, more rounded shape. This adaptation of the lens makes it possible to adjust the normal eye in youth for all distances greater than 13 centimeters. As old age comes on, the lens becomes less elastic and then cannot be focused for the nearer objects. Nearsighted eyes have an optical system adjusted for nearer objects but not for the more remote; farsighted eyes, on the contrary, cannot be adjusted for near objects.

As the retina is the essential part of the eye for reading, it may deserve a little more description. The rods and cones are the sensitive elements. They are somewhat different in shape, the rods are longer and thinner and have a smaller diameter in the outer section than at the base, while the cones are approximately the same diameter until near the apex. The rods are .040-.060 millimeter long and .002-.004 millimeter thick. The cones are .020-.040 millimeter long and .004-.006 millimeter thick. The distribution of the two is somewhat irregular. There are only cones in

# THE SENSES INVOLVED IN SPEECH 85

the fovea in the middle of the retina and only rods at the periphery. The cones gradually diminish in frequency from the fovea outward.

Two areas of the retina may be described in more detail. The first is the point of entrance of the optic nerve. Here there are only nerve fibers with no rods or cones. In consequence no visual sensations are aroused here; it is the blind spot. The second and more important is the fovea, mentioned above. It is especially well developed and constitutes the point of clearest vision. Two factors apparently contribute to make it effective. First, the cones which here replace the rods altogether are much thinner and so can be packed more closely. They are of about the dimensions of the rods in other parts of the retina, .040-.060 millimeter long and .002-.004 millimeter in diameter. Second, the other elements of the retina are in the fovea not directly between the light and the cones; the fibers and cells are drawn to one side here. In consequence, not so much light is absorbed by the nervous elements and the blood vessels. About the fovea and in it is a yellow pigment which has led to giving this the name, *yellow spot*. This region is that most used in vision and serves as a point of reference for the rest of the retina. Whenever any object attracts attention, the eye is at once turned so that its image falls upon the yellow spot. In reading, the fovea is moved along the line to take in the different letters.

*The Sensation.*—The organs that receive the impressions are the rods and cones. Some sort of chemical process is started in them by the light waves. Study of the phenomena of vision indicates that there are six different sorts of processes that may be aroused in the cones: four of these correspond to colors, red, yellow, green, and blue, and two to the brightnesses ranging from black through gray to white. From these simple processes all the others are compounded. These processes are retinal or physiological processes and have no direct relation to the wave lengths. Thus pure bluish green spectral color arouses two physiological processes, the blue process and the green process, and these combine to constitute the blue-green color. A mixture of a pure green light with a pure blue light may produce the same effect. The evidence that has led to the assumption of these four primary physiological processes, and many of the phenomena that are explained by them, do not concern us here, since reading primarily involves black and white alone. The appreciation of brightnesses is assigned to a separate organ or is given two processes, since each of the pairs of processes is assumed to involve but one organ, on the basis of a number of important facts. It is known that certain people who are blind to colors can, nevertheless, see black, white, and gray. In the dark, this is true for every one. It is further generally assumed that there are two sorts of organs for grays, one which is used in the twilight, the other in bright daylight. Twilight vision is assigned to the rods, daylight to the cones. No difference ordinarily can be noticed between the qualities of the grays however. The degree of brightness varies with the intensity of the light. In faint light, brightness depends also upon the rate of adaptation of the retina. After excluding light from the eyes for an hour, it has been found that the retina is one thousand times as sensitive as in the light-adapted eye. This is assumed to be due to the presence of the visual purple, a chemical substance that is found in the rods. In an animal killed after some time in the dark the retina is purple; when killed in daylight the retina is yellow in color.

*Reading and the Phenomena of Vision.*—More important for us than the qualitative aspects of vision are the facts of spatial discrimination by the eye. Legibility of letters depends upon the distance that separates the lines physically

# THE SENSES INVOLVED IN SPEECH

and, physiologically, upon the distance between two lines that the eye may discriminate. Experiments show that two ordinary lines or dots can be seen as two when they are separated by a distance of .004-.006 millimeter on the retina. Letters, then, might have lines about .06 millimeter apart and still be distinguished at 25 centimeters. At 50 centimeters for the normal eye it would require a separation of the lines by about .12 millimeter, and a proportionate increase is required for greater distances. This marks the point where reading would be just possible, and much greater distances are used in practice. It is interesting to note that the distance that separates the centers of two cones in the fovea is from .002-.004 millimeter. This may not limit the acuteness of vision, however, as under favorable circumstances, divergence from continuity in a straight line that amounts to only .001 millimeter can be noted.

These distances hold only for favorable conditions of illumination. In faint light the distances must be much increased, and also for very bright light. For faint light this may be due to the fact that the rods are the visual organ, and rods are lacking in the fovea, the point of clearest vision. The rods, too, have much less accurate discrimination than the cones. It is also true that all differences are discriminated more easily in the middle range of intensities. This is one phase of the phenomenon known as the upper and lower deviation from Weber's law. Weber's law itself states that a certain percentage of the total stimulus may be distinguished. For light this proportion is $\frac{1}{100}$. This means that two grays are just noticeably different when one reflects 100, the other 101 units, or when one reflects 200, the other 202 units. In a very bright light this difference must be very much greater, if it is to be perceived. The fact that it is impossible to read in very dark rooms and difficult to read in the bright sunlight may be regarded as belonging to the same general group of phenomena. The indistinctness in very bright light may be explained by assuming that there is a degree of excitation beyond which the sense organ cannot easily respond. The indistinctness in faint light may be referred to the fact that there is always some excitation of the retina that blurs the stimulation from the printed page by increasing the total activation to the point where the difference between page and print is below the just noticeable difference. This is in addition to the greater separation of the rods on the retina.

Another point that is of interest in connection with reading is the character of the illumination. The pupil acts very much as a diaphragm on a camera. When the light is strong, the pupil narrows reflexly; when faint, it widens. The small pupil gives better definition, but this may be counteracted by excluding so much of the light that differences cannot be clearly made out. It has been found that the reaction of the pupil depends upon the maximum illumination of any point rather than upon the average illumination. A single bright light in any part of the field, then, may close the pupil to the point that not sufficient light will enter from the page, if the illumination there be less than sufficient to make accurate reading possible. To avoid this, rooms should be evenly lighted, if possible by diffuse light.

The values given for the distance that must separate the lines if the letters are to be read hold, too, only for the center of the retina, the fovea. The acuity of vision diminishes very rapidly as one gets farther away from that point. At 5 degrees from the center the acuity is one-fourth as great as at the center, while at 35 degrees it has diminished to one-hundredth. Letters that can be seen distinctly when directly fixated cannot be distinguished when one

## THE SENSES INVOLVED IN SPEECH 89

looks a little to the side. This fact plays some part in determining the amount that may be read at one glance, although other factors compensate for it in some degree.

On the whole, then, the sensory factors that influence reading are to be found in the closeness with which cones and rods are placed upon the retina, upon the relative intensities of the black and white surfaces that constitute the letters, and upon the conditions of illumination. These in turn depend upon the part of the retina that is stimulated; upon whether the discrimination is by rods or cones, the cones discriminating more accurately than the rods; and upon whether the adaptation of the eye is to an evenly lighted surface or to an irregularly lighted one. These factors are also interrelated. Whether rods or cones are used in the discrimination of a letter depends upon the intensity of the light; and if the light is so faint that the cones are not excited, the fovea cannot be used in the discrimination, since there are no rods in the fovea. It should be added that the more important factors in reading are the associative and other mental operations that must be considered in a later chapter.

We may say just a word about the kinæsthetic sensations or the sensations from the muscles and other parts of the moving organ that give information of the position of the parts and extent of the movement. The organ for these sensations is provided by sense endings between the fibers of the muscles and tendons. When the muscle fibers contract, they thicken and exert a cross pressure upon the sensory ends. The degree of pressure indicates the amount of contraction, and the distribution of the contraction through different muscles and sets of muscles gives the awareness of the position of the member as a whole. The position of the tongue, for example, is known from the amount of sensation received and the way those sensations are distributed in the body of the tongue. The other movements that are involved in speech are appreciated in the same way. One knows what word is spoken by its feeling in the throat, and one may think of a word in terms of these kinæsthetic impressions. It is the importance of these sensations in appreciation of speech that justifies mention of them in this connection.

## REFERENCES

HARTRIDGE, H.—"A Vindication of the Resonance Hypothesis of Audition," *British Journal of Psychology,* Vol. 12 (1921), pp. 142-146.
HELMHOLTZ, H. L. F.—*Sensations of Tone,* Trans. by Havelock Ellis (New York, Longmans, Green, 1912).
———, *Physiological Optics* (Optical Society of America, 1924).
OGDEN, R. M.—*Hearing* (New York, Harcourt, Brace, 1924).
PILLSBURY, W. B.—*Fundamentals of Psychology* (New York, Macmillan, 1922), Chaps. IV, V and VI.

# CHAPTER V

### MENTAL PROCESSES IN SPEECH

THE real problems of language center about the ways in which the *processes* that we have been considering act. If we may state the matter metaphorically, we have been dealing up to this point with mechanisms that are used when we speak. We have considered the sounding apparatus by which words are produced: the sense organs through which sounds are heard, words are read, and by which we appreciate the sounds as they are made by the speaker; and the nervous system that receives impressions from these sense organs and initiates the movements that are made by the speech organs in making the sounds. We must now deal with the way in which these mechanisms are used and discover the laws that determine the responses and the effect that they have upon the listener or reader. We must seek to answer the questions as to why the brain sends a stimulus to the muscles that contract to produce the spoken sounds, why the orator thinks of the words that sway an audience, and why the remark of a friend evokes just the response that it does. For an answer to such questions we must turn from the anatomy and physiology of language to the more specifically psychological problems. For after all, language is primarily a mental phenomenon and on its practical side one of the most important mental phenomena.

### THE PROBLEMS OF THE PSYCHOLOGIST

For the psychologist, the problem of language has two aspects. He is interested to see how the ordinary psychological laws find expression in language and also to determine the effects that words and language in general exert upon the purely mental phenomena. The first of these problems may be approached on the assumption that man thinks first and then expresses his thought in words, by some sort of translation. To understand this, it is necessary to know how words present themselves in the consciousness of the individual, how they are related to ideas of another type than the verbal, how the ideas originate and how they arouse the words as images, how the movements of speech are evoked by these ideas, and finally how the listener or reader translates the words that he hears or the words that he sees into thoughts of his own. Speech has its origin in the mind of the speaker or writer, and the process of communication is completed only when the word uttered or spoken arouses an idea in the listener or reader.

We must not assume, however, that thought and the word are altogether distinct. As will be seen as we go farther, words are an essential element in the development of thought, and in many cases thought and the word are identical. Much of thinking cannot be understood at all unless we consider language. In much of thinking, thought does not precede words, but thinking is in words; the two are simultaneous. We must consider the influence of words on thought as well as of thought on words. For our discussions in this chapter, it will be simpler to speak as if thought and language were distinct, with the warning that the assumption is only provisional. We can then discuss the relation of thought and language in detail in a later chapter.

### THE PHYSICAL BASIS OF MEMORY

Any explanation of a mental process or of speech must take into consideration the fact that experiences in some

## MENTAL PROCESSES IN SPEECH

way leave an effect upon the individual and tend to have that effect revived after the passage of time. All now assume that this retention is due to some lasting effect upon the nervous system, and the revival is an expression of the tendency to respond in a certain way that was induced by the earlier action. The law of habit and the law of memory or persistence and revival of effects are in large part identical.

On the action side, a movement once made in response to a given stimulus tends to be repeated whenever that stimulus presents itself and, when repeated frequently enough, becomes the invariable consequent of that stimulation. This is regarded as due to a change wrought in the nervous system by the connecting of sensory and motor neurones in the brain. In the same way, when two nerve tracts or groups of neurones in sensory areas are simultaneously aroused, they tend to become connected in such a way that when one of the two is excited at a later time the other is also stimulated. What persists in memory and imagination is this after effect of the earlier excitation. It is assumed that when two groups of neurones, whether near or remote in the cortex, are stimulated in close succession, the synapses [1] between them become permanently more open so that the excitation of either group is likely to call the other group into action. The connection between the two groups increases with the frequency with which they act together and with the intensity of each at the time of the original excitation, and decreases with the lapse of time after the original connection. All rote learning consists in repeating the selection to be learned until each word or phrase serves to suggest the one that immediately follows it. Two objects frequently seen together are connected also, and when one appears, it at once calls up the other.

---
[1] See p. 26.

## 94    THE PSYCHOLOGY OF LANGUAGE

These connections are assumed to be due to changes in the connections between nerve elements. It is generally assumed that when the two groups of neurones are active at the same time, the resistance of the synapses between them becomes reduced, and that the reduction in resistance results in the transfer of the impression from either when it is aroused to the other group.

The basis of all association on this assumption would be found in the physical changes induced in the nervous system by the spread of impulses. This change is increased with each repetition of the two neurones and, when once formed, persists in gradually diminishing force for a long time. It might even be asserted that the physical basis of all memory is to be found in these changes induced in the synapses by the simultaneous action of the neurones concerned. Certain it is that, if memories are dispositions left in the neurones themselves, they could not be aroused except through the synapses. Since the synapses are required for making the connections and the bond becomes stronger at each repetition, it has been thought simplest to assign the conscious process as well as the association to the synapses. All memories and processes of imagination, all the elements of revived experiences, in fact, are assigned to these changes in the synapses, changes in the bonds between neurones. Every experience, then, must be connected with some other experience; it is associated by these nervous bonds with the experiences that precede and that succeed it and with the other simultaneous experiences of which it forms a part. Not only this, but experiments have shown that there is a bond of union between experiences that are separated from one another by several intervening conscious processes; these associations, however, grow weaker the farther apart the two experiences connected lie in the temporal series. Through these bonds all knowledge is bound together by a network of associations which makes possible all use of that knowledge.

#### THE LAWS OF ASSOCIATION

Upon this connection all recall, indeed the entire course of thought, depends. It is not possible to recall anything except when some experience that has been associated with it precedes it in consciousness. All recall is a process of retracing old paths of connection. Nothing comes into consciousness except by virtue of its original setting. This may seem an overstatement in view of the fact that one frequently does not follow the original train of experiences very far, but may leap from the events of one day to those of another remote from it in time. Even in these cases, however, it will be found that the incident immediately preceding the turn in the process of recall had also been connected with the events of the second series as well as with the first, or some object had the double series of connections in past experience. Recall can always be traced to some earlier connection. The only exception is to be found in cases in which the chain of thought is broken by the irruption of some sensation, or when some vivid experience from the immediate past that has been keeping active the neurones involved in its perception suddenly breaks in when for some reason the connections between the elements of the original train become weak. These two cases belong in the same class. Each may start a new train of thought.

While all recall is dependent upon the earlier associations, the strength of these connections alone does not altogether determine what shall be recalled. It has been said that each experience has been connected at different times with many other experiences. A little observation of the actual course of thought is sufficient to convince one that any experience may at different times recall any one of several experiences earlier connected with it. It will be seen that now one of its associates, now another, succeeds it in the mental stream. This selection of associates can in itself be referred to laws. A study of recall under experimental conditions shows that while recall depends upon the immediate connections in past experience, the selection of some one link rather than another depends upon the wider connections of experiences. The simplest of these wider connections is to be found in the earlier ideas in the same series.

In the recall of a line of poetry the word that shall follow any given word depends not only upon the word itself but also upon the words that have preceded that word. This connection between words in a series that are not contiguous has been often demonstrated, and the earlier words undoubtedly have some influence in deciding which of several words shall be called up by any particular single word. Thus in James's instance, where the same word occurs in two lines of poetry, one does not switch from one to the other because the earlier words in the lines serve to call up the right associate in each line. In

I, the heir of all *the ages,* in the foremost files of time

and

Yet I doubt not through *the ages* one increasing purpose runs

not alone "the ages" which is associated both with "in the foremost" and also with "one increasing" serves to arouse the association, but all the words that have preceded exert their influence and serve to decide between the associates that would be equally strong in themselves. "I, the heir of

## MENTAL PROCESSES IN SPEECH

all," through its association with "in the foremost" makes that come to consciousness and keeps out the rival. But in all serious thinking, there are other more fundamental, if more remote, influences that are important in determining the selection of associates. One of these that has been studied experimentally is the wider mental context or the purpose that dominates at the moment. When, for example, I am looking for an illustration of the control factors in association, as I was a moment ago, the one line of "Locksley Hall" serves to recall the other one quoted and the passage in James where the illustration is used. Were I attempting to recite the poem as a whole or to illustrate the evolution of knowledge, in fact, did I have any other purpose whatever, one of these lines would call up the one that followed it in the poem as a whole. Probably this wider purpose also has a part in the selection of associates within the line. Certainly it can be shown to have a great influence in the control of associates under other conditions. In detailed experiments by Watt and others, it has been shown that the task that is set, the purpose or the general problem before one at the moment, is a determining factor in controlling the selection of the associate. Thus if one is shown *dog* after one has been asked to name the genus of the animals in a series, *animal* or *mammal* will be given; while if one has been asked to name a special kind of the animal named, some one of the breeds of dog will be mentioned. Similar results are found if one is asked in one case to name a synonym, in another an antonym. In either case it will be found that the word suggested will be in harmony with the purpose or request. This purpose acts immediately; the first word that appears will correspond to it. It is only when an association not in harmony with the purpose is extraordinarily strong that it will be possible to overcome the influence of the purpose.

In ordinary thought and speech the same control is exerted by the general intention of what is to be said. If one is talking to a class, the particular topic in hand serves to select the right associates from the words that might possibly press into mind. The context or what has gone before in the discourse of the day and in the course itself, together with the problems to be treated in the course as a whole, constitutes the controlling purpose. In one sense these purposes constitute a hierarchy in which each more general controls all of the less general, the more remote dominates the less remote, and so on down to the immediate purpose that is dominant in a sentence or small group of sentences. It is this dominance of purpose and of groups of purposes that makes speaking rational or sensible. When the order of words is determined purely by the associative connections, one talks nonsense. This is characteristic of the speech of the insane. In the control of associations in speech, then, two factors must be recognized. The one is the closeness of the associations between the elements that constitute the discourse or the thought; the other, the wider control by the immediate purpose of the moment and by the more remote purposes that the immediate ones tend to subserve. These purposes in their turn are taken from society, from the family, from the school, and from general education. They are themselves suggested by an object or event seen some time earlier or by other purposes which have just been fulfilled. In short, the purposes are associated and called up in very much the same way as are ideas or words themselves. In one sense they may be regarded as merely larger organizations of experience that exert a directive force over the connections or associations between single experiences and smaller groups of experiences.

## MENTAL PROCESSES IN SPEECH

### RELATIONS BETWEEN THOUGHT AND LANGUAGE

Both thought and language are subject to these laws of association under more general control. In the preceding section no distinction has been made between them, and none need be made so far as the laws of mental action are concerned. It may contribute to clearness, however, to consider the different kinds of mental states that can carry the thought, and the possible differences between thought and language. If we take the second of the two problems first, it may be said that on occasion three different relations may be found: (1) Thought may precede language in definite and detailed imagery and then be translated into language as a separate process; (2) the only content of thought may be the language; or (3) there may be a mixture of the two. This intermediate condition which is probably the most frequent may consist of an alternation between thought in language and thought in images, in which some parts are imaged, others represented in language alone; or there may be a general idea of what is to be said in the vaguest, most symbolic terms, and this may be developed in words directly. No statistics are at hand to determine the relative frequency of the three. It is probable, from somewhat meager data, that one thinks in images alone only when dealing with material that is not easily represented in words, as in musical composition or in designing an instrument of original form. Words alone are most frequently used where the matter is very abstract and images are not at all relevant. In most cases there is a mixture of the two. Nearly always there is a foreshadowing of the general idea to be developed. The content of this foreshadowing may be itself a word, or it may take almost any form, varying with the individual and with the subject. When the speaker is dealing with concrete objects or descriptions, there is frequently, if not usually, some picture or image of the thing to be described, and the words are suggested by the images. Each of these statements must be regarded as true only for certain classes of individuals. They vary greatly from individual to individual and may be regarded as wholly true only for the author.

### MENTAL IMAGERY

Mental imagery in general has been found to be very different for different individuals. Galton long ago observed that certain people were predominantly visual in all of their thought processes, others predominantly auditory, etc. This means that when one man recalls an object, it stands in memory preëminently as it was seen; while for the other man the object is thought of in terms of the sound that the object makes, the way the thinker acts when he uses it, or by the words that are used in indicating or naming it. Galton classified individuals, with reference to the sense that dominated his memory, into *visuals, audiles,* and *kinæsthetic.* This absolute classification is unfortunate, in so far as it may seem to make it appear that each man has but a single sense in which he recalls all of his experiences. Nearly all men make use at times of at least three senses in recall, although one is usually more important for one man, another for another. At the same time, a man may have one sense most prominent in his recall and still have only very vague ideas of the objects that he recalls through that sense. Thus one man may think almost entirely in visual terms and still have only vague outlines of the objects of which he thinks. His pictures may be less clear than those of another man who thinks mostly in sounds. The type of memory image that dominates in an individual has considerable influence upon the effectiveness of the man and modifies both the capacity for language and his ability in certain professions. Visual images, auditory memories, and kinæsthetic impressions are the main vehicles for recall. The other senses very infrequently supply material for thought or memory. It is with difficulty that one can recall an odor or a taste with great vividness. One may see the orange that was eaten for breakfast, one may even remember that it was luscious, indeed the mouth may water with the thought; but it is very rarely that the specific tastes or smells reinstate themselves. Professor Griffitts found in a study of students that nearly 90 per cent made most use of visual imagery. For the others about 6 per cent used sounds most; and 4 per cent kinæsthetic imagery, that is, thought of the way they must move in response to the object. No one of the several hundred tested was altogether limited in his memory to one sense. The figures given indicate only what sense was used most in recall or thought.

We are more directly interested in the way in which words are thought. These may replace concrete imagery in thinking of objects, and they join with concrete images in practically every one in thinking. Obviously one may reproduce words as they are seen, as they are heard, or as one would feel them in the muscles of speech. All are used. Again Professor Griffitts' experiments on students show that 35 per cent of the students thought of words as they saw them most frequently, 31 per cent made most use of sounds, and 25 per cent had the kinæsthetic images most frequent. The predominance of visual imagery is in part due to the nature of the experiment that was used in Professor Griffitts' opinion. One should put together the auditory and kinæsthetic, as they usually interact and are somewhat difficult to distinguish. If we accept these two statements, it would follow that most people ordinarily think of words in auditory and kinæsthetic terms, what is frequently called *inner speech*. Less frequently visual terms are used. Practically all individuals have all three types of verbal imagery at command in some degree. Our percentages above indicate only the number of persons who use the particular sense most frequently. Any individual will use the imagery that is most suited to the problem in hand. When one is thinking what one is to say, inner speech predominates. When a question of spelling dominates, the word will be more frequently thought visually. That holds of writing in general.

In the kinæsthetic way of presenting either objects or words, there is always the possibility that the actual mental content may be sensations from muscles as they are actually contracted rather than memories of old contractions. Watson has emphasized this as the only relic of what the orthodox psychologists call thought or consciousness. He insists that actual movements of the tongue and related organs constitute the only vehicle of memory, although he does not say how they influence the behavior of the individuals that make them. We must admit that at times these movements are actually made and that the sensations that are derived from the contracting muscles contribute to the ideas of inner speech. It would be real talking to one's self with slight movements. In addition, and probably a larger component of inner speech in most individuals, one has the mere reinstatement of the memories of old movements, the revival of the kinæsthetic sensation and not of the movements themselves. These fuse readily with the auditory memories, because they have been usually associated with them in actual experience. While one will be more prominent for one individual and the other for another, both will be present in each thought of the word. The

## MENTAL PROCESSES IN SPEECH

actual sensations from the moving vocal organs are even more difficult to distinguish from the revived images. Both certainly may be present and both unite in the common image.

In discussing the ways of presenting thoughts, it may be well to mention that certain individuals have insisted that it is possible to deal with pure thought without images. We can take up the discussion of this possibility later in connection with thought and language. Here it may be considered as a reduction in the degree of distinctness of thought imagery. The series would diminish in clearness from specific images of an object in one or more of the sense groups in which it was first presented to a word that has come to represent the object, and finally to a mere reference to the object without specific imagery. Each of these, with the exception of the last, may be presented in one of the three more prominent senses. We find that individuals differ markedly in the degree to which they make use of each of these more general types and also in the specific sense that they prefer for the recall of each of the other divisions. Children are, on the whole, more given to concrete images. Some of them may have what Jaensch calls *eidetic images*, in that they have images so vivid that they may be confused with the actual objects. They grade down from that to individuals whose imagery is so schematic that they have difficulty in deciding from what sense it comes. Galton found that imagery tended to become less concrete and vivid with age. Older men, particularly men who dealt with abstract problems, tended to use words much more than the younger men.

The differences may be important for practice. Griffitts found that men who did well in geometry, in art, and in history in college made more use of visual imagery than did the average man. Failure in engineering courses, he found, in one man, to depend upon an inability to use visual imagery. The reader will find it interesting to study his own imagery as he thinks spontaneously or as he tries to recall concrete events, with the purpose of determining what form the memories are likely to take. It will be particularly illuminating to compare the imagery for the recall of specific events with that used by one or more friends. It will be seen that all may attain approximately the same ends by very different means. One may think an object in one type of image; another in entirely different sensory terms, and still mean exactly the same object.

### REFERENCES

GALTON, FRANCIS.—*Inquiry into Human Faculty* (New York, Dutton, 1908), pp. 57-128.
GRIFFITTS, C. H.—"Individual Differences in Iimagery," *Psychological Monographs,* Vol. 37, No. 3.

## CHAPTER VI

### MOTOR PROCESSES IN SPEECH

ANOTHER problem that offers material for psychology in connection with the language processes is the way in which words find expression. To understand the closeness of the relation between words and their utterance, one must first appreciate the general law that every sensation tends to pass over into movement and that every movement is made on the basis of some sensation or sensory excitation. As was seen in discussing the physical basis of mind, all nerve currents run from the sense organ through the nervous system to the motor nerves and muscles. In connection with memory and thought processes, the same law holds. Each idea tends to find an outlet in action, and in connection with speech each word that is spoken has a thought or a thought word behind it that arouses it. In the explanation of any action two questions, then, naturally arise: One is how the particular idea has become connected with the movement in question; the other, what the conditions are under which the idea will call out that movement.

#### CONNECTION OF IDEA WITH MOVEMENT

The process of connecting an idea with its corresponding movement seems to be closely related to the formation of association. When idea and movement have been frequently connected, the nerve tracts involved tend to grow together and then the idea at once arouses the spoken word. In the child of educated parents, even, the process of learning is one of trial and error, as it is called technically. From a very early stage, the child makes all sorts of sounds with his vocal organs. The character of the sounds is determined in the first place by hereditary connections and the structure of the organs. Within those limits, however, the order and character of the sounds depend very largely upon chance. The child tries one after another all of the sounds in its repertoire. Some pass apparently unnoticed because of lack of all interesting peculiarities.

Occasionally one attracts attention and is repeated because of that. What sort of sound shall attract attention and so be repeated and learned depends upon several different factors. Some of the gurgles and poppings of the lips seem to owe their interest to the intensity of the sound or to its peculiar character. Many other sounds take on interest from the connections in which they are heard. Most important of these are the words that are spoken by parents and friends. Those that are used most frequently in connection with the child get distinguished on account of their frequency of repetition. When these words that have thus been identified in advance are spoken by chance by the child himself, he is attracted by them and recalls them, and the very attempt to recall them serves to repeat them as motor processes. Added to this is the incentive that comes from social approval as the early words are spoken, the smiles that they draw from the admiring members of the family, and the pleasing way in which they are taken up and repeated. To this must be added the fact that if the word comes at a time when there is desire for the object that is designated, that desire is gratified as a result of speech. These pleasant results from speaking still further tend to impress it, to lead to its repetition until finally it is fully and completely learned. Later, the rewards from saying the words tend to induce a repetition of

## MOTOR PROCESSES IN SPEECH

them and renew the connection to the full sufficiently often to make it a permanent acquisition. Thus a chance selection from among chance movements finally results in establishing connections between idea and verbal expression, and this constitutes learning to speak.

It has been suggested by many authorities that imitation furnishes the real explanation of learning to talk, but when carefully studied it will be seen that there is really no separate and specific impulse to imitate. Perhaps it would be better to say that while the final result is imitation, that result is attained, not through a blind instinct or impulse to imitate everything, but comes as a secondary result of attending to certain things, on the one hand, and from the tendency to speak out sounds that are attended to, on the other. Imitation is not indiscriminate in the first place, and when one looks to the processes that control it one finds that it is made up of two parts. The first is the tendency to be interested in any movement that it has frequently seen made by others or any word spoken by others, and to repeat any movement that attracts attention and holds it. Chance and instincts supply these movements. The organism must wait for them to appear in the natural course of events; they cannot be hurried by any mental or physical process. Imitation is not a single force, process, or instinct; it is but the expression of several processes that work to the given end. They are named from the result that they accomplish rather' than from the forces that produce that result.

DISTINCTION BETWEEN SPEECH AND THOUGHT IN WORDS

After speech has been learned, talking is simply thinking in words with the intention of expressing one's self. The first essential is that the words shall be suggested. When once suggested the speaking begins. If speech is defined in this way, the question at once arises: What makes the difference between speaking and thinking in words? It is probably safer to approach the problem from the assumption that speaking aloud is the simpler and more usual operation and that silence is the artificial condition. The silence that is imposed is from secondary considerations. One desires not to warn an enemy of his presence, or wishes to spare a friend some remark that he thinks might cause him pain. These or some similar considerations lead to an inhibition of the usual motor accompaniments, and one thinks without talking. If one prefers to put the question, in what seems to the civilized individual the more natural way, as to why one suddenly begins to speak where previously thought had been in words not spoken, the answer must be found in some new factor in the appreciated situation. It is remembered that this thought contains information that $M$ was asking for yesterday, or that one was thinking of asking $M$ this question when it came up last night and another friend had said that he would probably know the answer. Now when $M$ presents himself, the conversation of the evening before is recalled and that is all that is necessary to make the question start the necessary movements of the vocal organs. Speaking is just thinking words with the additional awareness that something is to be gained by permitting the words to find expression in sound, or that nothing is to be gained by keeping quiet.

### INCENTIVES TO SPEECH

The first essential to speech is something to say. This to be effective is ordinarily formulated in definite words. In addition to picturing the words or having something to

## MOTOR PROCESSES IN SPEECH

say, there must ordinarily be some specific incentive to speech. This may be merely conventional. It may be a time when one is expected to talk. This happens when one is tête-à-tête even with a comparative stranger in a room at a social gathering where one is under observation. Again, as was illustrated above, it often happens that some earlier incident has made speech with that particular man desirable when he is next seen, and then one seeks out an occasion for private conversation with him. Again speech under other circumstances provides a way to the attainment of some definite end, and thus the idea itself, the sight of the individual, and thought of the end to be attained lead to the conversation. In every case, there is some incentive to speech, although it often corresponds to the purpose in the last discussion. It is something of a remote or incidental character that makes desirable the expression of the thought that is in mind in a general idea or in explicit words.

DETERMINATION OF THE CHARACTER OF EXPRESSION

Not only do the circumstances and context determine that the word or phrase shall be spoken, but they also determine the way it shall be spoken, whether loud or low, and even the form of the expression. If the individual to be addressed is at a distance, one will unconsciously speak the words in a loud tone; while if the person be near or the circumstances make for secrecy, the same sentence will be spoken in low tones. If the person spoken to is deaf or does not understand the language, there is a tendency to speak loudly in spite of the fact that if the listener is a foreigner, shouting or speaking in loud tones will have no influence upon the appreciation. Each emotion has its influence upon the loudness of each tone and upon the way the statement will be phrased. In brief, the loudness of the tones and the peculiarities of expression mirror not merely the thought of the individual but the distance of the listener, and the emotional and other related moods of the speaker.

While, then, the idea in its whole context and purpose, together with the emotion that the speaker is under, plays a part in determining what is to be said, there are other more physiological processes that also in part determine the character of the expression. These, too, are seldom lacking in the control of normal speech. Thus, one is guided more or less unconsciously by the sound of the words that are spoken. When one's voice becomes too loud or too high pitched, it is brought down to the usual intensity and register. The adjustment is not done consciously, nor is one aware of the departure from the normal or usual; but the ear almost reflexly or automatically checks the loud and the high tones and brings them down to the usual and normal. The lack of this control in the deaf or the hard of hearing makes itself felt in the monotonous lack of intonation that those individuals show in their conversation. The control may be emphasized also by the fact that the deaf are also dumb except when they have been taught to speak by special methods in which the fingers or electrical methods of making words visible come to replace the ears as a means of guiding the voice. The voice will be raised also, if the person addressed indicates that he does not understand. The voice will gradually be adjusted until the speaker sees that the listener can just hear.

Another influence adjusting the tone is furnished by the sensations that come from the moving muscle, the kinæsthetic sensations, that were discussed in Chapter IV. These give an indication of the position of the muscle and serve as one of the incentives to the reflex processes that they may exert themselves in the right direction and right degree to

## MOTOR PROCESSES IN SPEECH

make the desired sound. These sensations, again, are appreciated only by their lack. One never knows directly that they control action, until it is found that movements are not accurately executed when there is loss of sensation from the muscles. Occasionally a child will lack the development of the sensory nerves in the vocal organs, and in consequence it will not be able to speak clearly, if at all. The fact that words are frequently remembered in terms of the kinæsthetic sensation is an indication that these sensations are an important factor in learning to speak and in controlling speech after it has once been learned.

Speech, then, is fundamentally the development of connections between ideas and movements that are very much like ordinary associations. They are like associations, too, in that links are often jumped. One occasionally finds that it is intended to say some one thing, and without any preliminary translation into words, one finds one's self speaking what one was thinking. More usually, particularly in important things, what is to be said is put into words first and then the word pictured in some way serves to call out the actual sounds. But as in associations, the shadings of meaning are the result of different purposes, more remote than the immediately preceding idea. Even the slight turns of speech grow out of these remote purposes, as do the loudness of the speech and some of the grammatical constructions. These two last depend upon the visual picture or other direct evidence of the distance of a listener. Each of these associations is formed with no definite appreciation that it is being formed and with no knowledge that it has been formed, with no consciousness of why the sounds are spoken as they are. The man has the notion of the end he is to attain but no knowledge at all of the way it is to be attained. All that is an unconscious outcome of the purpose.

# CHAPTER VII

## THE ORIGIN OF LANGUAGES

THE problem of how languages originated is one that has been much discussed at many different periods, and since the evidence in favor of all theories has been frequently highly speculative, it is a topic that has given rise to much bad temper and may even be said to have fallen into disrepute. It is said that the French Academy some half century ago voted to hear no more papers on this topic. We may venture some brief statement of the more important theories for the light that they throw upon some of the attitudes that have been taken toward the problem of language and for their value in enabling us to emphasize certain phases of our own discussion.

### OLDER THEORIES

The older theories were mostly alike in that they assumed that the problem was one of the origin of single words and also that the thought was already present in some form before speech began. Thus both Max Müller and Whitney started with the common assumption that men's minds were filled with the ideas or concepts and that they were consciously struggling to discover some means of communication. Three theories were presented in the controversy between these scholars and have been prominent in all of the older discussions. These are the onomatopœic, the interjectional, and a theory that the sounds are the expression of a natural response or ringing out of the man correspond-

## THE ORIGIN OF LANGUAGES

ing to the tone that is peculiar to any object when it may be struck. These theories have been nicknamed by their opponents the "bowwow theory," for it assumes that the names that are given objects and particularly animals are an imitation of the sounds that they make, and the childish name for a dog was one of the frequent illustrations; the "pooh-pooh theory," as it stated that words were the development from the natural exclamations that were called out by the event;[1] and finally Müller's own theory was referred to as the "dingdong theory," from the emphasis it placed on the ringing out of some natural sound from the individual.

Each of the theories needs to be liberally interpreted. The naming from imitation plays a relatively small part in the words that any fully developed language exhibits, and those few are usually considerably modified from the assumed original form. The pure interjectional theory is in much the same case. True, as shall be seen later, emotions constantly give rise to meaningful expressions, but few specific names of objects or even of mental states can be traced to these expressions. The third theory is so vague as to explain everything and so nothing. What Max Müller calls a faculty for giving articulate expression to the rational conceptions of his mind would need no further elaboration but, on the other hand, explains nothing, since it really says that man speaks because he speaks. It assumes, too, that man has rational conceptions before he begins to talk, while probably he develops the two together. True, if you permit a more metaphorical interpretation, many words seem particularly appropriate even if they do not imitate a sound, represent an expression of emotion, or

---

[1] See Max Müller, *The Science of Language* (Longmans, Green, 1885), Lecture lx; W. D. Whitney, *Language and the Study of Language* (C. Scribner's Sons, 5th ed., 1867), pp. 426 ff.

constitute a peculiar ringing out of an object. To speak of a path as zigzag seems appropriate; but unless the prominence of the z's be emphasized, it has no particular similarity to the line represented. There is certainly no similarity in the sounds. Similarly, all enjoy the line.

The vorpal blade went snicker snack

but what constitutes the especial appropriateness is very difficult to say. One would need to go to the vague explanation that appears now and again in psychological explanations that the feeling aroused by the sounds is similar to the feeling aroused by the thing described, and this is little more than to say again that the sound seems appropriate.

Each of these theories is insufficient. Either it must be taken in such general form that it loses all specific meaning, or explains so few words as to be of little value. All the words in all of the modern languages that can be definitely explained by all of them together are an extremely small percentage of the whole. The greatest objection, however, is to the whole spirit of the theories. They assume that language is an intentional invention of a man who had the full capacity of the normal man of to-day and who already had clearly in mind the ideas that he was to express, and that the whole problem consists in imagining how two men at this stage of development might have discovered some means of communicating these ideas already fully developed in the minds of both. The rudiments of communication probably had been fairly well developed before that stage of mental development had been reached. As Wundt has said, animals are silent because they have nothing to say and many of the ideas to be expressed come only after the expression has been fairly well developed. A second objection to all of the theories is that they assume that

# THE ORIGIN OF LANGUAGES

words develop in isolation and are the units of communication, while it is much more likely that sentences and larger units developed first and words came to be completely recognized only after language had been committed to writing for some time.

### THE THEORY OF WUNDT

To these theories we may oppose such a modern theory as that advocated by Wundt, which attempts to connect the origin of language with known facts of the development of mental processes in the higher animals and the lower forms of mankind. The fundamental principle from which all of these theories start is that every excitation and every idea tend to induce some movement. These movements have been most fully studied in connection with expressions of emotion, but are also seen in practically every mental state. Wundt argues that each taste quality has a facial expression that is peculiar to it alone and that this expression may be regarded as the result of a definite nervous connection between a given sense ending on the tongue and certain of the facial muscles. After frequent observations, this group of contractions would come to mean that the other individual was tasting a given quality, and later would probably call out a memory of the same taste quality in the onlooker. Each mental state may be assumed to evoke a similar specific response that will be seen or heard or appreciated in some other way. The simplest form of communication consists in the revival through association in the hearer or observer of the mental state that has caused the sound or the facial expression or gesture. In such a type of theory the expressions would be aroused by excitations before they were fully understood, and the mental state aroused in the recipient need be no more definite than it was in the agent in order to induce appropriate actions. The actions or expressions of themselves would aid in understanding the situation and might lead to effective coöperation long before the individuals had reached the stage of development that would make possible an understanding of the situation in the concepts that both Max Müller and Whitney presuppose.

Granting, then, that these simple instinctive expressions constitute the simplest forms of communication, and that from them the more complex forms develop as the race develops something to say, the first problem is how these simplest connections between excitation and response arise. As was said in the preceding chapter, the connections between sensation or idea and the movements may be divided into two groups: (1) instincts that have been developed in the race and are complete in the individual at birth, and (2) acquired connections that are formed by the process of trial and error and deepened by repetitions into habits. The expression of emotions is altogether instinctive. They may be said to depend upon the survival in some slight degree of movements once useful that have lost their significance or application. The facial expressions of anger have been said to be reminiscent of the movements made by animals that fight with their teeth in actually chewing the body of their opponents. In man the movements have become useless but are repeated, because the connections in the nervous system, between certain ideas or groups of sensations that correspond to situations, and these movements, have been persistently inherited in somewhat weakened form. Now when the situation presents itself, the movements are stimulated at once. These instinctive movements are made by the limbs, by the muscles of the trunk, by the muscles of the internal organs, of the walls of the stomach, of the blood vessels in all parts of the body,

# THE ORIGIN OF LANGUAGES 117

as well as by the muscles of the face. It is generally assumed that the movements are selected when once they have been developed by the survival of the individuals who have acquired them. The individuals who make suitable movements live and their movements persist and the tendency to make them is passed on. They continue to be inherited so far as they are not detrimental in later and more advanced stages of developments, but probably in constantly diminishing strength.

Wundt argues that speech as well as gesture and other simple forms of communication finds its origin in these instinctive expressive movements. The problem in its more special forms must face the question how these particular movements could have been survivals of movements that were once useful. Movements of the vocal organs themselves do occur in forms that are partly expressive in connection with other movements. In man, for example, any vigorous downward movement of the arms tends to contract the chest walls and produce an explosive expulsion of air. As this passes through the larynx it tends to give rise to the *haa* that is heard in workmen who are wielding a heavy ax or sledgehammer. The panting movements after running to exhaustion or other similar vigorous exercise also give rise to characteristic sounds. These are easily observed in man and arise from no definite intention to express thought. It would probably be possible to find other sounds that arise similarly as by-products of other movements, which involve no contractions of the vocal organs themselves.

### THE ORIGIN OF MOVEMENTS OF ARTICULATION

More important, however, are the cases in which the movements of making articulate sounds are not mere

## 118    THE PSYCHOLOGY OF LANGUAGE

mechanical results or accompaniments of other movements but are connected with them in the nervous system, *i.e.*, arise because of nervous connections between a set of movements and the muscles of articulation. These are very numerous and are to be found in almost all animals. The howl of the dog as he runs from fear, or the angry bark he makes as he rushes upon an intruder or his prey, seems to be part of a single complex of movements. The same remark may be made of the twitter of birds or the hissing of the cat and of many of the sounds of all animals that are provided with vocal organs. These sounds would fall under the general law of overflow of motor impulses: that a nervous impulse when strong takes not merely the paths that are part of the usual complex, but spreads to related muscles. Even this would not answer all of the questions, however, as there is nothing in the statement to determine how these muscles originally came to be connected. One can view the vocalization as part of an emotional expression. They are, then, parts of many complexes of expression; but it is difficult to explain them on the theory of emotional expression given above—that they are weakened remnants or reminiscences of earlier purposeful movements. It is not possible to find movements that might once have been useful of which these vocal movements might be regarded as descendants. One cannot think of any use to which the vocal organs, the cords of the larynx, etc., might have been put that is not connected in some way with expression. While one can then easily see that vocal movements are more essentially part of expression in many animals, it is not easy to see how they can be descended from any series of movements that are useful but not in some way expressive.

It becomes necessary, then, to raise the question whether **expressive movements** themselves are of value for survival,

# THE ORIGIN OF LANGUAGES

for if of survival value there would be no trouble in understanding how they might have been perpetuated once they made their appearance. This, then, offers relatively little difficulty. In all animals that coöperate in any way in defense or offense, a means of communication however primitive would have its value. The bleat of the sheep seems to call the flock together for protection or to start all in flight. On the other hand, the howl of the wolf calls the pack and gives the benefit of the help of all the others. All social animals would be more fitted to survive if possessed of even rudimentary means of expressing emotions. Even in sounds less definitely valuable for coöperation, one can see survival value in the sounds that lead to mating, as possibly the songs of birds or the call of the bull moose. It can readily be seen how the male bird with an attractive call might secure a mate where others fail, and so perpetuate his kind. One can see, too, how the hyena with a loud call might secure more food than one with none or with rudimentary organs for producing sound, and so be more likely to live. There can be no doubt that means of communication would make possible coöperation and so success and survival. It must be assumed that the first man was provided with instinctive vocal calls, some few of which may have been remnants of formerly useful movements that survived in weakened forms, but many also that were instinctive expressions of mental states, reactions to the environment that had developed and been transmitted primarily because they enabled individuals to coöperate.

The form that these expressions might take would be indefinite in character and number. The last group in particular would depend for their character largely upon chance. There is no sufficient evidence in comparative anatomy or embryology to determine why the larynx and other vocal organs of the respiratory tube should have developed into means of communication rather than some outgrowth and modification of the partridge's wing or the locust's wings and legs. The fact of the gradual predominance of the respiratory tract as the seat of the organs of communication makes it probable that this was the most convenient. The detailed causes for the development and for the transmission of just the motor responses and expressions that we find cannot be traced. It suffices for our purpose to recognize the fact that the most primitive forms of communications are closely related to other forms of emotional expression and can easily be conceived to be sufficiently numerous to afford a basis for the selection by chance of a number of distinguishable tones.

### PROCESS BY WHICH MEANING IS ATTRIBUTED TO SOUND

Another problem to understand is the process by which these sounds when developed took on meaning, since without meaning they would of themselves have no value. It is probable that this also came very slowly. At first in man as in the higher animals a sound was no more than a vague indication of the character of response needed for a situation. A danger call means flee; a call for help, approach. Or when the animals are close to each other, one general kind of sound or tone means anger, that attack is coming; another characteristic group of sounds indicates a friendly attitude, that approach is safe or desirable. The characteristics of fundamental emotions seem fairly common. From experience with domestic animals one can recognize moods in the animals at the zoo. When among individuals who speak a language totally strange to one, the emotional attitude of individuals can be appreciated from their intonations and emphasis, even when no word is familiar and one cannot see the speaker to read his emo-

## THE ORIGIN OF LANGUAGES

tions from facial expression or attitude. These tones, inflections, and differences in emphasis are probably the first and most primitive vocal expressions of feeling. They persist in and through the different sounds that give the more developed and more concrete meanings expressed in the words of different languages.

These first vocal expressions took on meaning for the listener because they came to be connected with different situations that were the same in the response required. So far as they were appreciated as identical with the sounds that the hearer had himself made in similar situations, they would, after a few repetitions, come to be associated with these different responses. One might even assume an instinctive response to them, that the response to the cry as well as the cry itself was instinctive; but it is not necessary. The frequency with which they are made by any individual of high or low development living under primitive conditions would serve quickly to form an association between the sound and the response demanded and, gradually, as the consciousness of the species developed would form the center for a cluster of recalled different situations.[2]

Before one can discuss the problem, one must decide upon the nature of early memories. How far this memory is to be regarded as a definite picture, how far it is to be regarded as a means of recalling or rearousing old motor responses, old motor attitudes, cannot be decided until we know more of the nature of the consciousness of animals and of men at the lower stages. In animals it is safe to assume that

---

[2] Mrs. De Laguna has published since the above was written a theory of similar character. She, too, begins with the assumption that language develops from the emotional expression as a cry that serves first to attract other members of the group, then becomes significant as a signal for approach or flight, and only later acquires a specific meaning as an indication of the presence of a particular object. See Grace A. De Laguna, *Speech* (1927).

mental states, if they exist, are pretty vague at first. From analogy, however, it is possible to construct two theories of the original animal mind. On the other hand, it seems that the primitive consciousness is of the concrete. The child apparently recalls specific single events and only later learns to combine them into general ideas, laws, or concepts. On this line of reasoning one might argue that the primitive mind is always of the concrete and, to push the analogy but a step, of clear-cut images. On the other hand, it seems that in learning movements or in watching a train of complicated events one is aware of the general outcome, of the vague general direction, before one has any knowledge at all of the separate concrete steps. One may recall the general line of approach by which one solved a mechanical puzzle, for example, and only later after many successes know much of anything about the separate movements by which the end was accomplished. In the same way, one may witness for the first time some rapidly following train of events, have a general notion that such and such things were going on, but have almost no definite clear-cut memory images. If one should argue from these experiences, it would seem that the primitive consciousness is somewhat vague and general and that clear-cut images are attained at an advanced stage. Neither analogy is complete and neither conclusion altogether convincing, particularly considering the presence of the contradictory rival analogy in the field against it.

One might with some success attempt to combine the two theories on the assumption that the disadvantages of both were combined in the more primitive or undeveloped adult mental states. Then the memories would be concrete but vague. A considerable amount of preliminary experience is necessary to permit one to think or even to see clearly, and at the same time this is not the vagueness

# THE ORIGIN OF LANGUAGES

of a general idea but of an unclear particular. It would follow, if we make this assumption, that the mental state aroused in an animal by a growl was not a clear-cut memory image of some former occasion in which the growl had been heard nor was it a generalized result of many definitely appreciated individual experiences with which the growl had been associated, but it was primarily the arousal, partly instinctive, of the appropriate attitude with some rags and tatters of mental states derived from earlier events but not yet clearly developed. The possibility of having clear ideas would develop side by side with the capacity for forming general notions and with the general notions themselves. It is altogether possible that animals might have a vague appreciation of the meaning of these primitive emotional expressions and the expressions themselves before any clear consciousness of individual instances or any capacity for general ideas as such had developed.

Following upon the most rudimentary appreciation and forms of expression as found in animals and as may be assumed to have existed in the earliest men or the prehuman predecessor of man, the question arises how it is possible for an individual or a race to have developed particular words for particular objects and actions. Here is where the real controversy begins and where there is little hope for agreement, as facts are absolutely lacking and analogies that may in some measure take the place of facts are hopelessly conflicting. A discussion of the problem may be excused on two grounds. The first is the universal interest in the subject and the numerous theories that have arisen in the attempt to satisfy that curiosity which may fairly be stated in any book on language. Second is the fact that theories may at least prepare the way for an appreciation of other more definite results that they may serve to illustrate and from which they have grown. Finally we may offer the very general excuse that where all men are blind, one man's vision is as good as another's.

One might be aided in tracing the development of language could one find any evidence of language in the animals. The nearest approach would be expected in the apes. Several studies have been made—by Boutan, by Garner, and, most recently, by Furness—of the question whether apes do communicate by language. All agree that they have a considerable range of different sounds, and that these are ordinarily used in the expression of the emotional attitude. There is a difference of opinion as to whether they are connected with specific objects or situations and so constitute a real language. Garner was of the opinion that they might and probably did, but his methods are not above suspicion. Furness succeeded in teaching an orang-utan to say the words *papa* and *cup* and to use them in connection with pleadings and spontaneous needs. *Papa* was attached to Furness himself and would be used when the animal was in trouble and needed assistance. *Cup* he used more rarely, when the animal was thirsty. The associations required a long time in the forming and their use was very infrequent.

Yerkes attempted for a long period to teach two young chimpanzees to imitate English words, entirely without success. He found that they used approximately the same sounds to indicate the same emotion or special conditions, such as hunger. These were altogether on the emotional level. They learned readily to obey commands as a dog does, but kept them at the dog's level, without repeating them or showing that they could be detached from the special setting in which they developed. Yerkes agrees with Boutan that apes do not advance beyond the level in which sounds are used as a means of emotional expres-

# THE ORIGIN OF LANGUAGES

sion instinctively developed. They cannot be taught to use words as signs for objects or as representatives of experiences not actually present. Starting with the most primitive form of communication, emotional expression, we would need to trace the development of language along two distinct lines: gesture and articulate speech. Both are involved in some degree in the original emotional expression and both develop by approximately the same laws. The original emotional response of an ape involves facial expressions, movements of the limbs, and vocal utterance. Of these, facial expression alone has not been developed to the point where it designates separate objects, acts, or thoughts, as well as emotional attitude. True, it is closely related to intellectual acts. One can determine much of the degree in which another individual is following a discourse from the facial expression. It may even serve as an index of a man's general intelligence, but it has never been developed into an independent system of signs that shall communicate ideas without other aids. For language proper its discussion has no purpose.

## THE DEVELOPMENT OF GESTURE LANGUAGES

The gesture languages are perhaps even more important than language in the proper sense in throwing light upon how meanings may become attached to sounds or to movements, since in most cases they have not been developed so far; they stand closer to the original state. One can even see the first step taken in the origination of these movements in adults, if one watches carefully, particularly when individuals with no common language are thrown together. Generally, under these circumstances, pointing to an object is used to call attention to it, if it is in sight, and then imitation of the movements to be made or of the use to which it is to be put suffices to make clear what is to be done with it. Most often the situation and pointing are sufficient. Again, frequently it is possible to discriminate between several objects that stand near each other by indicating the purpose to which the one desired may be put. A salt shaker, if the communication is at the table, will be indicated by shaking, the pepper mill by turning, and so on throughout the list. These, of course, are not directly the outcome of an emotion, and then, too, they are the product of human minds at a considerably advanced stage of development. They are made by individuals accustomed to communicate. The pointing itself might very well be instinctive, or at least a frequent accompaniment of an emotion when the object that caused the emotion is at a distance. In fact, as a means of attracting attention, pointing seems to verge on the instinctive. It arises early in the child as a means of designating an object of enjoyment or of wrath; and, on the other hand, attention, turning the eyes, etc., seem to follow very closely and easily upon the movement. Based on this common, if not instinctive, act more special sorts of designation follow. In ordinary use these do not reach the stage of a real language. What is needed in addition is a development of connections between signs that shall be constant, if not arbitrary, and which shall be established with some degree of permanence. This we may conjecture would make its appearance in time on the basis of chance advances that proved valuable in practice. One might imagine that systems of this sort might originate by design on the part of some individual.

As a matter of fact, we have excellent instances of each. Among the Indians of the plains of western America there is a fully developed language of signs which originated spontaneously and which is understood by many tribes with no

# THE ORIGIN OF LANGUAGES

common language. In the deaf and dumb alphabet we have an instance of a sign language that has developed by human ingenuity. The former is of considerable value in throwing light on the nature of speech development. The other may be mentioned briefly. Thus, when the member of one tribe meets a member of another, he will indicate a man by a finger held up; a man on horseback by two fingers held apart with a finger of the other hand held between as a horse between the legs; a white man by putting a hand to the head, thumb out, to represent the brim of a hat, etc.

### THE DEVELOPMENT OF ARTICULATE SPEECH

Somewhat similar must have been the process of acquiring meaning that vocal sounds underwent in the beginning. Some were probably imitative sounds that early became specialized as the onomatopœic theory demands. In other cases, the sound that came to represent an object or an act was probably the result of pure chance, as can be seen in the case of the development of certain slang expressions. It is hard to venture on slang phrases that are altogether new. The word *swank*, that has come into general use in England as the equivalent perhaps of the American *swagger* or *cheek*, might seem to have no particular origin and seems to most Englishmen who use it to be an original expression, but it is found in the same sense in Scotch. Undoubtedly certain of these phrases seem appropriate for no assignable reason whenever they are used by chance and so once used are taken up and repeated. Instances of this sort might be brought under the dingdong theory: the sounds may be regarded as rung out of the individual who first uses them. The more essential element in the process, however, is the response they meet in the listener. What gives these words their appeal is very difficult to say; that they have it is alone certain. Sometimes vague resemblances can be traced; occasionally, perhaps, instinctive connections can be made out; but most often one can be certain of the appeal but not of the reason for it.

Starting from relatively few roots, the meanings can be seen to undergo various sorts of changes, that in the sum total may become very great, in spite of the fact that each change is of itself very small. These shifts of meaning constitute the problem of the semasiologist and must be left to a later connection. Many of their laws are well established and the problem itself constitutes one of the most fascinating fields in the history of language. Once a meaning is established, it is fairly easy to study its spread; but the original fixing of meanings took place for the most part before the recorded beginnings of language study. It is only in the occasional appearances of slang phrases that the real beginnings are open to study, and, as has been said above, the only thing that can be said of them is that some one happens to hit upon a sound that appeals to his hearers as appropriate, and it is usually not possible to say why it is hit upon or why it should appeal as appropriate. Sometimes analogies may be traced, sometimes it seems to be an instinctive response to a situation, but more usually no one of these can be definitely made out. Once started, frequent use fixes associations and the sound obtains meaning.

## CHAPTER VIII

### LANGUAGE RECEPTORS: READING AND LISTENING

#### THE NATURE OF PERCEPTION

THE final stage of speech, the stage without which all the others are valueless, is the appreciation of the spoken message on the part of the person addressed. This falls in the classification of psychological processes under the head of perception. The ordinary psychological formula for perception is that some sensation is received and amplified by association with earlier memories to make a real object or thing. Every perception involves a large percentage of memory or imagination processes that are added to, or aroused by, some sensation from the outside world. The essential part of perception is this supplementing of the newly entering sensation by older associations. The supplementing processes are usually fully developed ideas or types rather than specific memories. One is concerned with the object in its general rather than its particular characteristics. As one writes, then, one sees the pen as a pen and is little concerned whether it is one's own pen. That may be easily taken for granted, or it may even not matter at all in the case in question.

These general laws may be easily illustrated in listening and in reading. In listening, in particular, what is heard is not the jumble of sounds that are emitted by the speaker but is rather an ordered interpretation that is put upon these sounds. This can be illustrated in many ways. First, it is rare for two people to pronounce the same word in the same way. People from different parts of the country have different ways of pronouncing almost every word, yet these differences are overlooked unless they are very unusual. The New Englander or New Yorker may at first notice oddities of speech in a Westerner, but these drop into the background after the first few days. One reads one's own dialectic peculiarities into the speech of the stranger, so that the other's are not even noticed. One is impressed by the meaning alone; the vehicle is not noticed in the least. This tendency to translate spoken words into one's own peculiar form can be still more clearly seen in listening to a foreign language with which one is not too familiar. One will replace the German words by English and not be quite sure what the German expression has been. Frequently, too, the process of interpretation goes still farther and one remembers only the general thought that has been expressed and not the shade of expression or the particular words that were used. This is not due to the forgetting merely, but to the fact that the words heard are translated into thoughts or into one's own words, while the spoken words in and of themselves neither make nor leave any distinct impression on the mind.

To understand the perception process, then, one must discover, (1) what the stimulus is that comes from the senses directly; (2) the materials that are added by association from the stored memories; and (3) the conditions that determine why one rather than another of the possible associates and memories should be supplied. Each of these factors may be seen to advantage in the interpretations of speech.

We may begin our analysis with reading, since that field has been more fully worked out. Historically, the knowledge of the reading process has developed from the observation of the mistakes made in ordinary reading to a study of the physiological processes involved and then to the psychological factors. It is a matter of common observation that misreadings are frequent. One of the most common is the overlooking of misprints. Hardly a book is printed that does not contain misprints, letters omitted, inserted, or substituted, and these misprints may even extend to words. This holds in spite of the care that authors, typesetters, and proofreaders may give to the corrections. This proofreader's illusion was investigated by Münsterberg, by Goldscheider and Müller,[1] and later by Pillsbury, partly with a view to determining the amount of the error and partly to determine the conditions under which it occurred.

PSYCHOLOGICAL FACTORS IN READING

Goldscheider and Müller developed their investigations from a study of the range of attention. They began their study with a view to determine how many objects of different sorts might be seen at once, with an exposure of one-fifth of a second, a time too short to permit of eye movement. They began with simple objects, dots and lines, and gradually extended their investigations through combinations of lines to letters and words. They found, what had been found by Cattell and others before, that what could be seen at a glance depended relatively little upon the actual physical character of the stimulus and much upon the earlier habits of the individual. Thus one could see as many lines as dots, and if the lines were arranged to make geometrical figures or the dots to form familiar groups, as many of these figures or groups could be seen as of the simpler elements. When this process was extended to words, it was found that as many letters could

---

[1] Goldscheider and Müller, "Zur Physiologie und Pathologie des Lesens," *Zeitschrift für klinische Medizin*, Vol. 23, p. 131.

be seen as dots and almost as many short words as dots. Evidently, then, the perception process depends only in part on the physical stimulus and in larger measure upon nonphysical factors. That these other factors are subjective rather than objective is evident from the fact that fewer unfamiliar objects than familiar can be seen with a short glance. That the unfamiliar will not act in the same way can be shown by replacing the Latin letters by Russian or Greek or by Chinese characters. The number of these that can be seen will be considerably less, although with practice it will rise rapidly. Where there is no subjective material to replace or supplement the sensation, the number of things seen at a glance will be relatively small. The physical stimulus serves, as has been said, only to call up some familiar object.

The tendency to overlook misprints also emphasizes the presence and importance of this subjective construction. Evidently what actually results from the construction is something real, some actual mental content. As the final result and the physiological stimulus are obviously not at one, the errors must be accounted for by the presence of both sensations and memories. The problem naturally arises how the mental construction is combined from the two different sorts of material. The studies by Pillsbury,[2] Zeitler,[3] and others indicate that the amount and the kind of error that may be overlooked vary very markedly with the individual and the conditions of observation. No general law can be given, but in single words with short exposures different subjects will overlook one misprint in from 10 per cent to 50 per cent of the cases. When the

---

[2] W. B. Pillsbury, "A Study in Apperception," *American Journal of Psychology*, Vol. 8, pp. 315-393.

[3] Zeitler; *Tachistoskopische Untersuchungen über das Lesen*. *Philosoph. Studien.* Vol. 16 (1899), pp. 380 ff.

number of misprints is increased, the percentage of times the mistakes are overlooked decreases, but it is not possible to say how many letters may be changed before the word cannot be read as intended without noticing the changes. After many changes the word may become more like other words than the one with which the experiment began. As regards the character of the misprint, it has been found that blurring of a letter is most likely to escape notice; next in order comes changing a letter; while omitting a letter is most likely to be noticed, probably because it changes the general appearance of the word.

All these results indicate that reading is largely of words as a whole rather than letter by letter. One does not see a few letters for themselves and supply others, but rather sees a certain shape of black and white and this immediately suggests a familiar word as a whole. The shape of the word is determined in part by the length of the word and by the relative position of the letters, in part by the detail of the letters at the beginning and end of the word. This furnishes the basis for the recall of the word proper, provides the cue for the associations that determine the word.

The further problem is to determine the conditions that decide what course the associations shall take and so the word that shall come. These are, of course, the laws of association with the subjective and objective conditions that have been discussed in the earlier chapter. The objective conditions here are to be found in the closeness of association between the shape of the black mass on the white ground and the word sound or other word image as a whole. This in turn depends upon the frequency with which the two have appeared together, the recency of these appearances, and the strength of the impression at the time. Of these factors, frequency and recency are by far the most important.

The subjective condition, or the mental context in which the word presents itself, is also very important. In isolated words this mental setting into which the word comes may be slightly changed artificially and, of course, varies spontaneously from moment to moment under the influence of various events. Münsterberg and later Pillsbury tried the effect of calling some words related to the word to be shown just before a mutilated word was exposed. This was found markedly to increase the percentage of times the word was recognized, particularly where the word was much mutilated, and also increased the percentage of misprints that were overlooked. In the experiments one could notice that chance factors played a considerable part. When an individual had been reading a foreign language just before the experiments, it was noted that the misreadings were likely to take on the characteristics of the language that had been read. In subjects coming to the experiments from classes in German, the *sch* combination appeared frequently. Still more slight and passing settings, such as the word that was in mind before the exposure, and similar things would also have their influence. Even in reading isolated words, it is possible to show that the process of reading is one of associating a previously developed mental unit with a group of letters or visual stimuli. The unit is a word with more or less meaning in whatever imagery the subject is accustomed to use in his thinking. The nature of this must be left to another connection.

#### PHYSIOLOGICAL FACTORS IN READING

Much to the point for an understanding of the normal and usual reading processes is the work that has been done on the physiological factors involved in reading in the natural context, by Erdmann and Dodge, Huey, Dearborn, and others. One of the most important points that they have established is that in reading the eye moves by jumps, instead of continuously. One does not run the eye smoothly over the line picking up letter by letter, but rather reading is by a series of snapshots of the line that is to be read. These snapshots vary in frequency and consequently in size with the matter read, the age of the reader, and other factors. For simple and familiar matter the eye may make only four reading pauses in a line; in reading proof the number is usually increased. Similarly, philosophical prose requires more frequent stops than a newspaper or a novel. The number is also larger in reading an unfamiliar language and is greater for children than for adults. These reading pauses have been measured in various ways. Delabarre and later Huey recorded them by attaching a light plaster cap to the eyeball and recording the movements graphically on smoked paper. Dodge and later Dearborn photographed the eye movements on a falling photographic plate. Dearborn has suggested more recently that they can be seen and counted roughly by placing a mirror on one page of an open book while the subject is reading the other. The observer can see the movements in the mirror and keep a record of the number per line.

Of these methods the photographic has the advantage over the earlier method of being painless, while it gives a permanent record with the possibility of making accurate measurements of the time relations. The simple direct observation, however, requires practically no apparatus and is sufficient to demonstrate the fact of the reading pause and many of the commoner bad habits in eye movements that are important for school hygiene. The results agree that the pauses last for approximately one-fifth of a second. Observations show that practically all reading takes place during the pauses and that nothing is seen during the movements of the eye from point to point. Occasionally the eye will drift slowly over part of a word during the pause, but this is the exception rather than the rule. It is evident that reading could not take place during rapid eye movement, since there would be nothing but a blur of after images. One could see no more than one does when looking at a rapidly revolving wheel or at a rapidly moving train.

An interesting problem with a bearing on the nature of the perception processes is why the blur is not seen even as a blur during ordinary eye movement. Various theories have been held. Holt suggests that there is a central inhibition, but this is only a phrase to indicate the fact. It may, however, be brought into line with the general psychological law that those things which have no meaning in themselves do not attract attention. In this list may be mentioned contrast colors, after images, and constant sensations from any sense or from any part of the body. So these blurred sensations while the eye is moving do not come to consciousness of themselves and are completely neglected. However, they may and probably do serve as a means of detecting and estimating the movements of the eye and particularly in deciding whether the eye or the field of vision is in motion. The neglect of the meaningless and the possibility of obtaining meaning or knowledge of the external world from psychological processes that themselves give rise to no definite sensations are facts that are important in all matters of perception and will be frequently required in the explanation of many matters in later chapters.

One other question remains to be discussed: What is the relation between the amount of material read and the extent of the retina that is sufficiently sensitive to discriminate letters? As was seen in Chapter IV, the sensitivity of the retina falls off very rapidly from the fovea toward the periphery. It has often been suggested that more is read in a single glance than can be clearly discriminated. That all that is read at a glance is not clearly seen is evident from many of the facts already mentioned. In rapid reading, ten to fifteen characters are read in a single glance, while of single isolated letters not more than five can be seen or recognized at one exposure of the same length. Dockeray carried on an interesting investigation to determine how large the portion of the retina about the fovea may be that is sufficiently sensitive to discriminate letters in isolation. To accomplish this he arranged letters in pairs equidistant from the fixation point and at different distances from that point. Thus he determined the maximum distance at which both letters could be discriminated simultaneously. The object of using two letters simultaneously was to make sure that the fixation point was held accurately. Obviously, if the eye shifts too much toward one of the letters, the other could not be read. An adjustment toward the exact center would alone make reading possible. By this method it was found that recognition of single letters is possible over the area of the retina employed in ordinary rapid reading. One might distinguish each letter that was read were no other letter present. However, it is clear from other evidence, namely, that derived from the overlooking of misprints and from the investigation of the range of attention, that one never does read letter by letter, but leaves much to be supplied by association. One could read with a larger area on the retina than is actually employed.

If we bring together the results of these different studies, our conclusion is that one reads by a series of glances, snapshots at the line. These snapshots last about one-fifth of a second and from four to ten are required to read each line, the number depending upon the familiarity and ease of the material to be read. At each glance or pause a few letters can be seen, usually the first and last of the words, and a general impression is obtained of the shape as constituted by high and low letters, the length of words, etc. On this basis the words as wholes are supplied by association from the stock of words. Nothing is seen during eye movements, but the words obtained in the different pauses unite to constitute the material read or furnish the basis for the continuous development or reconstruction of the words and thought of the author. In this process of reconstruction, the same laws hold as in the reading of single isolated words.

### READING FOR WORDS AND READING FOR SENSE

One must distinguish at least two sorts of reading, reading for words and for thought. These are not always distinct; they may fuse in different degrees, but they suffice as a basis of discussion of types of reading. The typical case of reading for words, or for words and letters, is proofreading. Here very much the same laws of supplementing hold as in reading isolated words, except that the subjective controlling influences are largely supplied by the context, by the preceding words rather than by the ideas that chance to be in the mind of the reader. More attention is given to the letters, as is evident from the larger number of pauses, and less is supplied than in other types of reading. Still there is supplementing, as is shown by the fact that misprints are overlooked. In reading of this kind, the supplementing is usually by words as visual units as they have been seen on the printed page with the separate letters more or less distinct, supplemented in many cases by the sounds the words would have if spoken. Even here the

## READING AND LISTENING

first awareness of a misprint is not so distinct as it would be did the visual impressions coming to consciousness correspond exactly to what is on the printed page. Usually one first has a feeling that something is wrong in the word and then looks at it more closely to discover what the defect may be. Supplementing is here due, for the most part, to associations between the image from the printed page and letters or word units.

At the other extreme stands reading for sense alone, in which the words may be entirely neglected except when the style is ambiguous. In the words of Quintilian, language is, then, but a medium through which one views the thought of the author and is appreciated for itself only when it shows imperfections. In this case, the supplementing may be not words at all, but ideas of a nonverbal character. One may become so lost in a description that the words are practically not noticed. Pictures or other content are suggested by the word and come to consciousness instead of the words—again an illustration of the law of perception that one may appreciate meanings which depend upon very definite sensory impressions without being aware of the sensory impressions themselves. The process of supplementation follows the same general laws as in the verbal reading. Associations of ideas with words develop in exactly the way as do associations of ideas with ideas or of words with words. The content of the idea varies with the mental type which was discussed in Chapter V. The visual-minded man may see pictures of the objects and events that are described; the audile is limited to the sounds of the events; the person of motor imagery will appreciate events very largely in terms of the feelings of his own movements. Besides this, other vaguer ways of presenting the experiences to himself are not uncommon and are probably mixed with the mental contents of the other types. These we may designate by the term pure thought and leave the discussion of what thought is in this use of the term to a later chapter. For our present purpose it suffices to assert that in reading for sense the words serve to call up ideas of whatever kind, and that the words are not consciously present or, at least, occupy a very subordinate position.

Granting, then, that words call up ideas by association, the problem of how the associations are aroused and controlled offers some new points or new illustrations of old laws. The objective or fundamental associations develop in exactly the same way that they do in simpler cases. The child learns that a word is the name of an object by hearing it spoken when he sees the object. Repetition stamps it in until sound and word become interchangeable. In learning to read, the printed symbol becomes associated with the spoken word in the same sort of repetition. At first the sight recalls the sound and the sound the object or the idea, but with growing familiarity, the process becomes short-circuited as all mental processes tend to do, and the object may come at once on seeing the word. This mechanical association is fundamental for sense reading of all other types.

But much more important are the wider control processes, called the subjective conditions, which were discussed in Chapter V. Their importance can most readily be made apparent by considering the different meanings that words may have in different contexts. There is no natural language in which all words have but one meaning at all times. Words are used in many different ways, and this fact is a stumbling-block to the beginner in any language. Think of the meanings of *so* or *high* or *grade*, to mention the first three words that occur to the writer, or of *gleich* in German. It is evident that the bare objective association cannot determine the meaning or the idea that the word will suggest. Evidently the determining element is to be found first of all in the context. Context in reading is of very far-reaching importance. First of all, it is constituted by the immediately preceding and succeeding words. The earlier words very evidently determine whether *so* is to be an intensifier or to denote similarity to some earlier quality or act. "He did so" and "He is so good" have the same value of the *so* largely fixed before the *so* appears, but the later words also have their effect. As is evident from the simple physiological processes in reading, understanding cannot be completed as the words appear, but rather reaches back from the later to earlier quite as much as from earlier to later. The various snapshots are pieced together after they have been made, and the earlier receive their interpretation from the later almost as frequently as the reverse. Whatever may be the order of reading aloud, reading for understanding must take place at a time subsequent to the mental reception of the sensory material and occur practically simultaneously for considerable amounts of material. Reading for understanding is not word by word but sentence by sentence or even by larger units, for frequently later sentences serve to render clear what was not understood on the first reading. The meaning of a word is determined by this total setting rather than by the word itself and its immediate setting.

But not only the immediate context determines the way in which the word shall be understood. The wider context is also important. How a sentence shall be understood depends on the preceding sentence and that on what is known of the subject before reading began. Here, too, one is frequently influenced by knowledge that comes later. A sentence may be understood only in the light of what is read on the next page or in the next chapter. Still more frequently one can make nothing of a chapter or part of a chapter in the middle of a book before the earlier chapters have been read. This incapacity to understand does not depend upon new and technical terms whose definitions are not known, but the interpretation will not be complete until the whole of the preceding chapter shall have been read and understood. This depends in part upon the new material that can be brought to bear upon the new by the old and in part upon the control of the associations by this wider knowledge. The interpretation that shall be put upon a sentence or wider selection very frequently depends on what has gone before in a work and in many involved subjects depends on other works of the same author. In all of the cases the interpretation may be regarded as a thought suggested by the word. The context, too, plays a part in determining to what language a word or phrase shall be ascribed. Many words as printed are identical in different languages, but the meaning of such a word in another language will seldom appear when one is reading English, and seldom will the English meaning present itself when one is reading a foreign language. Context is again the determining factor.

Intermediate between reading for words and reading for sense are all degrees of intermixture. Most usual, perhaps, is the case in which one reads words and seems with the consciousness of the words to have the meaning in pictures or other mental content added to them. Most reading is probably of this intermediate type. In some cases mere clear appreciation of the words seems to constitute the entire meaning. In such cases there seems to be a gain in translating the visual symbol into auditory or motor imagery. The meaning or thought seems to be appreciated when that translation has been made without other sensory content. Why this should be and in what the satisfaction

## READING AND LISTENING

consists we shall have to consider in a later chapter. Particularly when forcing one's self to read when sleepy or more interested in something else does it seem to be an advantage to reproduce words definitely in the motor or auditory or other imagery that ordinarily precedes one's own speech. The same effect of using motor or auditory images as an aid to understanding may be seen in reading an unfamiliar language. One may not understand the visual symbols for themselves but will at one stage of familiarity understand when they are translated into the motor (as in my case) or auditory imagery of the mother tongue. At the next stage of familiarity one will understand when they are translated into the motor imagery of the language itself. The writer, for example, can understand German when pronounced or thought in the original, although French is usually translated into English as it is read, while English is appreciated by translation into visual imagery or into thought of a more general character, although occasionally in difficult passages internal speech may be the predominant characteristic even in English.

Still more rapid reading may consist in the arousal of pictures that give the whole sense. In that case one really reads only an occasional sentence or idea and supplies the rest. This is possible only when the material is very familiar and one is willing to take chances on missing much of what is said. Then on the basis of a sentence or a section here and there or even of prominent single words, one fills in the remainder and constructs the total discourse. In a sense this is different only in degree from the other forms of reading, but it is an extreme difference in degree that makes certain some omissions, while the other forms of reading can be regarded as giving all the important details. These different forms of reading may be regarded as varying in the sort of mental material that is used to supplement the printed symbols and in the relative amount of supplementation and sensation that is present in the word. Another principle of classification may be based upon the way in which the reader attends. When one is reading for words, those and those alone come to consciousness. Anyone may read proof accurately and know little or nothing of the sense when finished. One may read to appreciate certain points in the style of an author and get that to the practical exclusion of all else, or, and this is more frequent, one may read for the content and get nothing or very little of the words or have little appreciation of the style of the author. Within each of these larger fields there may be still further specialization. One may read a book for the author's opinion on some one point and get a very complete account of that without learning much of anything else. This last becomes partly selective memory, but it is also in part a matter of selection and supplementing in reading. One may, however, read an author to determine some particular point in his style as, for example, how a Latin author uses the subjunctive, and get nothing much else. The selection in each of these instances depends in part upon what is selected from the stimuli offered, but also in part largely upon the associated ideas that are called out or permitted to enter into consciousness. In many of these different sorts of reading, exactly the same sensations might be received from the eye, but the resulting effect upon consciousness would be entirely different.

We may bring together the results of the discussion of reading in a few simple laws: (1) Reading is by a series of snapshots taken during the pauses in eye movements, that last for a fifth of a second. Each line requires from two to six or eight reading pauses depending upon the familiarity of the material. (2) During these pauses only a few words and the general form of the words are seen. These suggest the word as a whole. (3) The supplementing of the parts seen is controlled by the associations that have been formed in the past between the visual form and the words controlled, by the immediate context, by the present purpose, and by the wider knowledge. Reading, then, is a process of reconstructing the meaning of the author on the basis of a few unseen symbols in the light of the knowledge of the reader and in terms of the purpose that may be guiding him at the moment.

LISTENING

The process of interpreting spoken language follows the same general laws, but we need not go into details as for reading, partly because it would be largely a repetition of the statements just made and partly because less work has been done upon listening. Bagley carried out one investigation to show that hearing is in large measure supplementation. He used a phonograph with which records had been made of inaccurate or blurred speech. In general, he found that these misplaced or disturbed sounds would be overlooked in much the same way as are misprints in reading. They are not noticed, and the full sentences are heard as if all were spoken clearly.

It is probable, too, that just as sentences are interpreted as wholes in reading, they are also appreciated as units in listening; at least, that interpreting does not keep pace with the sounds always but runs backward from some point. This is clear from the fact that the interpretation put upon many sounds depends upon words that come later in the sentence. Even in attentive listening, particularly to the sounds of a foreign language, the word spoken dawns gradually after the sentence is completed. Frequently, too, one interpretation will be put upon a sound at first and later when the whole sentence is heard, it will be seen that a quite different word was meant. Interpretation may lag a sentence behind hearing. In writing from dictation, this can be clearly seen.

The process and laws of supplementing also hold for listening. The sound must supply relatively little, as can be seen from the small amount that can be detected in an unknown tongue. One cannot repeat sentences. One cannot even recognize as the same a sentence from a foreign language when it is repeated in close succession. What supplements the word heard shall vary almost as much as the ideas that are added to the letters seen in reading. It probably depends again much upon the individual type of mind and upon the material. Probably in most people the sentences of the mother tongue are supplemented directly by the thought of objects in whatever imagery is natural to the individual. Some get visual pictures, others auditory, others motor, others verbal, and still others even less definite imagery. Probably in the mother tongue the visual imagery of printed words comes only occasionally when there is some question of spelling or other difficulty. When listening to a foreign language that is more familiar from reading, the visual images come more frequently to the aid of the sounds heard. The material that is supplied as one listens, then, is, like that supplied in reading, of many different kinds; but as in reading what attracts attention, what finally comes to consciousness, is the idea. The elements are added in the process of understanding rather than in the perception of the words alone.

The conditions that determine what shall be added to the bare sounds, that decide how the sentence or the larger whole shall be understood, are not at all different from those that determine the way in which what is read shall

## READING AND LISTENING

be appreciated and understood. All goes back to the associations that have been forming ever since the child began to notice language. The connection between the word *bottle* and the object is made by having the two enter consciousness together. Frequently similar connections are established for each word and its meaning or meanings; for each word has not one meaning but many, and the appreciation of language depends primarily upon the number of connections that have been established in this way. But what meaning shall be given to a word depends upon its context, and this in listening as in reading must be understood to mean not merely the other words in the sentence but also the wider setting, the previous discussion and the earlier intercourse of speaker and hearer and even much of the more general knowledge of the listener. Practically all that has been said of the influence of the context in reading may be applied here.

This completes the round of speech from thought to thought. All speech finds its origin in the mind of some individual, and its goal in the thought of some other individual. Intermediate are the motor processes of the speaker, the physical manifestation, and the perception processes of the other individuals. The stages, in the processes of transmission other than these three, cannot be completely isolated. Thought might be said to be translated into language, that is, given expression in language; perceived by the reader or hearer; and again translated into thought. As has been seen, however, these finer shadings cannot be regarded as distinct, since thought and language in the minds of speaker and hearer are frequently inseparable and even indistinguishable.

We may make clear many of the general principles involved in the statements of the preceding chapters, if we do what we can to trace the development of language and also illustrate the process by the learning of an artificial language, telegraphy, on which much work has been done. Learning the telegraphic language is a good illustration, since one starts with material that has never had meaning and gives it meaning artificially. As is well known, the Morse code is a series of dots and dashes that are arranged arbitrarily to represent certain letters. As a result of long use the telegrapher comes to receive a train of ideas from a series of these symbols in much the same way that we do from a speech. Bryan and Harter [4] traced the process of learning to understand the telegraphic language from the beginning to great proficiency. It ran very closely parallel to learning to read. At first the operator looks for single letters and requires some time before he can recognize them. At a later stage words form the object of his observation, and later he reads by sentences as wholes. When the letters are first learned the separate dots and dashes must be noted. Since groups of five and six come too rapidly to be counted, they must be appreciated as units and distinguished in that way. For a considerable time there is likely to be confusion between the down stroke and the upstroke. The one marks the beginning, the other the end of the symbol. To confuse them frequently means to interchange letters. For a long time one can send more rapidly than one can receive; but, with increasing practice, the receiving line crosses the sending line and then continues above it. To bring the sender's rate up to the receiver's, abbreviated codes have been devised; and it is said that the expert may become so familiar with this that he thinks in it. The receiver, while receiving 80 to 85 words a minute and transcribing them upon the typewriter, may think about the material he is receiving or about anything else that

---

[4] Bryan and Harter, "Studies on the Telegraphic Language," *Psychological Review*, Vol. 6 (1899), pp. 345-375.

interests him. His work is done automatically and his attention is free for other things.

In this work associative processes play much the same part as in reading. The receiver may supply words that he thinks are coming when the actual words are different. To avoid this as much as possible, the expert operator usually lags a number of words behind the sender. The beginner is ordinarily one letter behind; later he may lag behind a whole word. A fair operator may be several words behind in connected discourse, while the expert prefers to be from six to twelve words behind. It is found that there is then less likelihood of supplying the wrong word. The memory span by dots is considerable in this case: ten words required by count on the average from 175 to 300 characters, and these must be held in mind at once. Where the material is not connected, as in series of figures, not so much can be retained. The most expert said that he can lag not more than six characters behind and then only if the numerals are set off in threes by commas. Where altogether disconnected, he tried to keep only three or four behind.

As in reading words, not the letter or word but the phrase is the unit. When the operator becomes able to grasp words as opposed to letters, his receiving curve makes a big jump, and another marked increase in speed is made when he can pass from word to phrase. Each of the ascents depends upon the formation of one of these language habits, a habit of associating wider wholes with ideas, or of attaching meaning to larger and larger units. It is only the few who attain freedom in the telegraphic language and can use it as they would the mother tongue. It takes ten years to become a thoroughly seasoned press despatcher. Bryan and Harter insist throughout on the fact that the telegrapher learns a new language. They say: "We have shown above that receiving is not translating either letter by letter or word by word into the mother tongue, but involves the use of a great array of higher language habits, that telegraphy is psychologically a distinct language, almost or quite as elaborate as the mother tongue." [5] The words and phrases become the unit and take on meaning just as do words in any spoken language. Here, as in language, the ideas are wider than the words or phrases, and to understand any statement it is necessary to consider it as itself a unit and part of a wider unit rather than as a complex of unitary words that stand by themselves. It is very striking from the standpoint of the later discussion that these arbitrary units can be made to take on meaning as completely and by the same laws as do words of everyday speech.

Many of the laws of learning a language and the general laws of perception are illustrated by the acquirement of lip reading on the part of the deaf, particularly by the adults who lose their hearing. At first the method used was to teach the laws of phonetics, particularly the movements of the lips that were involved in the different words. This method proved relatively slow and on the whole unsatisfactory. The knowledge of the muscles and of the movements did not seem to be readily translated into words or ideas. More recently, Brauchmann, of Jena, suggested that it was essential that the patient should be taught to connect the sight of the facial movement with the feeling of his own vocal organs as he pronounced the words. A group to be instructed would sit looking at the face of the instructor and all would pronounce the series of syllables and then sentences together aloud. The method is being extended in its use and has proved itself an advance upon the older more analytic method of learning.

Its sponsor believes that the reason for its success is that

---

[5] *Ibid.*, p. 358.

all men may learn to think in kinæsthetic terms and that immediate translation of sight of the lip movements into one's own movements eliminates the use of visual words and so saves time and confusion. Probably the kinæsthetic elements are not so generally used as he believes and are no more truly the carriers of thought than sounds, as was said in Chapter V. The success of the method probably is due, in the first place, to the directness with which the translation is made to thought. One forms a connection with the picture of the words spoken as wholes and is not distracted by wondering how the sounds are produced or by other analytic operations. In the second place, pronouncing the words serves to keep the student active and interested. He has something to do that interests him, and he keeps his attention upon the face. The details are connected with the appropriate word without being distinguished for themselves. At first the connection is between the sight and the feeling of the word in the throat, but this soon changes to a connection between the picture of the lips and the meaning of the whole. It is another illustration of the law that differences in experiences that are not definitely analyzed may serve to arouse different total associates, and so be interpreted correctly when the details are not discriminated.

### REFERENCES

DEARBORN, W. F.—*The Psychology of Reading* (New York, The Science Press, 1906).
ERDMANN and DODGE.—*Ueber das Lesen* (Halle, Niemeyer, 1898).
GRAY, W. S.—*Types of Reading Ability* (Chicago, University of Chicago Press, 1917).
HUEY, E. B.—*The Psychology and Pedagogy of Reading* (New York, Macmillan, 1908).
JUDD, C. H.—*Reading, Its Nature and Development* (Chicago, University of Chicago Press, 1918).

## CHAPTER IX

**THOUGHT AND LANGUAGE: WORDS AND THEIR MEANINGS**

THROUGHOUT the preceding discussion, in speaking of the connections of language to thought, we have asserted that thought is translated into speech and that, in the process of understanding, speech is translated back into thought; but whenever the question as to what thought in itself is has come up, an answer has been deferred. Before we can go farther this problem must be faced and an attempt made to reach a definite basis upon which to construct the *later more linguistic* theories.

### WORDS, IMAGES, AND THOUGHT

So far we have seen that there are two sorts of mental content that may in a measure be opposed and in a measure be referred one to another. *Words* are one sort of mental content that frequently carry thought or at least are present during thought, while *images*, the persistent remnants of sensations, are also often in evidence as one thinks and frequently seem to be the only content of thought, that is,— to constitute thought. As has been seen, these two forms of mental elements are not really different in last analysis, since words are in their components—words as they have been seen upon the printed or written page, or words as they have been heard, or words as they have been felt in one's own utterance. They are, in short, merely visual, auditory, or kinæsthetic images. These, all will agree, are present in consciousness while one thinks. Some would assert that they are the only elements present during thought. Others insist that other more directly representative elements are the essential factors in thought. Still others take an intermediate position, that the images must be present, but that the essential elements of thought are not to be found in their mere presence, but in elements or functions that are added to and different from the images themselves. When one thinks: "All men are born free and equal," the first would assert that the words alone constitute the thought, the second that one must have a mental picture of masses of men without shackles, the third that neither alone is adequate, that the thought is something still different.

There are numerous objections at present to the assumption that images alone constitute thought or that words alone are sufficient to explain thought. One may, perhaps, best approach the problem, if one first brings together the differences that, as all agree, hold between image on the one side and thought on the other. (1) In the first place, images as images are usually concrete, are mere mental elements that stand for themselves alone and can never represent any general ideas or groups of objects. This is the old distinction that was recognized by the scholastics and by the logicians in introducing the notion of the concept or general idea. (2) Mental content may be vague or indefinite as opposed to thought which should always be perfectly clear and definite. This distinction opposes thought to the feeling or intuitive processes rather than to images as such, but still in the development of mind the way seems to be frequently from the confused to the clear and definite, from the confusion of bare impression to the orderliness and clear-cutness of thought. (3) In thought one frequently deals with relations, in space, in time, in intensity, of the passive sort, and with such more active relations as cause and effect. These are not images but, nevertheless, constitute a large part of the content of thought. (4) All thought has reference to something besides itself. It is representative of processes and things that exist outside of mind or at least of things outside of the mental content itself. It means these other things; it is not merely existent. In brief, thought always deals with meaning, not merely with content.

Each of these distinctions between image and thought has been made the basis of a theory of thought by some individual at some time in the history of the discussion of the subject, and most theories have assumed these distinctions as important features that must be explained in a theory of thought.

1. What a concept is and what makes it a concept has had the longest history. One of the rival scholastic schools found the solution in the word, another found it in realities that existed independently of the mind. Both of these views were based upon considerations that had little meaning for psychology. The statement that concepts were only words that had received a general use or reference is the only one that can be given any concrete application to the mental states as they actually exist. That view has been often revived under various names and undoubtedly contains a germ of truth. Frequently the word does serve as a general term. One has that and that alone in mind as one thinks some general idea. But in many instances it can be noticed, in actual practice, that one may have general notions when words are not present, and that words are frequently no more general than the concrete ideas themselves. Furthermore, thought is in itself not necessarily general. One must admit concrete as well as abstract elements in thought. From a study of the actual mental content, a general idea may be almost any mental content.

## WORDS AND THEIR MEANINGS 155

Furthermore, one may insist that a general idea is, as a mental content, always particular, that there is something in addition to its character that makes it general as opposed to the particular idea. In other words, one cannot find the solution in the character of the content but rather in the function that the idea fulfills. It is general because of what it does rather than of what it is. An idea is general because of what it means or represents. This conclusion disposes of the problem of the general or universal character of thought for the present to come up again under our third head of what it is that makes any mental content mean that which it is not.

2. The vagueness of the ordinary sensory content shows itself primarily in the instances in which one has a preliminary awareness or plan that is gradually ordered by reference to definite notions. One frequently has a foreshadowing of a statement in cases that require considerable time and effort to organize into clear-cut form. A whole theory may first present itself in this way, in fact, frequently does; while to formulate it, not to speak of giving evidence for it, may require a very long time. Similarly, unclear masses of mental content characterize much of the more rudimentary mental operations. When a patient is coming out from under an anæsthetic, the consciousness is full of queer sounds, of unorganized and bizarrely arranged colors and forms, which seem to have no definite parts and no particular order. In the process of recovery the thought becomes clear. A definite mental content gradually takes the place of the indefinite. It is probable that the early stages of mental development as seen in the child or savage show similar vagueness. Discrimination in the infant is at first probably almost entirely lacking. Only with increasing age does clearness develop. Similarly, there is evidence that while the savage has clear perception of

concrete elements, he lacks capacity for a wide grasp that shall bring clearly before him the general relations of what he sees. As in the instance cited by Stout, the savage finds his way from one natural object to another along his path but can't tell at all whether his course has been east or west. There is a general confusion with clearness of detail. This function of thought in giving clearness and definiteness may be performed by some single image or it may be given by expression in words. To be able to formulate an idea verbally may of itself suffice to clear it up, or may be taken as evidence that it is already cleared up.

3. The ideas of relation are, all agree, not represented in consciousness by any distinct images. James was among the first to call attention to the importance of ideas of *but* and *if* and *and*. These are evidently important to thought but have no distinct content. The same may be said of the notions of spatial and quantitative relations, such as *greater* or *equal to, above* and *below, before* and *after,* and the active relation of cause and effect. Here one might turn to the word and assert that one could think these relations only in verbal form. True we have words for most of the relations, but a little observation shows that one can also think them before the word comes and even when the word is not present at all. Occasionally imagery develops to represent them—Titchener, for example, asserts that he pictures *together* by a rubber band—but these images are obviously, like the word, only representative of the relation and are not the relation itself. These related elements have been called feelings, or it has been asserted that they are elements of consciousness that must be accepted as immediately given and added to the other elements of consciousness that we have been enumerating. Others still would take them over into the realm of pure thought and assert that they, with many other higher men-

tal operations, have only slight connection with the images ordinarily used and are not at all dependent upon them for their existence. How we are to dispose of these relational elements in consciousness must be left over to a later point, but it is clear that they serve to distinguish thought as such from the simple images.

4. The last mark that distinguishes images from thought is that in thought all has meaning, while images as images may or may not mean anything, and are always treated as if they had no meaning. Meaning itself may be more easily described than defined. The best instances of meaning are to be found in words themselves. Normally these have no place in consciousness except in so far as they stand for ideas or things that they are for the most part not at all like. Through use and convention they have come to represent objects and various relational and other thought processes, and thereby they change from sounds or visual impressions without sense to become very real elements of thought. The feeling of meaning is very distinct, very characteristic. One can appreciate it best in comparing the attitude toward a new word in a foreign language with the same word in the mother tongue, or, still better, the attitude toward the succession of sounds that constitutes a foreign language with the ordered meaningful sentences of English or of the same language when it has become familiar. Professor James's experiment of staring at a word like *language,* for example, in the sentence above, until it no longer has meaning is also instructive in bringing out the differences. At first it is the word with its meaning, but as one looks the meaning drops out more and more until finally it becomes just the black outline on the white page and the meaning has apparently disappeared. As was seen in the discussion of the learning of the telegraphic language, any series of mental impressions

may be made to take on meaning by being used frequently as representatives of something else. Gestures do this with great ease. The emotional excitement induced by the thumb on the nose of the small boy is altogether out of relation to the simplicity of the act itself. The more elaborate gestures of the highly developed gesture languages or the finger language of the deaf show the same tendency. Meaning is something very real and something that may be added to any mental content. In the broadest sense all mental content has meaning in the fully developed consciousness. The meaningless image is largely a hypothetical element used to emphasize the meaningfulness of the usual mental elements. We think always of a perception as representing a thing outside, and it is this that constitutes its meaning. Memory images and images of imagination always refer in the same way to objects that have existed or will exist and it is this reference that constitutes their meaning. The cases in which the meaning is general, in which the idea refers to general notions rather than to particular things, is but a special instance of this general phenomenon characteristic of all sensible mental content. Meaning may be said to be characteristic of all thought, probably its most constant and important characteristic.

### THEORIES OF THOUGHT

Theories that would take into account these four characteristics of thought may be divided into four groups, including one that is not now given much prominence. These are (1) the theory that thought and language are identical, a theory that may be regarded as descended from the nominalists, but whose best-known modern sponsor was Max Müller; (2) the sensationalistic theory, that thinking it always in terms of concrete sensations; (3) the new theory of Binet, the Würzburg school, and Woodworth that thinking is altogether different in character from the ordinary imagery; and (4) an eclectic point of view (advanced by Pillsbury) which would make thought a function of imagery and in some degree dependent upon it but with peculiar characteristics that admit most of the contentions of the believers in pure thought.

The first theory as expressed by Max Müller asserts that there can be no thought without words and, on the other hand, that there are no words without thought. One argument is that two things so unlike could not have come together by chance and, therefore, must be essentially parts of the same process. They must be for practical purposes identical. A stronger bit of evidence is, perhaps, Max Müller's assertion that it is impossible to have an idea of an object without having the corresponding word in mind and his challenge to his readers to think anything without having the word at once present itself. If you think *table* you are sure to have the word in mind, together with or immediately after the object. Neither of these arguments is irrefutable. The first is too evidently special pleading to require consideration. The second is easily explained by the laws of habit and association. One nearly always thinks with the intention of communicating ideas in some way and so ordinarily the words are present. This is nearly always true when one is talking or preparing to write, and at other times the possibility of speech or other utterance is always so near that words are likely to occur to one with the thought. Furthermore, the challenge in itself is sufficient to bring the word. It is a well-known psychological principle that suggestions work just as well from the negative as from the positive side. The endeavor to prevent an idea from presenting itself is quite as likely to suggest it to mind as is the desire to think it. As a matter of fact, the best modern investigators agree that there are ideas that come without language, ideas for which we have no words even, but they occur when one is more concerned in solving problems for themselves than in questioning whether one does or does not think in words. While we must admit, then, that most thinking is in words, and that it is usually a good test of the clearness of thought to be able to put it in words, thought without words is by no means infrequent.

The second theory, which would find the explanation of meaning, of relations, and of the other characteristics of thought mentioned above in sensations of various sorts, is best represented among modern writers by Titchener.[1] His main thesis is that the meaning of one idea or mental content is to be found in some other idea or sensory mental content. In its inspiration it must be considered largely as a protest against the assertions of recent writers of the Würzburg school that thought is a peculiar and new sort of mental content. He would find it, on the contrary, in the ordinary mental content, in mental imagery of the concrete sort. Just what he means is not quite clear from his writings. Some of the ideas that mark the meaning of relations are other concrete images. *But* is described as "a flashing picture of a bald crown, with a fringe of hair below, and a massive black shoulder," which is traced to having sat behind a vigorous speaker with these characteristics who made use of the word. In an earlier paper, as was said above, he described his image of relations like *together* as a picture of objects bound together with rubber bands. In more general terms, he would make meaning depend upon kinæsthetic sensations. Each individual is

---

[1] Titchener's main thesis is given in the *Experimental Psychology of the Thought Processes* (New York, Macmillan, 1909).

described as taking a definite motor attitude toward any object from the beginning, and this attitude in the developed individual gives meaning to the sensations or images that call them out. This meaning may later be transferred to sensations and ideas of other sorts, and may even be due to unconscious processes. In this way he would explain imageless thought so far as he would admit it to exist at all.

From this side his position is fairly clear. Anything that is in the mind with any mental content that has meaning comes to constitute its meaning. On the other hand, he would make meaning depend in part or at times upon slight irradiations of associations and upon conscious sets, upon physiological processes that are not conscious for themselves. How far this explanation is to replace or supplement the other is not fully stated. Certainly he looks with favor on Ach's [2] theory that meaning may be due to partially aroused associations and admits that Watt's purpose or problem plays some part in the determination or control of meaning. On the other hand, he definitely asserts that the meaning of one idea may be just another idea, and the instances he gives seem to permit the second idea to be entirely irrelevant to the specific character of the meaning that they carry. This latter view would make the second content the vehicle of the meaning of the first without reference to any special characteristics it may have. The first view, if intended to supplant the second, finds the meaning in partially aroused associates or in other peculiar elements, in what James called the fringe. The general tenor of Titchener's work and the criticisms that have been passed upon it by others all make it probable that meaning, relations, and the other properties of thought are to

---

[2] Ach, N. *Ueber die Willenstätigkeit und das Denken* (Göttingen, Vandenhoeck and Ruprecht, 1905).

be found and explained in terms of the ordinary mental imagery.

The third view would make thought altogether or largely imageless in character and would oppose it to imagery of the ordinary type and to words. The theory was developed independently by Binet [3] in France, Woodworth [4] in America, and Külpe and his students in Germany, not to mention earlier suggestions of the fact by Stout in England. In essentials it may be traced back to the scholastics and to Descartes. Briefly, it asserts that thinking may and usually does take place without imagery of any sort. At its fullest development thought is one sort of mental content; the ordinary memories and images, an entirely different sort. This thought material is not described in any way, except negatively: it is not like images of sense or memory. The belief in this form of mental content has developed in several ways and in connection with different sorts of mental operations. Ach found, in working with movements required in reaction times, that no definable mental state necessarily preceded the movement. The stimulus and the intention of making the movement were all that was required in most cases and the intention either was the purpose at the moment or grew out of that purpose. Woodworth noticed the same fact at about the same time and independently.

Soon after, Bühler,[5] then a student at Würzburg, found that many times when subjects were asked to pass on the truth or falsity of complicated statements, the decision came to mind without imagery of any kind, often without

---

[3] Binet, *L'étude expérimentale de l'intelligence* (Paris, Schleicher Frères, 1903).
[4] R. S. Woodworth, "Imageless Thought," *Journal of Philosophy, Psychology and Scientific Method*, Vol. 3, No. 106, pp. 703 ff.
[5] Bühler, "Tatsachen und Probleme zu einer Psychologie der Denkvorgänge," *Archiv. für die gesamte Psychologie*, Vol. 9 (1907), p. 363 f.

# WORDS AND THEIR MEANINGS 163

even a word. It seemed to be a naked thought. Bühler recognizes three types of pure thought: first, what he calls the consciousness of rules. By this he means appreciation of the method by which a problem may be solved without knowledge of the details of the solution. This came frequently in cases in which an individual was asked to remember how a problem has been solved at an earlier time. It is also seen when one lays out a plan of campaign suited to a number of different individual circumstances. His second form was the consciousness of relation. This needs no discussion. The third he calls intentions, which is almost, if not quite, identical with meanings as discussed above. In several of his instances a whole series of ideas or thoughts is covered in an instant and correctly passed upon. The consciousness of the moment represents, but does not reproduce, more than could be covered by a written chapter. These are instances of very broad meanings or ideas of things intended, but it is also used in narrower senses in cases in which one has bare ideas of meanings that might be represented by single or relatively few words or images. These imageless thoughts are then to be regarded as substitutes for images or words in most of the more important activities of the mental life. They are not to be explained in terms of images or sensations, but are an entirely different sort of mental content that cannot be more nearly described or defined. They can only be indicated in the actual mental operations.

It seems possible to give a fourth theory of thought that shall combine in a measure the advantages of each of the others and shall at the same time escape most of their disadvantages. As a first step, it is well to bring together the features of the three preceding theories that are common to all. All would admit that words may in themselves be the vehicles of thought without the presence of images. All but the adherents of the first theory, on the other hand, insist that words are not the only vehicles of thought. Even the chief exponent of the theory, Max Müller, insists that not all words, but only those that are understood by the speaker or listener, can be the bearers of thought, and avoids the obvious difficulty in the restriction by asserting that only these can be regarded as language. Evidently not words in themselves, but something added to the words that makes them understood by the individual, or some attribute peculiar to words that have meaning for him, can be regarded as determining thought.

Very much the same thing may be said of the theory that finds the vehicle of thought in sensations or other concrete imagery. Images are ordinarily (some would insist, always) present in the thought processes. Clear thinking may be carried on in images. In fact, much of the clearest thinking on concrete problems is imaginal. Images are frequently representative of abstract or general thinking. Probably they are the most frequent accompaniments or bearers of conceptual thinking. As Titchener insists, they also often do duty for relations in our ordinary thought. Usually, too, they are the mental content that carry the meaning. Another question is whether the images have meaning because they are images or whether like words they have meaning because of some peculiar characteristic that is present at certain times and absent at others. Certainly images or sensations may be as devoid of meaning as words. An entirely new object may offer a perfectly clear group of sensations but be quite as free from meaning as a word in an unknown tongue. In both cases, meaning is reduced to a minimum, even if still present in some slight degree. Even where one image constitutes the meaning of another, it is not its meaning merely as a second image. One frequently knows that one thing is related to another, yet does not know the meaning of either. Something more than the image is necessary, just as something more than the word, if one is to have real thought processes of any kind. The problem is to determine what that something else is.

If one is to seek the characteristic of thought in an entirely different sort of content, this content must at least be capable of description or definition in other than negative terms to be of real value. To speak of this content as imageless does not of itself tell anything at all of what it really is. At most it recognizes the problem and states that the solution cannot be given in terms of the recognized material of consciousness. It obviously must give way to any positive solution of the problems. If it is to stand at all, it needs to be extended to show the relations of the pure thought elements to the ordinary images and sensations, since all its supporters assume that thought does in some way grow out of the ordinary sensational experience. All of the advocates, too, admit that thinking often does go on in images or words. Only rarely does one find the imageless form of thinking. It is obvious, then, that one must first seek an explanation of thinking in words and images, then discover under what conditions, and, if possible, how the ordinary forms of thought are transformed into the imageless variety, and how the imaged and the imageless are related.

### THE PROBLEM OF MEANING

Each of the different views, then, really resolves itself, on analysis, into the problem of how one mental state can mean something which it is not. The problem of the concept is how a concrete mental process may seem an abstract idea or how a single mental element may represent a number of objects. The problem of relation is how a static single element may mean a dynamic relation or static relation between two things. The problem of clear thought in a wilderness of detail is how a simple picture or succession of pictures may be typical of a mass of experiences and so represent it clearly in spite of the manifold of concrete simple events. The foreshadowing idea that gives the consciousness of intention or of rule or a notion of the general direction that thought is to take in advance of any real solution is again a problem of the way in which a sketch of what Beaunis calls "the mother idea" may represent the complete involved solution. If we can solve the problem of meaning, we shall have solved the problem of thought in all of its essentials. The only other problem is how we develop abstract notions like those of force, of space, and of time, and of the various relations which are never given in any single concrete experience. This is also related to the problem of meaning and may be postponed until we have done with the latter.

As a preliminary, one must see that the problem of meaning is a universal one in mind. No experience, no matter how concrete, is completely devoid of meaning. Some words in a foreign language may pass for mere jargon, but they are at least given the meaning of human sounds, with some understanding of the emotional attitude of the speaker. They stand on a plane higher than the indefinite buzzing that greets one on the return from the narcosis of an anæsthetic. It seems probable that meaningless impressions would not be appreciated at all; they certainly would not be remembered. Meaning has all degrees from the vaguest general appreciation of some experience to the fullest scientific understanding of an object. Some light may be thrown upon one condition of meaning by the fact that it grows with experience of the object

In question. When one has a complicated experience for the first time, it is all confusion, nothing stands out from the rest, it cannot be adequately described or remembered. With repetitions, parts come to stand out from the whole, the order in which the parts occur is recalled or recognized, and with many repetitions one finally relates part to part, knows the order of the succession, can prophesy from one part what is to follow, and, if it is in any degree subject to human control, one learns what must be done to induce the desired changes at the right time. In this sense, meaning grows with experience and may fairly be said to grow out of experience.

Complete meaning of any event usually involves something more than this repetition and gradual disentanglement of its parts, and the consequent relating of part to part. One obtains a complete understanding, so far as that is ever obtained, only by connecting any object or event with all other objects or events. One understands natural phenomena by connecting them with the laws established in physics or biology. On the other hand, physical phenomena are understood in the light of natural phenomena. When Franklin proved that lightning is electricity, he threw as much light on the nature of electricity as on the nature of lightning. Similarly, each instance of appreciating identities or similarities between groups of events in different fields gives an explanation to both of the events related. This, on the whole, is the type of meaning that is given to mental states or events by scientific investigation. It consists in referring one thing to another and that to something else. Even when the movement is in a circle, as happens not infrequently, each of the members of the chain or circle gains meaning from its connections and relations. This is the sort of meaning that attaches to words. An association is formed between the word and some object,

## 168  THE PSYCHOLOGY OF LANGUAGE

event, or relation. This association serves to give it meaning. The meaning may be given, if the object itself is understood, by one association. Fuller meaning comes, however, from seeing or hearing the word used in a number of different concrete applications, each of which adds something to the total meaning of the word at any particular time. Meaning is everywhere present in consciousness. Sometimes it is extremely vague and may sink to approximate zero, but an idea without meaning has no real existence. It is appreciated only as confusion; it is not remembered; it cannot enter into relations with consciousness. This meaningless condition is approached only by ideas that have entered consciousness for the first time. As they appear more frequently, they come gradually to take on more and more meaning. As they enter into wider connections, meaning increases and reaches a maximum when the idea is connected with all possible relevant experiences. The problem of meaning is one that occurs not in connection with reasoning or with language alone. It is a universal problem and must also be faced, if one is to understand perception, memory, action, or any of the other simplest mental states.

### MEANING AND ACTION

Meaning or the thought process in general can best be understood from its similarities with other mental operations. One of the most closely related processes and one that is also most familiar is action. Both Ach and Woodworth seem to have come to their conclusion that thought may go on without images from a study of the mental states that precede and initiate action. It was usually previously asserted that an idea of the act must be present in consciousness to start a movement of any sort. Some asserted that this must be a definite kinæsthetic image of the member to be moved. To move a finger one must think how the finger feels while making the movement. Both these authors found, on the contrary, that these images were rarely present when the movement was made. It might be argued, and, indeed, has at times been argued, that the image must have been present at some time in the process of learning. Bair,[6] in tracing the process by which one learned to move the ear, however, found that there was no necessary connection between the kinæsthetic sensation and the movement, that the sensation and the movement must be connected by some chance, if the idea was to serve as an excitant for the movement. While there is no single cue to movement, it does seem to be true that ordinarily one requires rather more elaborate imagery to start a movement in the beginning and that, after the movement has become more practiced and is better learned, this dies away. This simplification consists in connecting a larger and larger number of constituent partial movements with a single idea or intention. When beginning to write, each stroke needs attention; when beginning to sew or crochet, each stitch; but with the practice the vague intention to write a letter on a certain subject may be all that is necessary to take one to the typewriter in the other room and complete the writing. The only exception is that one usually must think when there are difficulties encountered in the way of expression or when a slip is made and an eraser is to be used. Each of these ideas is rather of the purpose to be accomplished than of the means to be used. Without our taking part in the controversy as to the character of the incentive to action, it may be asserted that one mental state comes to replace many. In a very active

---

[6] Blair, "The Development of Voluntary Control," *Psychological Review*, Vol. 8 (1901), pp. 474-510.

sense it may be said to represent them. So far as function is concerned, it may be said to mean them.

A second characteristic is the tendency for imagery to disappear, for the movement to be less and less in response to some conscious process, or to be less and less preceded or foreshadowed in consciousness and to recur more and more frequently directly upon some stimulus or excitation from the outside world. Thus Ach found, in his study of the antecedents of the movements required for pressing a key in response to a stimulus of any sort, that at first one might need some idea of the finger to be moved, but that sooner or later this would fall away and the movement result at once. If one were told to press a key with the first finger if red were shown, and with the ring finger if white appeared, at first when the card was presented the subject would need to think in some way of the first finger before the movement would be made. After a number of trials, this idea would drop away and the movement would come at once upon the exposure of the color designated. This, of course, is what takes place in the habit formation of daily life.

Still another feature that came out of the work of Ach was the influence of the determining purpose in the execution of the action. In the experiment cited above, if it was decided in advance that one should press the key with the first finger when red was shown, that movement came, at first, after thought, later automatically. If the instructions were to press with the middle finger for red, that movement was made. The attitude of mind determined by the instructions served to determine what movement should be made when the stimulus was given. This is the mental attitude, the correlate of the context that we found in Chapter VI to be active in controlling associations. Where the act is more complicated, it may be represented by some vague imagery plus the feeling that it can be executed. This feeling that it can be performed is the essential antecedent by any act, according to Woodworth, Thorndike, Ach, and Messer. This feeling or intention is partly made up of, in part determined by, the purpose or attitude, and partly is made up of vague memories that the act has been executed before, partly of partial activity of the nerve tracts that are to initiate the movement.

MEANING AND PERCEPTION

Similar instances are to be found in the simple cognitive processes. Even in perception, what is seen is not the mere mass of sensations from the eye that are entering consciousness, but is more a mass of irradiating experiences that are suggested by the bare sensations. The sound of a voice takes its value from the partially aroused associations with other occasions on which the voice has been heard. These in part take the definite form of the face or of the name of the individual; but more depends upon a vague arousal of associates, or upon the awareness that one could recall many of the earlier experiences with that man if one cared to. Altogether these have the same form as the intention of making a movement or the confidence that it can be made. In some cases the partial arousal of movements, or the suggestion of movements that might be made, has some effect upon the process. Berkeley long ago asserted that one saw distance in terms of the movements that would be necessary to reach the object. While this is not the only element involved in the idea of distance and probably not the most essential element, it may play some part in the total experience. Certain it is that distance is not a single sensation, but is rather a complex of experiences, most of which are not definitely conscious, but rather partially aroused associates of the sensation that is presented. Consciousness is always in greater part dependent on these added elements than upon the mere sensations. In this it is like the intention to act.

### MEANING AND RECOGNITION

The recognition process follows still more closely the course of the development of meaning. When an object presents itself for the first time, it arouses no associates. It seems altogether strange even when one recognizes its class sufficiently to give it general classification and so meaning. The process of recognition runs its course in very much the same way as the ideas that precede movement. At first an object or person is given a place by definite events or places that he calls up through association. You recall the place where the person has been seen before, his name and profession. You give the memory the setting it had when it first came to consciousness. The setting or the associates are called up in a very definite and complete form. As objects become more familiar, the clearness and definiteness of the reference diminish. The reference becomes more general. One thinks vaguely of the time or region in which the memory originated. With more complete acquaintance, the ideas of reference largely die away. The object is taken for granted as familiar, and no particular ideas are needed to evoke it or arise in connection with it. If we make the usual interpretation, it is seen that the development is the same as in movement with the single exception that the ideas and associates follow the original excitation instead of preceding the movement. At first the entering impression is given a place by associates it calls up. These are as clear and definite as the idea itself. As the familiarity increases, the associates are less

# WORDS AND THEIR MEANINGS 173

distinctly conscious; the reference is to a general class. Finally, they disappear altogether; one is immediately aware that the object or idea is familiar, but no reason or occasion for it is conscious. On the same assumptions that are made in connection with action, it seems that the associates that are at first fully aroused later become less and less fully conscious, until finally one has only the modification of consciousness that comes with partially opened association paths. The final stage corresponds to the automatic movement in which the movement is made through the same stimuli and by the action of the same nerve paths as the fully conscious movement, but consciousness has dropped away altogether. The intermediate stage of thought is the correlate of the period of automatization of action in which one is conscious of the general intention of moving, without any idea of the physiological processes that are to direct the movement. At the same time, the knowledge of the movement to be made is complete. In each case partially open association paths carry the knowledge.

### THE DEVELOPMENT OF MEANINGS

The development of meanings of all kinds follows very much the same general laws. If we take the process of learning a foreign language, the meanings of the words, when language is taught by the older methods, are caught at first only when they can be translated into their equivalents in the mother tongue. Gradually one catches the shade of the meaning that is distinct from the corresponding word in one's native speech. Then the reference is to objects and experiences that are mirrored directly, with no conscious presence of the familiar language. Finally, as in one's own language, the words and phrases have meaning for themselves without reference to anything else. At this stage the partially opened association paths replace the complete associations. There is an awareness of the meaning that is as effective in use as the definite conscious reference. As was seen in the earlier chapter, learning the telegraphic language goes through the same stages: first mere clicks that are long and short; then a grouping of the clicks with reference to the letters they stand for and only a painfully slow assembling of the letters to form words; then the word becomes the unit, later the sentence, but with constant reference to the ordinary speech; and, finally, all associates drop out but pictures and ideas. These come at once, and the dots and dashes may be said to constitute a real language with full meaning.

### MEANING IN THE EVOLUTION OF LANGUAGE

The evolution of meaning can be traced in the development of the race and in the individual. As was seen in the discussion of the origin of languages, when some movement of the hand or some vocal utterance first became connected with an object or thing, it took on meaning and its meaning developed and changed as associates were added. The study of the development of words is a study of the associates a word has. Usually a word originally designates an object or an act and then is extended to include the act as well as the object and the tool or individual that produces the act or is affected by the act. Later, some one part of the object or some one function of the object becomes predominant, the others disappear, and the word has a new meaning. But throughout the course of the development, it is the series of associates that are suggested by the word that constitutes its meaning. The same holds in the acquirement of language by the child. The word has a meaning that corresponds to its associates. At first, the reference is indefinite and somewhat uncertain. *Puss* is made to cover all small animals, but the meaning is dependent upon the associates and the associates determine the character and extent of the meaning. As the vocabulary grows and experiences accumulate, the meanings of the words change with them. Again it may be said in the child that the associates are at first definitely conscious and gradually fade away with increased familiarity with the objects.

More striking is the phase of the meaning of words in which not one but many objects or classes of objects are represented by the word. It is apparently almost universally true that in the savage languages and in the less developed languages in general, words and phrases at first refer to particular objects and acts. The Klamath Indian has no single word for run but a different one for the running of each animal, as the German has a different word for *eat* for the man and for the animal. Other languages have no single word for *brother* but different words for older and younger brother. It is only relatively late that the more general terms make their appearance, and even then the more particular terms are slow to disappear. One sees them in the specific names for the young and for the male and female of familiar animals that have persisted down to the present. In a sense, every word other than the names for individuals is general. They refer to classes of objects that are in some respect different from each other, rather than to a single object. *Dog* is only less general than *animal*, because it refers to fewer individuals and to individuals in some degree less different from one another. The very essence of language implies the representation of more than one individual. Here again one may assert that the general meaning is determined by the associations that have been formed with the word and that are more or less active when the word is spoken or heard. When one individual is meant, the associations are restricted more closely; when many individuals, less closely. John Brown has one associate, American has more, man a still greater number, and these associates, while seldom explicit, are effective in determining the meaning.

## MEANING IN IMAGERY

Most images other than words are similarly representative. One practically never thinks an object or event in complete detail. In fact, experiment seems to indicate that it is impossible for any event to be represented or imagined in its full completeness. As was seen in discussing imagery, even the most favored individuals do not have as many different kinds of imagery as of sensations. The range of images is insufficient to reproduce objects. As a matter of fact, if one will watch carefully the imagery as any object is recalled or remembered, it will be seen that everything is represented very schematically. Details are very largely lacking; rough outlines are made to do duty for much more than they reproduce. In other cases one is satisfied with the merest reference to the object or event; the resemblance between idea and thing is reduced to a minimum. One is sure that he could think it if necessary and is content with that assurance. This bare reference is apparently of the same sort whether it refers to a single object, to a group of objects, or to an abstract quality. In any case one may believe that it is due to the aura or fringe, which again is itself due to partially open association paths. The openness gives the certainty that the corresponding images might be recalled. One link in the chain does duty for the whole chain as is the case with the preliminaries of action. One may thus think man in general in terms of some representative man, as well as think of him as an individual. The imagery may be the same in both cases, but the irradiating associations, and consequently the meaning, would be different. The image that represents triangles in general is usually some particular triangle, if it is not a word, and the representation is based upon the belief that any other triangle would do as well in the situation in question. In short, images as well as words may be general and owe their generality to the same conditions. When very unlike the thing represented, they act as coins or symbols and have the same relation to it as words. If an image did not mean something beyond itself, it would be almost valueless. The mere content is little like anything in the world without or within, and is probably never twice alike even when the same thing is meant.

A SOLUTION OF THE PROBLEM OF THOUGHT

When once it is accepted that all mental contents are valuable rather for their meanings or references than for themselves, all the problems of thought are solved at a stroke. It is just as easy for an image or a word to mean a number of objects as to mean one, to mean a quality or a group of qualities as to mean a material object of the simplest kind. It is also just as comprehensible that it should stand for the relation or a general intention as for the things related or for a particular act. This possibility of reference is the same for ideas in what we call meaning as is the reference involved in the act of recognition, the interpretation in perception, or the intention in action. If it is a marvel in the case of meaning, it is just as much a marvel in the simpler process; and, if one refuses to admit that mental states have a value beyond themselves, they are worthless for the explanation of any mental process whatsoever. The physiological basis of the reference is apparently the same in each case also. It is probably to be found, in part at least, in the open or partially open association paths. Furthermore, one finds in each case that the processes are at first fully conscious and then gradually become less and less conscious with repetition. If one may close with a definition, let it be asserted that mental states have meaning because of the associations that have been formed about them; the nature of the meaning is determined by these associates whether fully or partially conscious. When associative reference is to many objects, one has a concept; when to a single object, a particular idea; when to the relation between two objects, the idea of relation in particular or in general. The reference alone marks the distinction. It is possible for the same mental state to be particular or general, thing or relation, according as the connections are of one kind or another.

It might well be asked what it is that is represented in certain obviously abstract terms or concepts such as, on the one hand, space, time, force, or, on the other, such relations as cause and effect or greater and less, or even in such a simple thing as the size that shall be accepted as standard when we see an object or even feel it. In each of these cases there is no single experience that can be regarded as real, nor can one say even that there is a group of experiences that together serves to give meaning to the particular experience that has meaning. Rather is the notion which is accepted as correct obtained by a process like the formation of a scientific hypothesis, by a series of trials and failures that are continued until a notion is attained that harmonizes with the facts. This happens even in the formation of percepts. Take the simplest case—the formation of the notion of the size of a simple object. The book that you hold in your hand casts an image upon the retina of perhaps 5 by 7 millimeters area. If you take the same

## WORDS AND THEIR MEANINGS 179

book across the room, it has the same size to all appearance, although it may cast an image not more than one-tenth as large. No matter how far away it may be, it always seems to have the same size in spite of the fact that its image changes with each distance. All objects are seen of a standard size, for the most part, with small objects of the size they would have at the distance at which they can be easily handled. Houses and similar large objects are usually thought of as of a size that can be conveniently appreciated or comprehended, the size that they will have when viewed at a distance that will permit them to be seen at a glance.

In the same way, one corrects the outlines of sides and tops of objects to allow for perspective. The true shape of a box has never been seen and cannot be seen from any position. It can only be reached by a process of mental construction not unlike that by which scientific theories are formed. Testing similar objects in corners and cutting and preparing objects of the sort serve to develop the idea of the object. In many cases it grows by a process of trial and error, until a construction is hit upon that satisfies the conditions. Those perceptions that persist under test conditions, or that are found to harmonize with various experiences, are accepted as real, while the others are rejected. One does not see after-images or contrast colors or similar optical phenomena, because, when tested, they are found not to have real existence. The empirical space forms develop in this way and it seems altogether probable that many of the more abstract notions of space and time, of force and energy, and the more static relations have a similar origin. They have developed out of experience, because it is found that they are needed to explain experience. But they are not like any single experience, since in many instances no single experience will satisfy the conditions. Just as the physicist thinks of vibrations where he sees colors or hears sound, so the common-sense observer reads right angles where he sees acute, thinks of time as running at the same rate instead of by uneven bounds, and ascribes causal efficacy to certain antecedents and mere antecedence to others. These abstract ideas or notions may be regarded as types, as ways of conceiving the world outside, which are necessary to make our experience consistent. When hit upon, they are accepted as real; while the single experiences that precede them are rejected as illusory, as unreal and untrue.

The way in which these types present themselves to consciousness varies from case to case. Where it is possible, they are constructed like architects' drawings. Triangles and squares are represented as they would be constructed. Space as a whole is pictured as mere emptiness, or a tri-dimensional system of references is called up. But in many cases some one thing is used as representative of a number of different things. The type image is of value rather more for its meaning than for its actual content. As Titchener's image of a relation is of two objects bound together by rubber bands, so time may be represented by a spatial image with verbal extensions or with meanings that are added or understood. Just as meanings refer not to things that have been seen, but to types or constructions, so the types to which they refer are sometimes constructions of a theoretical character that cannot be pictured definitely but which are thought of by reference to sets of thoughts. So it is very difficult to say exactly what one has in mind when one thinks force or cause, but one knows perfectly what is meant. There is something of kinæsthetic imagery in both cases. One feels the muscles contract as the idea presents itself. But this is not necessarily the essence of the idea; rather is it a means of referring to the elements. They typify all force, all the active life and its relations, by representing one form and meaning all others. These types which have been developed in the endeavor to give consistency to experience as a whole are accepted by the individual as the fundamental realities. For common sense they are the real things that persist amid the illusions of sense perception. In some cases they have a definite pictorial representation in which there are no inconsistencies; in others there is but a core of mental content with a wide fringe of reference.

Thus the circle is complete. The concrete imagery refers to abstract types which even in perception are accepted as more real than the immediate sense experience. When one asks what the type or abstract idea is in itself, one finds that it in turn may be merely a reference, the appreciated possibility of making a construction that will satisfy the conditions of experience. Thus the concrete image derives its value for thought from its reference to the type, the precipitate from experience. When one attempts to discover the characteristics of the type, it may be an actual mental construction, but it may also be a reference, a reference to a construction which is merely felt to be possible rather than actually made. The real value of the mental process for thought is its meaning, and the meaning is a reference not to one experience but to many, and these experiences are not definitely present in consciousness, but are only felt to be capable of being called up.

As a result of the process of testing, corrected ideas of separate objects develop, and these separate things are also put together to make wider wholes. Thus every man has an ordered system of experiences. For the primitive man this is extremely simple and filled with references to unknown forces. Personification or anthropomorphism is the fundamental principle of explanation. Nevertheless, this system of knowledge, this interpretation of natural phenomena, is accepted as a fundamental part of reality, since it is needed to bring order out of the chaos of immediate experience. The man of science has other constructions which fulfill the same function, but more adequately, we believe, since they take into consideration a much larger number of facts, harmonize a larger number of experiences more completely than do the primitive explanations. The system of knowledge is, however, a means of bringing order into the various experiences. Its laws are developed by chance trial and error, as are the types of separate objects in perception. The systems are constantly changing for the individual and for science as a whole, but each is accepted as true while it exists, and only changes when some new construction is found more fully to harmonize with the experiences. Such laws as the conservation of energy and Grimm's law are constructions of this character. Energy itself, ether, gravitation, are, as things and forces, on the same basis as the square top of the table, typical constructions that have value as means of harmonizing concrete experiences. Each of these constructions is accepted as very real and has a great value in perception, in memory, and in all of the concrete mental processes.

All the four theories of thought with which we started may be said to fall into one. Thinking may go on in words or in images equally well, but that which makes both images and words capable of carrying thought is not their peculiar structure but their reference, and the reference in either case is not to other words or images, but to types, to organized experiences, and to their representatives. But this reference to types does not serve to distinguish thought processes from the simpler mental states, for the simplest percepts and memories are also shot through with types, with references to these abstract thoughts. No consciousness is entirely without this typical meaning, although growth in intelligence is marked by progress from the relatively meaningless to the meaningful.

The problem of thought without images is not so easy. All careful observers agree that there are certain instances of thought without words or without adequate images. To make this a peculiar phenomenon would make a break in structure with no corresponding break in function. No one argues that imageless thought is necessarily more adequate than thought in images or words. All admit that images may be present and that when they are present the thought fulfills exactly the same function as when they are absent. There is no reason given why they should be absent. Their absence has no more virtue than their presence. The differences seem altogether fortuitous, even if we admit all the claims of their advocates.

At least four analogies might be drawn between thought processes and other processes which would make it seem probable that thought should be less imaginal after much practice than before and which would make it possible for the imageless thought to be the limiting stage of all thought. It has been indicated that the conscious accompaniments of movement gradually disappear until in automatic acts no consciousness need be present. The same holds of the recognition process. At first one recognizes by calling up definite associates. Later one is sure that a face is familiar with a vague setting or with no setting, but recognition is still assured. Titchener brings forward what he calls the *stimulus error* to explain the fact that mental contents are overlooked. This term designates the tendency to keep attention fixed upon the meaning of the mental state, usually the object that it represents, rather than upon the mental state itself. One does not appreciate how little of what one reads is actually seen, because one is interested in the matter rather than in the sensations that represent it. In thinking one is always concerned with the result and the meaning that is intended at different stages of the process rather than with the mental imagery itself. One does not notice the lack of visual or auditory imagery until attention is called to it, because facts are adequately represented by the imagery that one has. Conversely, one is very likely to say there is no image present when one is thinking, since one is concerned always with the meaning, never with the content. Even the most skilled observers are likely to lose themselves in the meanings of their mental images and not be sure of the images themselves. Still another suggestion is made recently by G. E. Müller, which is, however, consistent with all of the others. This is that there are always ideas that may become unclear or not accurately representative.[7] When one thinks that a certain reference is in a part of a book but can't say exactly where, it may be that imagery consists of a finger running over a part of a page in a definite place in the book. It is sufficiently indefinite to be overlooked or so apparently inappropriate as to be forgotten. All considerations make it probable that the so-called imageless thought is a development or degeneration from thinking in images, and that the images may in many cases be present but be overlooked owing to their vagueness or to the interest in the meaning or the reference.

In brief, the essence of all thought processes is to be found in the fact of meaning. Meaning in its turn is due to the associations that are aroused by the mental content or, when associations are not fully aroused, by the partially open association paths. The meaning of a word is primarily the associates that it partially arouses and which give it color. When the associates that are excited change,

---

[7] "Zur Analyse der Gedachtnisstatigkeit und des Vorstellungsverlaufes," *Zeitschrift für Psychologie*, Ergänzungsband 9, 2$^t$er Teil, pp. 505-567.

the meaning of the word changes. This can be seen in the historical development of words which will be discussed in a later chapter. Meaning in this sense constitutes the real essence of mental processes. It alone gives value to a mental state, be it image or word. With it any structure is valuable, and the structure is a matter of indifference and is often neglected. Without it the most wonderful imagery is nonsense or delusion.

Accepting the view that it is the meaning of mental processes, not their structure, that is important, all the thought problems vanish. A concept is no more difficult to understand than a percept, an abstract idea than a concrete. One means a number of objects on the type of a particular one; the other means a single one understood in the light of many. Relations can be meant as readily as structures. General intentions and plans for work or an order of procedure may be referred to as simply as single things. The so-called complicated processes are seen to be really not more complicated than the simplest perceptions and images, when once the latter have been completely analyzed. There is not much more of the abstract, of the type, in the one than in the other. The usefulness of each is derived from the same element. The train of thought is a series of ordered references to the outside world. The outside world, in turn, is for the subject a harmonious system of types that has been developed through the reaction of thought and perception to give consistency to experience. It is a train of thought, this succession of meanings that precedes speech. It is our next problem to see how it is translated into words, bearing in mind the fact that part of it is already in words when first it presents itself to consciousness.

In the study of the relation of thought to language, one may assume that what one means by thought is some form of this system of meanings; by language, either the words as mental images or the actual motor processes and sounds heard that are called out by the thought. It is by no means easy to make sure exactly what goes on in the individual mind when one speaks. This is in large part due to the fact that one is much more concerned with the outcome, with what is being said and the effect that it shall have upon the hearer, than with the mental operations. In consequence of this, those who have written on the subject have for the most part advanced theories of a purely speculative character, based on what they thought should go on rather than upon actual observation of the process.

### REFERENCES

DELACROIX, H.—*La langage et la pensée* (Paris, F. Alcan, 1924), pp. 361-398.

PILLSBURY, W. B.—*Psychology of Reasoning* (New York, Appleton, 1910), Chaps. III and V.

TITCHENER, E. B.—*Experimental Psychology of the Thought Processes* (New York, Macmillan, 1909).

# CHAPTER X

## THE MENTAL ANTECEDENTS OF SPEECH

It was said in discussing speech as a motor process that an idea of some sort always started the mechanism of speech. It also appeared that one must distinguish in some degree, at least, between ideas and words as incentives to vocal utterance. When we make this distinction in the light of the discussion of the last chapter, two problems must be considered: (1) How does thought get translated into words as one prepares to speak? (2) What bearing does this have upon actual vocal expression? The first of these problems is by far the more important, since, so far as consciousness is concerned, having the word is practically the only condition necessary for its utterance. In attempting a statement of the problem, it is necessary to distinguish different cases. With reference to the relation between thought and language, one must have noticed that there are many instances in one's own experience in which the problem could not arise at all. Very frequently one talks without noticeable antecedent imagery. In other cases one has a vague notion of what is to be said in advance of talking, but no definite words or separate images that correspond to the words. In other cases words are presented and judgment passed on them before they are uttered, and there is also the general notion of what is to be said in addition to the words, and before the separate words develop. In still other cases the processes reach a maximum of fullness. There is first the anticipatory intention, then a further elaboration as thought, then translation into words, and finally the vocal utterance. This most complete form is the least frequently noticed, but since it is possible and actually does occur, it may perhaps be made the type for discussion and explanation.

## WUNDT'S THEORY OF THE ANALYTIC DEVELOPMENT OF SENTENCES

A theory that can be made a starting point for discussion is offered by Wundt's assertion that the process of the development of the sentence in preparation for speech is nearly always analytic rather than synthetic. He insists that there is ordinarily in mind a complete idea of what is to be said before the sentence is formulated and, furthermore, that the way from the anticipatory total idea to the sentence is ordinarily one of analysis. The idea is present in all its entirety before the sentence or its anticipatory thought elements present themselves. These part ideas or words are selected or analyzed from the total idea, and at the same time they are thus selected, they are seen to have certain relations to each other. By the very process of analysis or by virtue of their earlier connections they have or are given certain relations to one another that determine their connections in the sentence as a whole. On this view, discrete thought would be only a process of elaborating what is earlier contained in a total idea. The advantage of this way of putting the problem, from Wundt's point of view, is that it avoids the necessity for raising the question of how the elements of the sentence are put together. They are found together. The question is only one of how they are made distinct in the total complex or matrix in which they are found.

Unfortunately, Wundt does not make very clear the nature of the preliminary idea. It is apparently for him something almost as definite as a real perception. If one examines one's own consciousness, there are occasions that seem to harmonize with this picture; but these come, for the most part, when one is describing some event or object from memory, rather than when thought is more constructive. Suppose, for example, one is endeavoring to describe a landscape. If one is of the visual type, one sees it at first in its entirety in the "mind's eye," and then selects one feature after another for description. The objects are all there before the processes of analysis and description. These two processes consist in selecting one feature after another and supplying the words that best describe them. But this is the only case in which introspection seems to justify the statement that there is a definite anticipatory idea that is analyzed and translated into words. Even here one might question whether the selection did not really add something to the picture that was at first in mind and whether the process was not, in part, one of recalling elements of the original picture as well as merely picking out one part after the other. Certain it is that the picture in mind before analysis into parts and the picture as analyzed are not identical. Indeed, Wundt says that the analyzed thought is clearer and more distinct; but besides this the process of analysis has enriched the content. It is difficult to determine whether recall through association has not played quite as important a part as has mere analysis. But even this slight justification for the preliminary idea as container of the material that is to be obtained and described in language is absent in all other forms of description. When one is describing an object through motor or auditory recall, it is not all in mind at once, but comes in a bit at a time. There is no question of analysis in that case. When one is thinking of anything abstract, again, it is not easy to see how the whole situation can be present in advance of its formulation and the work of thought consist in nothing but analysis. Here is where construction must take place, if thought is at all constructive. Wundt, on the contrary, would make the mere description more thoroughly and completely construction and the more abstract thought the more analytical process. He distinguishes two forms of sentence structure, the analytic and synthetic. The analytic is used for the most part in abstract speech. The synthetic or purely associative predominates in the descriptive forms. Evidently, the process that to introspection seems more analytical, namely, where the idea to be expressed is present as a whole before it is broken up for description, is characteristic of the associative sentences predicated by Wundt.

But while one cannot take Wundt's description as seriously as he means it, still he emphasizes certain important features of the preliminaries of speech that must be taken account of in any theory or description. First, while we cannot agree that the idea to be expressed is always definitely present in consciousness in advance of analysis and expression, yet it is certainly true that there is some foreshadowing of what is to be said before it is definitely prepared for expression. In the second place, it must be admitted that the same elements that give an inkling of what is coming also furnish the conditions that serve to unite the different elements of thought and of the sentence, or, more accurately, make the elements really belong together from the beginning rather than be separate at first and require to be put together as is sometimes assumed by writers on language. On the other hand, it is logically impossible that the idea can both be present in advance of analysis and be developed by thinking. As a matter of fact, give this description the most liberal latitude possible in interpretation, and still it is very seldom that the actual process of preparing thought for utterance takes the form that Wundt indicates of a total idea, an analysis of that total idea, and then a translation of the parts into words.

### PRELIMINARY INTENTION

One must, in any discussion of the speech process, go even farther than Wundt in insisting that any particular speech element can be understood only in its setting, in the general situation of the man at the moment, and in the general context of the individual thinker before any sentence is spoken. One sentence grows out of another, and still farther back one idea is the outgrowth of earlier ideas, so that one cannot understand any single step or stage in a discourse unless one considers what has gone before it in the discourse, the general social situation in which the speaker finds himself, as well as the more remote bits of knowledge, and the earlier connections with the members of the group to whom he is speaking. If one were to sketch a list of the factors that are involved in thinking, one would have to begin with a statement of the problem, and this could only be stated if one were to go back to a fairly general purpose that had been developed gradually in the experience of the thinker. I am writing this sentence now as a result of my intention to discuss the mental antecedents of sentences in general. That intention has developed gradually out of other problems, as the result of reading and observation that raised the question whether one thinks before one speaks and how far thinking precedes this speaking and what form it takes. If one drops into this attitude for some purely nonprofessional train of thought, there is a fairly complete break in the train of ideas. The new series began where one was working last week or yesterday on the same problem, but all that is remembered of what has been said before has its influence on the train of thought at the present moment. The first controlling influence on speech, then, is the group of antecedent experiences that in a sense constitutes this attitude and in a sense controls the attitude, which is renewed and aroused as I sit down to the typewriter with the intention of doing a little work on this particular topic.

But it is not implied that this intention necessarily carries with it the full details of all that is to be said. Much of the intention is no more than a general idea of the problem to be solved. There are vague references to Wundt and the feeling that his theory is incomplete and one-sided. Notions are current of the influence of meaning and the possibility that the Würzburg schools and Woodworth's naked-thought theory may play a part in the matter, that in any case they are all wrestling with the same problem and are probably all aware of the same group of facts and may really mean the same thing as a solution, except that they are taking partial views of the total processes, and each is prevented from seeing the truth in the other's view by the different methods of approach. These different ideas are not clearly represented at one time. In fact, all that may be clear is that one must analyze this preliminary idea. The elements flit in and out as the process of analysis proceeds and before anything is formulated in words, before satisfaction with the result is sufficient to make it possible to formulate the attempt in words. There is nearly always some preliminary idea. One knows that a certain notion is to come, one does not have a definite presentation of it. One knows *that,* but not *what.* One nearly always has the belief that it is sufficiently clear to

## MENTAL ANTECEDENTS OF SPEECH

stand formulation before the words begin to make their appearance, but it is not analyzed. The different parts are not represented as distinct, and there is no foreshadowing of the form of the sentence before writing takes place, and still less before one speaks, even in the somewhat formal process of lecturing without notes. What Wundt calls the total idea proves on analysis to be nothing more than this intention to say something when one begins to express any bit of abstract thinking, and need be no more than that in connection with more concrete mental operations.

The form that this intention to say something takes, varies from individual to individual and from moment to moment. In the experiments of Bühler and others it seems to be nothing more than the satisfaction that the subject is ready to speak, and this may be no more than the removing of inhibitions. In any case it comes in no particular imagery, certainly no imagery that a critical observer would say was adequate to what was to be said. In fact, we may say in the light of present controversy that the total idea is nothing more than something that *means* what is to be said, rather than anything that resembles or *is* what is to be said. It can only be asserted in the most metaphorical sense that this is analyzed in the process of speaking. There is really nothing there to analyze, in the sense that one can analyze a painting or a landscape that is present in the world outside. In most cases one would not know that there had been anything in mind unless the formulation in words had taken place. Certainly one would not have known what was in mind were it not for the expression, and could one give to anyone else an accurate description of the mental content that preceded the sentence, he himself would not recognize it as the matrix from which the sentence had been chipped.

## 194    THE PSYCHOLOGY OF LANGUAGE

### FORMULATION OF THE IDEA IN WORDS

On the negative side, it seems that Wundt's description of the processes that precede speech is not adequate. How, then, does this intention become fulfilled, how do the vague foreshadowings of what is to be said actually take form? As has been implied above, this varies greatly with the material to be expressed. In the case of more abstract thinking which we have started to analyze, it appears that the formulation of the idea first takes place in words. There is the preliminary intention, which may be sufficient for several sentences. Then the words come as a result of association, first with the idea, then as a consequence of the connection between the words themselves under the influence of the more general purpose or intention.

It is more of a problem what determines the associations that start the sentence. The first idea of a series put into words may come from the preceding sentence; it may come from the preceding train of ideas; it may be due to the fact that it seems to require particularly accurate statement or analysis; or it may be determined by the social environment at the moment. Someone may have appeared; or it may chance that the idea that has presented itself promises to be particularly interesting to the companion with whom one has been sitting or walking in silence; or more frequently where one has been with someone else, it may be in response to a question. The response to a social need, immediate or possible, present or in prospect, constitutes the most usual incentive. But very much of our more serious thinking is given the verbal form for the sake apparently of definiteness and of being tested as to its truth in that form. Part of the test may be that it is merely more definitely formulated and thus can be evaluated in its details. In rarer cases it may be put in the conventional forms of logic; more frequently, in the unconventional, but more habitual, forms that have been found to be adequate in practice. Often, too, the formulation is given that it may be ready for an imaginary audience, and the result accepted or rejected as past experience has shown the ordinary auditor or customary audience would accept or reject an argument of that form. In consequence of these different factors, much, if not most, of adult thought, particularly serious abstract thought, is in words, even when the individual is alone and has no intention of preparing a discourse for future delivery to an audience.

Granted the general intention to express something, the preliminary intention to express some particular thing, which is indicated by a most general mental content that means that thing in the vaguest way, nothing seems to intervene between that and the appearance of the words in consciousness. If one is talking or the situation is one that demands or permits expression, the words come at once. Occasionally, the formulation in words is slightly in advance of actual expression; but that need not be the case and, ordinarily, is not, unless one is talking in dictation or unless some other circumstance demands unusual slowness of speech. Most of the description of what intervenes between thought and formulation in language is of this negative character. No idea, or at least but the vaguest and apparently the most inadequate idea, precedes the appearance of the words, or even the actual speech or writing. There is never, or extremely rarely, a sequence of ideas that comes before speech that can be said to be sufficiently detailed to be translated into words. Speech comes as a result of the intention and of the conditions under which thinking takes place, and for no reason other than that the situation and fulfillment of the intention to speak demand the words.

In the large, it may be said that the cerebral or mental mechanism of itself gives forth the words that are appropriate. What one can be seen to do is to pass upon this product as to its adequateness to the purpose in hand. This judgment may be passed either after the intention has been formulated in words, but before expression, or in ordinary conversation after the words have actually been spoken. In writing, it is more usually the case that one thinks what is to be said first and then writes only after the sentence has passed inspection. In conversation one may reject an entire sentiment that presses for expression. One less frequently may notice that one has a word in thought just ready to speak that is not suitable, that will not pass the subjective censor; but much more often than in writing one actually gives expression to a thought and then sees that it is not what was intended. One must then modify it, usually with an apology that that was not what was meant.

### PROCESS OF CENSORING LANGUAGE

Two further problems naturally arise in connection with the general question of how thought passes over into words: (1) the one already mentioned and postponed, what is it that determines the word that shall come to mind? and (2) how is one able to pass upon the expression that is thought of or that has been spoken to determine that it is or is not what one desired to say? Both processes are alike in that they cannot be definitely observed by the speaker, but can only be studied indirectly through observing under what circumstances they go wrong and under what circumstances they lead to desired results.

The process of censoring is not unlike the processes of recognition and of passing upon the truth or falsity of a statement that has been heard. It is like the criticisms that are passed upon works of art, upon æsthetic creations, or upon a conclusion that has been attained. It probably depends, like all of the others, upon the wide-reaching associates that have been developed in past experience, which are aroused, sometimes completely, sometimes latently or partially, by the words as they are suggested or uttered. Often one notes that a word that has been thought of in one connection, under the influence of one mental attitude or setting, will arouse an entirely different group of associates in a mind dominated for the moment by another idea. The second possible setting suddenly presents itself just after the phrase has been used, and the associations that result are seen to be not at all in harmony with the intention that is controlling the expression as a whole. On the purely formal side, one may become aware, after the formulation, that some definite rule of grammar has been violated, or some other accepted generalization of good practice may suggest itself, with which the statement made will not square. On the whole, however, the judgment is passed in terms of unformulated past experience. The sentence pleases or does not please at once. Then on the side of mere expression, one usually looks first to see what it is that does not please, that is awkward or worse; then discovers the part of the expression that is wrong; and finally may decide how this is wrong and why, by reference to rules and canons of good taste. It is striking that in this, as in so many similar judgments, the recognition that something is wrong is likely to come before the appreciation of what it is that offends; just as in the simpler comparisons or judgments one can tell that two sensations are different, before it is possible to say how they are different. One can

## 198  THE PSYCHOLOGY OF LANGUAGE

say that one tone is different from another before he can say which is higher. In passing on the truth or falsity of an argument, it is nearly always the case that one decides that the formulation is not correct before it can be said what is wrong, and it is only still later that one can say why it is wrong.

The same process can be traced, in much the same way as for language, in the judgment of a picture, a house, or any work of art. One first is impressed that it is unsatisfactory or inadequate, then turns to the analysis of detail, and finally makes reference to accepted rules of practice, if one knows them, to justify one's criticism. The first vague dissatisfaction comes not only first, but much more frequently than either of the actions. One is frequently certain that a statute or a sentence is unsatisfactory without ever being able to refer the dissatisfaction to its causes. The occasion for the dissatisfaction is to be found in some group of factors that do not come clearly to consciousness. The same group of associates that cluster around a mental state to give it meaning also seem to be active in censoring the products of consciousness. They are not of themselves conscious in this activity any more than they are in the meaning; but, nevertheless, they are the final arbiters of expression, as they are the final determinants of meaning. It is not at all unlikely that the same set of associates that in one case gives meaning to the words or phrase as it presents itself in the discourse also serves to decide that it is appropriate or the reverse, when the expression is censored. Usually the expression merely passes muster; there is even no explicit thought as to whether it is or is not satisfactory; but when some false note is sounded it is usually because a new set of associates, different from those which gave it meaning, is aroused to pass upon it. From the standpoint of instruction, the most effective means of improving the taste seems to be not in giving rules in explicit formulation, but in acquiring familiarity with the best in expression, with the best in literature, with the approved in conversation. This experience and this alone will give the background against which one's own language may be judged. Practice in recognizing solecisms will help, but unless the other background is present, unless there is a wide experience with correct expression, the censorship is likely to be lax or perverted. Rules, too, have their place but are helpful for the most part only after some skill in detecting inaccuracies has been developed; they are used only to justify a correction or rejection of a defective form, not to detect it.

Decision as to whether the meaning is adequately expressed rests upon exactly the same basis and follows the same course. It is much more closely related to meaning than is decision on the grammatical accuracy or æsthetic qualities of the expression. If there is conflict between the associates that a phrase suggests and the intention of the speaker, the phrase is immediately rejected. One tries again, if the phrase has not been spoken, and may keep trying until some group of words presents itself that satisfies the censor. Then expression proceeds. If one is conversing or speaking before an audience, it is necessary to withdraw the statement. One says, "That is not what I meant," and substitutes another expression, or the meaning is made clear by a series of explanatory statements that seem to elucidate, but which may merely annul and replace the original statement. The process of judging is largely concealed; one sees only the result. The experiences that happen to be active at the moment pass upon the statement. One can be sure that these are active only because one sees that phrases that are accepted change with the accumulation of experience. The method by which they pass upon it, one cannot see. A statement is rejected at once or accepted at once; one only occasionally sees why. So far as the process can be traced, it appears to lie in the fact that when expressed the phrase arouses associates that were not aroused by the intention, or, as was said, it is seen that it might suggest ideas that were not suggested by the intention or the other mental content, whatever it may have been, that preceded the speech. These associates are seen not to harmonize with the intention, although the words as viewed in the first way suggested nothing incompatible with the earlier intention. But the process of deciding whether these associates are or are not in harmony with the intention is exactly the same as that which rejects the phrase. In each case earlier experience passes immediately upon its fitness. Only its effects are seen.

### FORMULATION OF LARGER UNITS OF SPEECH

Taking up the first problem, that of determining the conditions which lead to the formulation of the phrases and sentences or larger wholes of speech, we find those conditions in large part concealed. Ultimately the process resolves itself into a matter of association under the control of the general setting, the intentions and what not that are prominent at the moment. The first association is between the intention and the form of sentence that is to be used. Such a difference as that which gives rise to the indicative or the interrogatory sentence, for example, must depend upon a connection between definite purpose and a definite arrangement of words. There is, of course, no explicit intention to use an interrogatory sentence, but the antecedents which make the speaker desire to obtain rather than to impart information lead to the appearance of the verb before the noun. There is, of course, nothing more than an habitual association between a desire of this sort and the particular arrangement of words, as is evident from the different expression of the question in different languages. The interrogatory mood governs the associations between the single words, and this attitude of mind, together with the particular need for information and an appreciation of the fact that the person present may supply the information, is sufficient to start the formulation or expression of the sentence. Once started, the connections between the words that have been used before in similar cases, guided always by the wider purpose or intention, serve to carry the sentence to its end.

Similar purposes and intentions serve to determine other matters of form of expression. Thus, as Owen has pointed out, there is practically no difference in the ideas expressed by the passive and the active voice. One is chosen rather than the other because of the prominence of one element or another in the thought to be expressed. If the speaker is interested in the thing acted upon, that is made the subject and thereby made prominent; if the agent or the action is of greater interest, that is made the subject. Aside from the immediate intention, one finds that a number of other circumstances may play a considerable part in determining the form of speech. Thus the prototype of all speech, the simple interjection, comes under the influence of emotion. An idea that might be expressed in a full sentence in usual circumstances calls out under surprise or anger or other strong emotion merely the single word and that in the form of an exclamation. Similarly, the distance of the hearer makes a difference in the form of expression. What would be expressed at length to one near at hand will be communicated in a word if the hearer is several hundred yards away. The shepherd cries, "Wolf!" to his master, while the summer visitor may express no more in a long and leisurely disquisition to his companion in the passing motor car.[1]

Once a particular form of expression is started in response to the intention, guided by the emotional attitude and external condition, the continuation of the expression, whether thought only or expressed, is largely due to associations between the words themselves. In a language spoken fluently no thought is required for a phrase once started. The words fuse by association into larger groups, sentences, or phrases, and these even may associate into groups. One of these groups may be touched off by an appropriate stimulus and when thus touched off runs to its conclusion of itself without conscious guidance, with no more than the censorship of the general intention or meaning, and even this is aroused only by a mistake of some sort. One returns a greeting, or will respond to a remark about the weather, without thinking or even without knowing that one has. The set phrase of response is merely associated as a whole with the phrase heard. Much the same relation is established in connected thought and discourse between general intention and special sentence and even between phrase and phrase. All is guided, however, by the general purpose that has led one to think and is subject to the censorship of past experience as to both matter and form. In the larger aspects, the different ideas suggest one another as large general ideas. Each of these may suggest a series of subordinate, but still general, ideas and these in turn less general ideas that again suggest the particular sentences. The ideas are of the vaguest sort and need not be more than intentions. These finally suggest sentences and then phrases and serve to evoke words.

---

[1] Edward T. Owen, "The Relations Expressed by the Passive Voice," *Transactions of Wisconsin Academy of Science, Arts, and Letters*, Vol. 17, Pt. 1, pp. 1-65.

## CRITICISM OF WUNDT'S THEORY

To go back to the discussion of Wundt's theory: in abstract thought, one cannot say that language comes as a result of the analysis of an idea present before speech begins. The most that can be said is that there is a general intention first, and that this general intention arouses a series of associates in verbal form. The analysis, if present, is only of a logical concept, not of an actually present idea, nor of any psychological entity. The results of these analyses are for the most part larger groups rather than single words. The words come by association with one another and with the general ideas. The course of each thought is really much more a development of its meaning than a mere analysis of what was present in it. What develops was in no sense present before the development.

Even if one considers the sort of thinking and speaking that most nearly follows the description that Wundt sets forth, the description of some object or scene that is held before the mind's eye, the process is necessarily not merely an analysis. If one attempts to recall and describe a scene from the past, even if a visualizer, one will have at first usually a comparatively vague outline of the scene, sometimes only a symbol for it. As one proceeds, the different parts of the scene become clear one after the other. It is very difficult to say whether these new elements are analyzed from the mass that is actually present or whether they are added by association with what was thought of before. In most cases the process is at least a mixed one; something is added by association even if something is analyzed from the preliminary idea. One may say quite confidently that in no case is there a preliminary idea from which the different ideas that are represented in the words are analyzed, without being added to or suggested by preliminary ideas.

## 204   THE PSYCHOLOGY OF LANGUAGE

Rather, we always have a preliminary purpose. The words to its attainment are suggested by earlier words, and these suggest others that were not present before the formulation. Wundt's views on sentence structure are doubtless based largely on his introspective analysis of his own speech habits. It is quite likely that the form of thought spoken of above as possible in the case of the description of something familiar is the form habitually followed by Wundt even in other kinds of thought.

It is interesting to note also the division that Wundt makes of sentences into groups, the apperceptive and associative. The one would be constituted of the sentences that correspond to the analysis of a preliminary idea, the other of instances in which subject is added to predicate by mere association. That one in which most comes from the preliminary idea was the apperceptive or closed form; that in which practically all was due to the addition of new elements, the associative or open. The former was used in abstract thought, the latter in description. We have seen, however, that in practice abstract thought usually is the result of associative additions. Description alone shows signs of a preliminary idea that can be analyzed. On the other hand, there is always a preliminary intention, a forewarning of what is to be said in a symbol with a meaning. The development of this meaning constitutes thinking and the formulation of the sentence, processes that go hand in hand. This holds both for abstract thought and for description. The intention at once guides and controls the associations that give rise to subordinate ideas and to their expression in words, and passes upon their adequacy to express the meaning, that is, to carry out the intention. There are differences in the degree to which the associations may be controlled by the purpose, but nothing more. The types of expression are fundamentally one. Classifications,

# MENTAL ANTECEDENTS OF SPEECH

in consequence, are bound to shade into one another rather than to have sharp lines of division. Nevertheless, the fundamental notions of the nature of a sentence which Wundt holds must be maintained against the older schools. The unit is a preliminary idea that develops in the sentence, and this preliminary idea or intention is itself determined by wider antecedent intentions and in its turn determines the later and subordinate meanings or intentions; the sentence and the words are subordinated to all. They are not the units as they have often been made. It is from this fact that the end of the sentence may control the beginning, as well as the beginning control the end. No part can be isolated from the whole, and in the whole must be considered the antecedent thought: large masses of the earlier experiences, the present environment, particularly the social environment, the emotional as well as the intellectual condition of the individual at the time of speaking.

### RELATION OF THE ACTUAL EXPRESSION TO THE THOUGHT

If we assume that the words have been formulated mentally and the sentence prepared for expression, there is still the problem of the relation of the actual expression to these thoughts. As was said before, one must distinguish at least three different cases: one, in which expression and thought are a unit. The thought comes to consciousness only as it is spoken; a second, in which thought and speech are distinct, but utterance comes a sufficiently long time after the thought to give full development to a whole thought before expression; and the third, in which speech merely lags behind thought, and one is thinking of what is to be said a little later as one speaks a sentence that has been formulated earlier. Here one is uttering a thought formulated in words a short time before and at the same time preparing another to be expressed later. The first offers few problems. The vocal organs act at once under the influence of the intention, the social environment, and the habitual connections of the movements of the vocal or writing organs. There is no internal speech, or internal speech and expression are practically one. All that has been said of the formulation of internal speech above could be repeated here, except that the word "habit" would replace the word "association."

For the second case also little discussion is needed. The formulated words arouse the vocal organs as they might in reading. It is a simple case of ideomotor action. The third requires a little more consideration. It would appear at first sight that, with the formulation of new sentences holding attention, they would be spoken rather than the words that had been decided upon some seconds or a minute before. It seems, however, that speaking the sentence earlier formulated goes on automatically. This is entirely similar to automatic action of any sort. One cuts a sheet while reading, talks while walking, eats while thinking of something far away. The automatic execution of a movement while attention is occupied with something else is an event of almost continuous occurrence. It shows only that the connection of vocal movements with ideas is extremely close and that probably many phrases or sentences constitute units that may be initiated as wholes by a single idea. The guidance of the vocal organs depends in part upon speech habits which make one movement start the next in the series, in part upon the fact that there is a primary memory of the words to be spoken, similar to the after-image or the tune that when first heard runs through one's head, that may act as an excitant of the movement when the first idea no longer occupies attention.

## MENTAL ANTECEDENTS OF SPEECH

The control of this automatic speech is frequently not so accurate as the control by fully conscious words. The plural subject is more likely to call out the singular verb, particularly when several singular nouns have been used since the subject was spoken. There is more likelihood that a word will be succeeded by one that has been frequently connected with it, rather than by the one that has been intended. Mistakes, in general, are more likely to occur under these conditions. In lecturing extemporaneously it is noticed that one frequently falls into this divided state of attention. While ordinarily all goes well, occasionally when one is too much interested in something that is coming, misspeaking occurs. Association takes the upper hand; control by intention and purpose is reduced. It is in case of slips that one obtains the best instance of the action of the censor. One may be apparently entirely wrapped up in the decision of some point that is to come, when suddenly a jarring note makes its appearance, attention turns at once to the words just pronounced that are still ringing in the ears (primary memory), sees what is wrong, and corrects it. Attention is attracted by the mistake, by the failure of the mechanism, where correct speech would attract no notice. That the two mental operations are not entirely distinct is shown, too, by the instances in which one will speak a word that should be spoken in connection with what is being formulated rather than what is being spoken. These mistakes are as frequent as those due to any other cause. It seems, then, that, while the automatic speech is distinct from the words that really dominate consciousness, it is sufficiently under control to have mistakes in expression detected at once by the dominant consciousness, and for words from the more prominent mental process to break into the series that is being actually spoken. While the two are essentially distinct and subject largely to different controls, constituting a form of partial dissociation, the line of separation is by no means complete. The partially conscious automatic operation may at any moment be brought to the bar of full consciousness, may be disturbed by the word processes that constitute the major operation, and is at all times largely subject to the control of the wider experience.

### REFERENCES

DELACROIX, H.—*La langage et la pensée* (Paris, F. Alcan, 1924), pp. 398-435.
WUNDT, WILHELM.—*Voelkerpsychologie* (Leipzig, Engelmann, 1900), Vol. I, Teil 1.

## CHAPTER XI

### SOUND CHANGES IN LANGUAGE

It has become clear from the preceding chapters that language is not stable, but that there is continual change both in the movements of the muscular tissue and in the ideas which the movements symbolize. This instability is abundantly testified to by the facts revealed in the historical study of language. Ever since the foundation of the Indian Empire, when the Sanskrit language was made familiar to the Western world and the science of comparative philology established, our greatest linguists have been devoting themselves to two tasks: namely (1) to determining what changes have taken place in those languages which were available to them for study; and (2) to discovering the nature of such changes and the causes that produce them.

#### HISTORICAL DATA OF COMPARATIVE PHILOLOGY

The first task has yielded most abundant material in the field of sound changes, especially since the rise of experimental phonetics. In all languages, ancient and modern, that have been studied innumerable changes have been recorded and described. Among these thousands of historical changes, we may select as illustrations the following typical examples: Modern English *here* was in Old English pronounced as two syllables, the first of which sounded about like Modern American *hay* without the *y;* the second, a trilled *r*. Old English *cyning* (with *y* rounded, as *u* in French *lune*) has become *king*. Old English *singan* (*s* like

210  THE PSYCHOLOGY OF LANGUAGE

*z* and *a* like *o* in American *hot*) has become *sing*. Old English *brōk* (pronounced nearly like contemporary English *broke*, but with a trilled *r*) has become *brook*. Old English *bryd* (*r* trilled and *y* about as in German *über*) has become *bride*. Old English *hlæfdige* (*hl* like voiceless *l*, *æ* like *a* in *man* but longer, *f* voiced like *v*, *g* like *y* in *yet*, final *e* like *é* in French *été*) has become *lady*. Latin *femina* has become French *femme* (the first *e* nearly like *a* in *man*, the second *e* silent).

It has been observed that changes like the above do not go on uniformly in all parts of the territory in which a language is spoken, but that the sounds change differently in different communities. The result is that nearly all languages are broken up into dialects. Most Americans know that a New Englander speaks somewhat differently from the people of the Middle West and that the Southerners speak still differently. Thus it becomes necessary to distinguish between two kinds of changes: local (geographical) and chronological. In addition to this, each class in a community, each profession or trade, in fine, each individual man, has its or his own language, which differs more or less from other communities, groups, and individuals.

Comparison and classification of the observed changes were begun early in the last century (soon after the "discovery" of Sanskrit) by such men as Bopp, Grimm, and Pott, with the result that certain striking correspondences were observed between the speech sounds of numerous European and Asiatic languages.[1] The following table illustrates these correspondences:

---

[1] These correspondences led to the conclusion that ancient Hindu (Sanskrit), Armenian (medieval and modern), Greek (ancient and modern), Latin (with the modern Romance languages), Celtic, Germanic (including English and Scandinavian), and the Balto-Slavic languages all descended in direct lines from a very ancient language, which was

## SOUND CHANGES IN LANGUAGE

### CORRESPONDENCES IN SPEECH SOUNDS

| SANSKRIT | GREEK | LATIN | ENGLISH | RUSSIAN |
|---|---|---|---|---|
| *bh*arāmi | *ph*erō | *f*erō | *b*ear, 'carry' | *b*eru |
| *bh*rātā | *ph*rāter | *f*rāter | *b*ro*th*er | *b*ra*t* |
| *p*ança | *p*ente | ...... | *f*ive | *p*iat' |
| *p*itā | *p*atēr | *p*ater | *f*ather | ..... |
| *b*ala | *b*elteron | dē-*b*ilis | ...... | *b*olii |
| ........ | ....... | ...... | *p*ool | *b*oloto |
| *dh*ā-man | *th*ēma | *f*ē-ci | *d*ee-*d* | *d*e-lo |
| *d*aça | *d*eka | *d*ecem | *t*en | *d*esiat' |
| ve*d*a | oi*d*a | vī*d*ī | wi*t* | ve*d*' |
| *t*rayas | *t*reis | *t*res | *th*ree | *t*ri |
| dir*gh*a | doli*kh*os | ...... | ......... | dol*g*o |
| *gh*arma | ....... | *f*ornos | *G*ornergrat | *g*oret' |
| *j*ānāmi | *gn*ōscō | *gn*ōscō | *k*now | *z*naiu |
| çrad-dhā | *k*ar*d*ia | *c*or*d*is | *h*ear*t* | *s*er*d*-tse |

The reader will observe the consistency:

```
Sanskrit bh  corresponds to Gk. ph, Lat. f,  Eng. b,  Russ. b
   "     b        "         "   "  b,   "  b,   "  p,   "  b
   "     p        "         "   "  p,   "  p,   "  f,   "  p
   "     dh       "         "   "  th,  "  f,   "  d,   "  d
   "     d        "         "   "  d,   "  d,   "  t,   "  d
   "     t        "         "   "  t,   "  t,   "  th,  "  t
   "     gh       "         "   "  kh,  "  h,   "  g,   "  g
   "     g        "         "   "  g,   "  g,   "  k,   "  g
   "     k        "         "   "  k,   "  k,   "  h,   "  k [2]
```

The correspondences in the vowels are just as regular, but are much more complicated, so that in the above table they present some apparent irregularity.

Very soon philologists began to reduce these regularities to formulas. One of the first of these formulas, or "sound

---

spoken somewhere between Scandinavia and the Himalaya Mountains (probably in the neighborhood of the Gulf of Finland) and which has been variously named Indo-Germanic, Indo-European, and Aryan. The last name has been discarded by scholars in this meaning.

[2] Illustrations of this last series are not given in the preceding table.

laws," to become firmly established was Grimm's law, which (somewhat simplified) runs: "The Indo-Germanic voiceless explosives *p, t, k* became in primitive Germanic the corresponding spirants, voiced explosives became the corresponding voiceless explosives, and the voiced aspirates became the corresponding voiced explosives." But there were still left certain cases that did not conform to Grimm's law. These seeming irregularities were finally in large part explained by Karl Verner and Karl Brugmann on the basis of accentual and other conditions. In the same way scholars have busied themselves in discovering the explanations of numerous other apparent anomalies and irregularities until finally, in the field where at first all seemed to be ruled only by chance and caprice, men have become more and more convinced that here, too, as in the fields of the physical and natural sciences, everything has taken place in accordance with laws, which, when precisely stated, will be found to hold without exceptions.

### NATURE AND CAUSES OF SOUND CHANGES

Under these circumstances it was natural that the energies of philologists—and chief credit is here due to German scholars—should be turned more and more from the mere accumulation of data to the second of the two tasks mentioned above; namely, to the investigation of the nature of these changes and the causes that brought them about. Fortunately, just at this critical period in the development of philological studies the science of psychology was transformed largely under the influence of the idea of evolution, while chemists, physiologists, and physicists made remarkable progress in the knowledge of the nature of nervous and muscular activity and of air vibrations. Philologists then began to avail themselves, albeit rather slowly, of the

# SOUND CHANGES IN LANGUAGE 213

results of these investigations of their fellow workers in other fields, and progress was made, at first slowly, but in recent years much more rapidly. The methods of language study were revolutionized. The work of the linguist was wedded with that of kindred fields of science. Formal logic, which for two thousand years had guided men's thinking, was rejected, metaphysics was banished, and exact scientific methods were applied to the study of speech sounds and meaning. Thus arose the branch of experimental phonetics and the new biologico-humanistic science of general linguistics.

It seems almost superfluous to call attention to the various futile attempts to explain sound changes that were advanced during the first three-quarters of the past century; and, indeed, it would be unnecessary to do so, were it not for the fact that even in the present day the ghosts of these ancient ideas appear now and then in unexpected ways and places. Most of these explanations assumed that the changes result from a conscious purpose on the part of men to avoid uneuphonic sounds or combinations of sounds and to replace sounds "difficult of production" by others less difficult or "more convenient." As it gradually became clear that no such purpose, conscious or unconscious, attends or precedes the production of speech sounds, the words "conscious" and "purpose" were dropped out of the discussion and such words as "tendency" and "inclination" began to appear in their stead. But "tendencies" and "inclinations" in their turn came to be recognized as offering no explanation at all, and as being but vague expressions which were themselves in need of explanation. Those who explained that difficulties in pronunciation led to the substitution of easier articulations were asked how it happened that these difficult pronunciations had come into existence in the first place. It was further observed that we are never conscious in ordinary speech of any difficulties in the pronunciation of words of our own vernacular, but only when we are learning the unfamiliar movements of a foreign language. Finally, it came to be realized that, while speaking, we give no thought to the pleasant or unpleasant character of the sounds. In general, speech sounds are pleasant or unpleasant to us—if, indeed, we at times reflect on our emotional attitude toward them—rather by reason of the associations connected with them than because of any qualities of the sound itself. Occasionally a sound occurring in a foreign language will seem ugly or unpleasant to us, but inquiry will generally reveal the fact that the foreigner himself finds no unpleasantness in it. Changes in speech sounds have also been said to be due to carelessness and laziness, but these again are vague general terms standing for complex psychophysical conditions. They explain nothing. They merely suggest new problems.

OBJECTS AND METHOD OF MODERN PHILOLOGICAL RESEARCH

Gradually the fantastic elements of the older explanations have been eliminated and those elements which rest upon some dimly felt or imperfectly understood scientific basis have been subjected to searching analysis in the hope of separating the true from the false. Thus the philologists, driven from one untenable position after another, have, on the one hand, settled down to a painstaking investigation of the structure and functioning of the speech organs along with a careful analysis of the speech sounds as air vibrations, and, on the other hand, to the investigation of the mental processes involved in speech, with the ultimate purpose of correlating in one consistent explanation the results of the two lines of study.

## MUSCULAR MOVEMENTS

The structure and physiology of the speech organs have been dealt with in Chapter III. It should be borne in mind that speech sounds in the precise sense of the term are auditory sensations, that is, states of consciousness attending physiological processes in the nervous system. These sensations are aroused by the air vibrations impinging on the outer membrane of the eardrum.[3] These vibrations are caused by the movements of the organs of speech. A full discussion of speech sounds and their changes, therefore, involves consideration of (1) the physical characteristics of air waves, (2) the psychology of hearing, (3) the central processes immediately preceding and attending speech, (4) the activity of the motor nerves, and (5) muscular movement. In this chapter we shall deal chiefly with the muscular movements as being the immediate cause of the air waves.

We must first dispel a very widespread misconception of speech sounds. A language is popularly regarded as made up of a limited number of speech sounds (thirty or forty), each distinct and constant, and represented by a sign (letter) which the layman often confuses with the sound itself. This confusion is occasioned primarily by three conditions: (1) While each individual speech sound, so-called, consists physically not of a single sound, but of a succession or group of sounds continuing ordinarily from one-tenth to one-half, three-fourths, or even an entire second, there is usually one portion of this sound series which stands out more prominently than the rest because of its loudness, pitch, or some other characteristic. (2) Owing to the fact that one's attention while speaking is directed mainly to the

---

[3] Vibrations are also transmitted to the ears through the tissues of the speaker's head. These must also be taken into account in some cases.

"Captive" as pronounced by J. F. Shepard

|  | First Pronunciation | Second Pronunciation | Third Pronunciation |
|---|---|---|---|
| 1. Duration of $a$ | .11 sec. | .14 sec. | .14 sec. |
| 2. Duration of $i$ | .20 sec. | .24 sec. | .19 sec. |
| 3. Number of vibrations of vocal lips in $a$ | 16 | 21 | 22 |
| 4. Number of vibrations of vocal lips in $i$ | 18 | 24 | 21 |
| 5. Pitch of $a$, vibrations per second | 145* | 150* | 157* |
| 6. Pitch of $i$, vibrations per second | 90† | 100† | 110.5† |
| 7. Duration of $c$ | .20 sec. | .13 sec. | .14 sec. |
| 8. Air emission on $c$ | 27.15 mm.‡ | 29.77 mm.‡ | 32.2 mm.‡ |
| 9. Air emission on $t$ | 13.65 mm. | 15 mm. | 17.2 mm. |
| 10. Air emission on $v$ | 28.9 mm. | 28.35 mm. | 25.7 mm. |

\* These three tones are about D, D sharp, and E, in the octave below middle C.
† About F sharp, G sharp, and a rather high A, in the second octave below middle C.
‡ Measured by the resolved vertical rise of the air pressure line.

thought content of the language and not upon the sounds, one disregards the less important portions of the group and either they do not catch one's attention at all, or, if they do, they remain in the dimmer background of consciousness. (3) The mental habit of building up types on the basis of one's individual, specific, concrete experiences tends still further to give an apparent uniformity to the continually varying individual experiences.

As soon as the attention is directed to the muscular movements (or, more broadly speaking, to the tissue movements) that constitute the basis of language, three characteristics of those movements immediately impress themselves upon us: (1) their extreme variety or "inaccuracy," (2) their complexity, and (3) their continuous character.

Judged from the point of view of tissue movements and air vibrations, the different sounds produced by any given

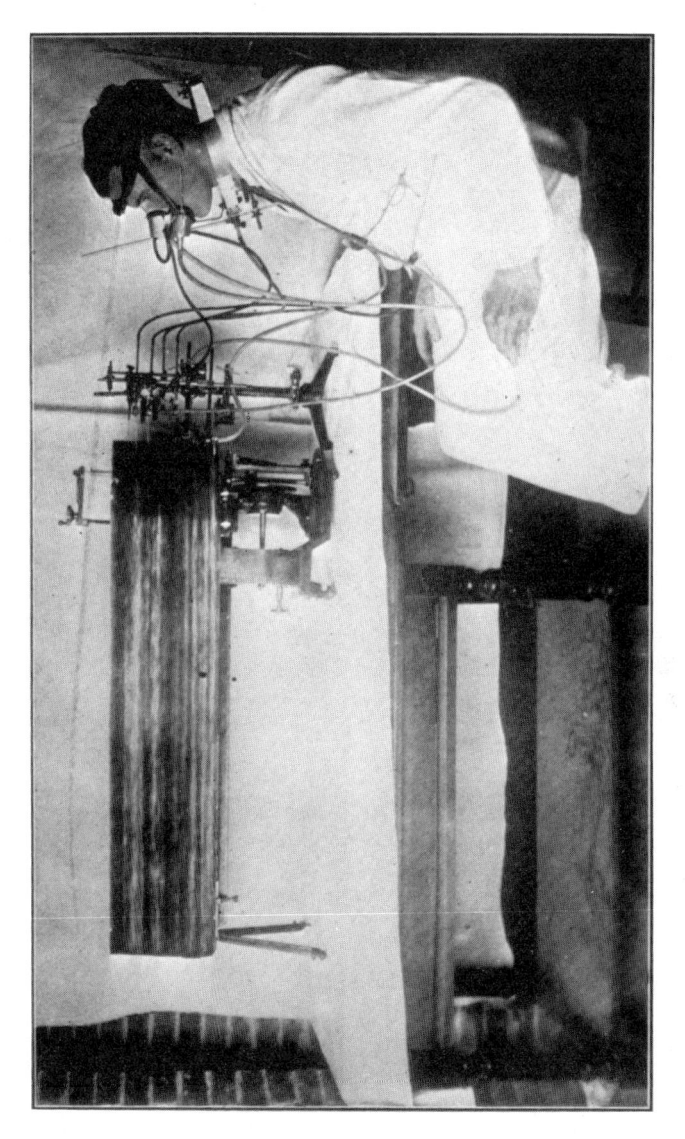

FIG. 14.—THE KYMOGRAPH WITH ACCESSORY PHONETIC RECORDING APPARATUS.

## SOUND CHANGES IN LANGUAGE

"Captive" as pronounced by C. L. Meader

|  | First Pronunciation | Second Pronunciation | Third Pronunciation |
|---|---|---|---|
| 1. Duration of $a$ | .09 sec. | .0875 sec. | .08 sec. |
| 2. Duration of $i$ | .23 sec. | .22 sec. | .233 sec. |
| 3. Number of vibrations of vocal lips in $a$ | 14.5 | 14 | .12 |
| 4. Number of vibrations of vocal lips in $i$ | 23 | 22 | 23 |
| 5. Pitch of $a$, vibrations per second | 166 vib. | 166 | 150 |
| 6. Pitch of $i$, vibrations per second | 100 | 100 | 99 |
| 7. Duration of $c$ | .09 sec. | .086 sec. | .073 sec. |
| 8. Air emission on $c$ | 38 mm. | 22.8 mm. | 26.8 mm. |
| 9. Air emission on $t$ | 21.5 mm. | 16.25 mm. | 16.45 mm. |
| 10. Air emission on $v$ | 16.5 mm. | 17.30 mm. | 17.9 mm. |

individual are innumerable. Indeed, they would be infinite if the life of the individual continued forever. This variety may easily be demonstrated by means of speech records made by instruments that accurately record. Such an instrument is shown in Figure 14. In this instrument, the kymograph, the principle of transmitting tissue movements by means of their effect on the air through rubber tubes and variously constructed recording instruments (tambours) is so employed as to transform the movements of the abdomen, chest, larynx, and vocal lips into vibrations of metal, straw, or feather pointers, the tips of which oscillate vertically over the surface of a soot-covered paper. These pointers describe curving lines on the surface of the paper. The measurement of the lines of such a record, in which the word "captive" was pronounced three times in succession at intervals of about one second by Professor John F. Shepard, gives the results in the table on page 216.

Many other variations are shown in the record, for example, those in the abdomen and chest lines, in the form of the vibrations of the vocal cords, in the movements of the larynx as a mass, in the nose pressure line, etc.

The corresponding values in a record of the same word as spoken by Professor C. L. Meader are shown on page 217.

If the showings of the two records be compared, the large amount of the variation between individuals is apparent. In other records of the pronunciation of this word by the same person, variations in pronunciation at different times would also be very marked.

These two records make it plain—and all similar records abundantly confirm the conclusion—(1) that it is impossible for an individual to repeat a given speech movement at will in exactly the same way in which he has previously performed it, and (2) that the speech movements of different individuals differ even more noticeably than do successive utterances of the same individual.[4] Similar variations are shown by palatograms, which record the contact areas of the tongue and palate. It may be seriously questioned whether one ever makes the same group of speech movements twice in a lifetime. If one does, the fact is to be attributed to chance rather than law. All systems of spelling according to sound make use of a comparatively small number of conventional symbols (letters) to represent sounds and thus encourage the naïve assumption that, as there are few letters, so there are few sounds.

Turning now from movements as recorded to the observations of the movements themselves, the following simple experiment will give one a clear idea of the variation in the degree and form of tongue movement, even when the sub-

---

[4] This is shown in part also by the fact that one can distinguish with ease and accuracy between the voices of different individuals, while only by special attention would the average layman note differences between successive pronunciations of the same word by the same individual.

ject is endeavoring to reproduce the same movement: Open the mouth fairly wide, extend the tongue slightly out of the mouth and raise it so that its upper surface a short distance behind the tip rests against the edge of the upper teeth. Note in a mirror the distance which the tip of the tongue extends beyond the teeth, or better, have some one measure the distance for you. Close the mouth and repeat the operation. How do the two measurements compare? Was the shape of the tip of the tongue the same? Was it pressed against the teeth with the same firmness in the two cases? Practice the experiment for some time to see how great a degree of accuracy of movement you can develop. Try the same experiment on a friend and note the result. Tests with unpracticed persons show variations as large as one-eighth to one-fourth inch. With practice, greater accuracy, but never perfect accuracy, can be attained.

The following experiment is equally instructive: Pronounce successively the vowels of the words *beat, bit, bait, bet, bat, boot, put, boat* and *pot* (as pronounced in America). Measure in the case of each vowel the distance between the edges of the upper and lower incisors, and record the measurements. Repeat the vowels and measurements and compare results. How do your results compare with the figures given on page 64? Make the test on a friend.

Some idea of the accuracy of control that can be voluntarily kept over the action of the vocal lips is suggested by the achievement of the amateur singer cited on page 55.

In the last experiment we were concerned with sounds produced in isolation from others. If we examine the special movements necessary to produce one sound, we shall see that they are extremely complex. Take for example the vowel *i* in *bit*. To produce this sound there is needed first an expiratory stream of air, which in normal breathing requires the relaxation of the muscles of the chest and the diaphragm and perhaps also the contraction of the abdominal muscles. Second, there is necessary such action of the eleven intrinsic muscles (counting the three distinct masses of the interarytenoidal muscle) of the larynx as will adjust the vocal lips to their proper position, form, and tension. There must also be action of the muscles controlling the position and form of the mouth and lips, and the necessary changes in the form and position of the tongue. For the pronunciation of such a single sound, nearly all the muscles of the trunk and head to the level of the ears may be used, not to mention the accompanying movements of other parts of the body that incidentally attend speech, such as the wider opening of the eyes, raising of the eyebrows, smiling, frowning, gesticulating with the arms, etc., which lend even greater complexity to the communicative movements.

Not only are these movements required, but they must also be of fairly definite range, and stand in certain temporal relations to each other. This last implies the *coördination* of the movements. The importance of such coördination [5] is realized when for some cause it is partly lacking, as in the case of a person whose control over the respiratory muscles is imperfect and who, under certain conditions, inhales during phonation. The result is a violent disturbance in the other muscular movements involved at the time; the entire system of movements is thrown into confusion. First, incoherent and meaningless sounds result, and very quickly the whole process is brought to a standstill.

Such isolated sounds as are spoken of above are, of course, not normal usage and consequently not normal

---

[5] For the nervous mechanism of coördination, see pp. 29, 36–39.

movements. The main reasons are (1) they are not pronounced with the emotional and ideational background that normally accompanies speech, and (2) in producing such isolated sounds, the speech organs start their movement from the rest or neutral position, that is, from the position which the larynx, vocal lips, jaw, tongue, and lips occupy in ordinary breathing, and pass back immediately to that position, whereas in normal speech they emerge from the movements of the sound next preceding them and pass on into the next following; unless, indeed, they immediately precede or follow a pause in discourse. It thus comes about, as is to be clearly observed in speech records, that the movements yielding a given vowel or consonant sound cannot be marked off sharply from the preceding and the following movements. Such transitions appear in all accurately made records of speech movements. In other words, speech movements are *continuous*. If, for example, a record of the vibrations of the vocal lips in pronouncing the word *Erie* be examined, it will be found that it is impossible to determine any point in the series of waves at which it may be positively said that the waves characteristic of *e* end and those characteristic of *r* begin, or at which the *r* waves cease and the *ie* waves begin. There is a gradual transition covering many waves, during which the characteristic *e* waves pass into *r* waves, and another in which the *r* waves pass over into *ie* waves. No break or sudden change appears at any point. An apparent exception is afforded by stop consonants, *p, b, t, d,* etc. Even without a record, one can almost assure one's self, by self-observation, of the continuous character of the tongue movement during the *t* in such a word as *batter* pronounced with ordinary rapidity. The tip of the tongue appears to move rapidly from the *a* region through to the *r* region and to touch only lightly upon the palate in pass-

## 222   THE PSYCHOLOGY OF LANGUAGE

ing through the *t* region. Far from resembling the successive separate jumps in the escapement of a timepiece, speech movements may more appropriately be compared to the waves on a broad expanse of ocean, rising and falling ceaselessly in endless variety, the one merging into the other, the lesser swept along by the greater, and the surface rising on the "tenth wave" with increased energy.

This continuous character of speech movements holds not only as between the adjacent movements of the same words, but also between successive words of the same sentence, and, indeed, not infrequently between successive sentences. The latter cases give rise to the so-called *sandhi* phenomena, which consist in the harmonization of the final movements of one word with the initial elements of the next, and the modification of the final elements of a word that is followed by a pause. This characteristic is conspicuous in all languages. The Hindu grammarians more than any others have indicated these variations in movement. It is familiar in French (compare the pronunciation of *je suis ici* with *je suis perdue*) and is conspicuous in English in such expressions as, for example, "Praise ye the Lord." [6]

A careful examination of speech records further shows that, although the organs are in continuous motion, there are certain points or, to be more exact, certain brief periods, within which movements of greater acoustic importance occur. For example, in the case of stop consonants mentioned in the last paragraph, the instant at which the tongue is snapped away from the roof of the mouth, although by no means the only distinctive mark of the stop consonant and perhaps not its most distinctive mark, is, nevertheless, of great moment acoustically. In the case of the vowels and liquids, the most characteristic parts should probably be regarded as those in which the wave form characteristic

---

[6] See p. 224.

## SOUND CHANGES IN LANGUAGE

of those vowels is most fully developed. It is not always easy to identify this point in a record. Doubtless it usually coincides with the point at which the greatest output of energy appears in the record. The case is sometimes complicated, however, by the presence of two or sometimes even three such regions of greater energy, yielding, to all appearances, very complex forms of accentuation. It is the auditory sensations corresponding to these particularly marked regions that are popularly spoken of as the sounds of a language.

The tissue movements corresponding to these regions are designated by the rather inaccurate term *positions*—inaccurate because it implies a static rather than dynamic view of language. We speak, for example, of the tongue, lip, or larynx position of the vowel *a* or the consonant *b*. As the above statements concerning the character of speech sounds imply, we must not suppose that these positions are points at which the organs rest for an instant, and then start onward towards the next position, although this may to a certain degree be true in some cases of rather slow or intentionally prolonged utterance. Of course, it is possible to maintain the tongue or the vocal ledges or other organ in practically the same position for some time, but such cases are rare exceptions in ordinary speech. They represent only what *can* be done and not what actually *is* done.

Contrasted with these positions are the acoustically less important regions. To these the rather vaguely used term *glide* is applied, although they include more than is commonly spoken of as glides. These glide movements are not less essential movements than the others. In other respects than acoustically they are important. Among them is one group of movements as yet little studied, namely, those occurring at the beginning of a sentence or after any pause and continuing up to the point at which the first audible sound waves occur. These movements which appear in the speech records analyzed above (page 217) in the curves of the abdominal, chest, larynx and mouth pressure lines, though acoustically unimportant, are kinæsthetically no less vital than the audible movements that succeed them. These silent movements occur not only at the beginning of discourse and after a pause, but are scattered all through the discourse.

It must not be inferred from the above statements concerning glides that each two successive letters are separated by a glide. As a matter of fact, they may *overlap* each other. For example, while the tip of the tongue is making a series of movements necessary to the production of a *t*, the base of the tongue may be executing the movements which constitute the vowel immediately following it. This phenomenon is observable in the series *teach, tack, Tom* and can be accurately studied in palatograms. It shows even more clearly in the series *kick, cape, Keplar, cash, could, coke, car*. Pronounce the words in the order in which they are given above and note by the sensations of touch the points at which the tongue touches the palate in each case. Pronounce in the order *car, kick, coke, Keplar, could, cash*. Pronounce naturally and fairly rapidly the sentences "Praised be the Lord" and "Praise ye the Lord." Ordinarily they come out "Praiz b . . ." and "Praizee . . ." (*z* as in *azure*). Parallel in main is the pronunciation of "Is your hat here?" and "Is this the place?" In "Praise ye . . ." and "Is your . . ." the overlapping consists in the simultaneous performance by the tongue of two different types of movement and the consequent slight adjustment of the two to each other. It is the same process that takes place in *palatalization*. Still more complicated are those forms of overlapping in which two different organs simul-

## SOUND CHANGES IN LANGUAGE

taneously perform movements characteristic of different sounds, that is, in which one organ executes the movements of one letter at the same time that another organ is making the movements that constitute a different sound, which we ordinarily think of as following the first. The movements of the vocal lips and tongue often overlap in this manner. A normal *s* sound is voiceless, that is, the vocal cords do not vibrate during its production; yet in actual speech the cords do often begin to vibrate for the following vowel during the execution of the *s* movement by the tongue. This yields a voiced *s*, yet not a *z*, which we ordinarily think and speak of as a voiced *s*, but a peculiarly sharp, clear and loud combination of *s* and *z*. This seems especially likely to occur, if the vowel following *s* chances to be *e* (pronounced as in *keep*), or a vowel related to it in movement. For the connection between this phenomenon and the transformation of Latin *spatium* and *sperare* into French *épée* and *espère*, see page 246.

### CAUSES OF VARIATION IN SPEECH MOVEMENTS

The variety and complexity of movement described above are not, of course, confined to speech movements, but are characteristic of muscular movement in general, so that the linguistic facts under discussion are to be explained in terms of the general physiological and psychological principles of muscular movement. Muscular movement never attains perfect accuracy and precision. Recall the fact that the most skillful baseball pitcher repeatedly fails to put the ball exactly where desired. The best marksmen show some inaccuracy. In these cases visual errors play an important part; but even after these have been discounted, there still remains a large residue of error that must be explained on other grounds. The constant variation of muscular movements is beautifully shown in ergograph records, and very suggestive comparisons may be made of such records and those of speech sounds.

In general, the causes of this variation may be grouped under three heads: (1) variations in the physiological (chemical and physical) conditions within the nerve and muscle cells; (2) inaccuracy of control exercised by the sensations (kinæsthetic, auditory, tactual, and visual); and (3) variety of the central processes (ideas and feelings) which immediately precede or accompany the speech movements which represent them.

1. *Physiological Conditions.*—The effect of temperature on muscular activity is fully recognized. Even the layman is familiar with the disturbances brought about in the speech processes by very cold weather. Three factors enter into the case: (a) the general low efficiency of muscle action when the tissue is exposed to subnormal temperatures (this is due to the slowing down of the metabolic processes); (b) the distortion in the shape of the mouth chamber due to the tendency to keep the mouth closed (it must be remembered that the nose and not the mouth is the specific breathing passage, as is shown by the fact that the organs of smell are located in the nose and as is illustrated by the fact that the breathing process is checked in horses if their nostrils are held shut); and (c) the shivering and chattering of the teeth brought on by the cold. It seems improbable that extreme cold produces many extensive permanent effects upon language, since muscle tissue speedily regains its normal condition on the return of a more normal temperature. Even in high altitudes where high temperatures prevail, the effect of the cold is minimized by the partial adjustment of the muscle tissue to the rigorous conditions. Furthermore, the fact that the muscles are rather deep-lying tissues serves to protect them

from the cold. The temperatures at which these serious effects are observed lie considerably below those prevailing in the environment of most of the inhabitants of the earth. On the other hand, the disturbances caused by supranormal temperatures begin at a point only slightly above those prevailing in summer in temperate zones.[7]

Investigators do not agree in detail as to the effect of temperature on muscular action. Gad and Hymans (1890) and Clopatt (1900) found in the case of frog muscle a maximum of efficiency as regards extent and rapidity of contraction at 30 degrees centigrade (86 degrees Fahrenheit), and observed that the efficiency fell with both a higher and lower temperature. Others disagree with this. Fick, for example, writing in 1882, Coleman and Papillon (1896), and Schenk (1900) failed to find 30 degrees an exceptionally favorable temperature. The optimum temperature for protoplasmic activity varies in different animals, but its average is about 35 degrees centigrade (95 degrees Fahrenheit), somewhat higher than the temperature just mentioned (frogs are cold-blooded animals) and not far from the normal temperature of the human body. It is a very common, in fact, almost universal experience, that an external temperature only a little higher than 98 degrees Fahrenheit causes a general depression and lack of buoyancy marked by sluggish and less accurate bodily movements, including those of the speech organs. These effects, though for the most part not permanent, are very extensive. A few degrees rise in internal temperature (fever) is usually attended by fatal consequences.

Fatigue also has a marked effect upon muscular action. The first effect of strong muscular activity is to increase

---

[7] These considerations render highly improbable the theory of the older philologists that climate plays an important part as a cause of sound changes.

the muscle's action, but after a short time the extent of the contraction begins to fall off, until it becomes at length very low and finally on complete exhaustion ceases entirely, in consequence partly of the using up of the protoplasm by the katabolic process and partly of the accumulation of waste products in the tissue. A period of rest reestablishes capacity for normal contraction. While the permanent effects of fatigue on the speech movements are probably less than those of temperature, they deserve especial mention, if for no other reason than that the question is one of great importance to singers and public speakers. The alternation of appeal and response and of question and answer in ordinary speech is a safeguard against fatigue. It is possible that the weakness of the post-tonic syllable in languages having a pronounced dynamic accent (as, for example, English and Russian) is due in part to the effect of fatigue, but other factors certainly play a large part.

Malnutrition and drugs have important effects upon speech movements. They are, however, for the most part temporary in the sense that they do not materially alter the character of the speech movements of an entire community, since, fortunately, extreme alcoholism and addiction to drugs are confined to few or, even in extreme cases, to a small minority of a community. The effect of such addictions on the speech of the individuals, however, is very great and often permanent, but on others it is negligible except in so far as the abnormalities are inheritable.[8]

The same general statements may be made of pathological and traumatic conditions, such as those occurring in apoplexy and syphilis.

Aside from the questions of the effect of temperature, etc.,

---

[8] The spermatozoa of a man who dies in an intoxicated condition exhibit a variety of physical deformities.

## SOUND CHANGES IN LANGUAGE

on muscular activity, there is a general law of muscle action. In accordance with this law, the extent of the variability, that is, the range of error, increases with the extent and energy of the movement. This law explains, in part at least, the fact that the muscles of the larynx, which are smaller and have a much smaller range of action than the tongue muscles, admit of higher degree of accuracy in adjustment than do the latter. For the same reason the action of the abdominal muscles during active expiration is even less accurate, nay even crude in comparison.

2. *Inaccuracy of Control.*—If one attempts to draw a straight line on a piece of paper up to a certain point previously determined, there is an initial innervation involving an adjustment of energy expenditure sufficient to carry the pencil at a fairly constant speed over a greater part of the distance to be traversed or even beyond the goal; but as the pencil tip approaches the goal, not only does the speed of the movement materially slacken, but corrections are introduced (implying new innervations) that in a high degree reduce the error of the original adjustment. Of these two kinds of control—initial innervation and secondary corrections—it seems unlikely that the latter plays an important part in speech movements, since they are observed to disappear when the time occupied by the total movement is less than about one-half second, a space of time which exceeds that occupied by all but a few speech movements. Furthermore, these secondary corrections are due to voluntary control, which is not exercised over the detailed movements, except in so far as they may be subject to modification by the loudness, tempo, and general level of pitch, or by other factors that influence the whole series of movements. In some movements connected with speech, as, for example, the copying of another's handwriting, this form of control is

continually exercised; but in ordinary cases, as in letter writing, such corrections largely disappear, since the voluntary control over the movements is reduced to a minimum. The details are no longer heeded, being purely mechanical, and the eye serves mainly to keep the writing approximately on the line and to check errors.

The high degree of accuracy that attends movements rhythmically repeated must also be held to have little permanent effect on the ordinary speech movements, owing to their great variety and complexity. However, in ordinary speech and especially in poetry and rhythmical prose, the indirect effect of rhythm on pitch and duration is very pronounced. To cite one illustration, a record of Milton's verse:

Hail, holy light! offspring of heav'n first-born

spoken by Meader shows that the word *light* was held (lengthened) sufficiently long to make up in time for the missing unaccented syllable.

Of much greater importance is the effect of the speed of utterance on the range, precision, and energy of the movement. The universal desire to be understood has operated to establish the habit, perhaps we may even add, a semiconscious tendency, to speak with a fair degree of precision, and the frequent queries, "What's that?" "I didn't understand you," serve to keep the habit perpetually reënforced. As soon as speech begins to flow quite rapidly, disturbances begin to set in, and the movements assume unusual forms. The disturbances result from several causes. We have seen in Chapter III that innervation of a motor nerve and the physiological act of muscle contraction require an appreciable period of time. It is further true that the speech movements approach in rapidity near to the limit of speed possible to muscular action. It

## SOUND CHANGES IN LANGUAGE

is evident, therefore, that, if the speed is materially increased, the movements cannot be carried out in the normal manner. At first these disturbances take the form of a reduction in the extent and energy of the movement, which is inevitably attended by a divergence from the normal range of kinæsthetic sensations and the consequent tendency toward the disturbance of the coördination of movement. The importance of maintaining the movements at their normal energy is reflected in the circumstance that, as soon as the speaker perceives that he is not understood, from whatever cause the difficulty may arise, his first impulse is to raise the voice and moderate its rapidity. It is true that in rapid speaking the output of energy is increased above normal, but notwithstanding this, the amount of energy available for each individual movement is decreased. On further increase of speed, the phenomenon of *regressive assimilation* (so-called) grows rapidly in frequency and extent. The sentences "Praise ye . . ." and "Is your . . ." serve as illustrations. The sentence "Give me that" spoken rapidly assumes the form which the layman would represent orthographically thus: *gimmi that,* and it would be assumed that an assimilation of the *v* to the *m* had taken place. In fact, it is not an assimilation. The *v* is, so to speak, almost entirely ironed out. It has completely disappeared. What is left is a modified *m*. The movements have been simplified by the omission of acoustically unimportant movements. As a matter of fact, there occurs in the normal, unhurried pronunciation of this sentence a regressive assimilation of *m* to *v*, which consists of the formation of the *m* while the lower lip is still in the *v* region, or, at least, before it has moved from it into the *m* region. The result is that, whereas in the pronunciation of *gimmi* the center of the area of contact of the two lips lies along the center of the crest of both, in the pronunciation of *givme* this line is shifted an eighth of an inch or more backward in the case of the upper lip and about the same distance forward in the case of the lower lip. Anyone can easily confirm this by observing the movements in his own case in a hand mirror. In pronouncing *givme* a point on the upper surface of the lower lip near its center describes a line which first rises upward and backward until the lip is brought to a stop against the teeth; then a nearly horizontal forward movement begins, which carries the lower lip to the nonmedial contact (mentioned above) with the upper lip. In the pronunciation *gimmi* the same point on the lower lip moves upward and slightly outward, instead of inward, until checked by its contact with the upper lip along the central line as above described. The rapid pronunciation *gimmi*, therefore, though not effecting a progressive assimilation, produces a related result in abolishing, so to speak, the regressive assimilation of the slower pronunciation. A still different type of *m* is produced in the word *comfort* by the fact that the lower lip moves well into the *f* region before the *m* sound is uttered. Unquestionably the central processes have much to do with these disturbances caused by rapidity of utterance. They find confirmation in other fields of muscular movement. A typewritten sheet shows that the typist wrote *He* for *The,* and wrote *sp* when starting the word *stop* and *ru* when starting *result*. When the speed of utterance becomes excessive, these deviations become so great as to cause violent disturbances of the auditory and kinæsthetic sensations, resulting in lack of coördination, hesitation, and ultimate stoppage of the speech process.

Unquestionably the effects of rate of utterance upon normal language are very great for the reasons that (*a*) rapid speech is of such exceedingly frequent occurrence; (*b*) physiologically and psychologically there is no sharp dividing line, but only gradual transitions between slow and rapid utterance; and (c) even with a slight increase of rate of utterance, noticeable variations make their appearance. A large part of the permanent historical transformations of language are of the same types as the changes effected by rapid utterance.

3. *The Central Processes.*—Marked variations in movement attended by conspicuous auditory variations are brought about by external environment. The energy output is adjusted to the distance between speaker and listener, to the presence of intervening objects, and to a variety of social conditions and circumstances.[9] The intonation and pitch of voice vary with the personal relations between speaker and listener. These external factors affect the speech organs through the reactions of various parts of the nervous system to the external stimuli, and so these effects need to be interpreted in terms of the central functions.

It is a matter of common observation that sudden disturbances of the flow of thought, whether they consist in a diverting of the ideas into other channels or in the marked alteration of the emotional tone, produce confusion in the speech movements. From this we should naturally infer that similar confusion of less extent results from less violent central disturbances. It is also recognized that the pitch of the voice varies with the variations of the emotions. This last problem has been investigated to some extent by accurate recording instruments. The investigations are rendered difficult by the fact that the emotions themselves have been so imperfectly analyzed and also by the fact that the artificially induced emotional states, to which the investigator is obliged for the most part to confine himself, probably differ from those that occur under

---

[9] Additional details may be found on p. 110.

the natural conditions of life. The whole question is bound up with the as yet imperfectly understood question of the relationship between thought and language.

The difficulties would be greatly reduced, if the connection between thought and expression ran only through the word images, but this is far from true. Some light is thrown on the problem by the fact that speech is only an imperfect expression of thought. The mental experiences of both an ideational and emotional nature find only partial expression through the vocal organs. The central experiences not finding their expression therein are reflected in the movements of the face and other parts of the body. "It was not what he said, but the way he said it." Oft-heard remarks like this show how diffuse the communicative processes are. The variations of which we are now speaking are significant variations and are, therefore, to be put into a separate category from the small variations discussed above, which entirely escape the notice of both speaker and listener. The difference between them, however, does not lie in any deep-seated divergence in the nature of the processes. All variations of speech movements, except those due to physiological conditions existing solely in the nonnervous tissues, are connected with corresponding nervous activity and therefore symptomatic of it. This difference between significant and nonsignificant variations in the sense here employed depends only on whether they can appreciably affect the sense organs of another person. The fact that one can either say to another "Come here" or can beckon him with the finger shows that the connection of the central processes with any particular group of movements is rather complex. In one situation the command may be used, in another the gesture. If the command is employed, there may be present also an impulse to move the hand. If the gesture is used, there may

# SOUND CHANGES IN LANGUAGE

also be present abortive movements of the vocal organs corresponding to the usual spoken words. Such movements are properly regarded as due to the influence of the central processes, although, like all other movements, they are subject to further variations due to physiological conditions of nerve and muscle not directly connected with the thought processes.

The central processes are also responsible for the so-called *analogical changes* in language. The analogical changes involve movements to which special meaning has come to be attached, as when a child says *goed* for *went*. The close association of the *d* movements (*-ed*) in certain connections, with the idea of past action, leads the child to make the movements in connection with *go*, as he and others make them in connection with *haul, call*, etc. Many English irregular verbs have thus become regular. The pronunciation *unánimity*, influenced by *unánimous*, is another example of the working of analogy. The process is also responsible for the origin of many new words, such as *Bryanism*.

### THE CONTROL OF SPEECH MOVEMENTS

No one of the individual variations above discussed and no one of the cumulative historical changes just mentioned can be explained as due to a single cause. The interrelations between nerve and muscle actions, whatever the precise nature of those interrelations may be, are so intimate, and the influence, direct or indirect, of the one form of activity on the other is so universally exerted, that it becomes impracticable to estimate with precision the part which each plays in the combined activity. Again, if we regard the nature of the nervous process involved in the formulation and utterance of the simplest idea, we shall find, as appears from the topographical description in Chapter II and from the functional description in Chapter VI, that this is of itself not a simple uniform process but a group of closely associated minor processes. Great difficulties and uncertainties attend not only the scientific investigation of these processes but also the interpretation of the pathological evidence derived from aphasia and kindred pathological disturbances of speech. In addition, it must be remarked that even after we have succeeded in assigning to each particular movement or variation of movement its corresponding nervous process, we should still have left undiscovered the conditions which produced the given nervous activity. To determine these, we must not limit ourselves to the examination of the nervous processes alone, but must go outside of the individual and search his material and social environment for the conditions that have contributed to the molding of his intellectual life and physical organism, and which have facilitated the spread of a given change to other members of his community.

*Kinæsthetic Sensations.*—The main factors that keep the variations of speech movements from assuming such proportions as to detract from the intelligibility and effectiveness of speech are the forms of control exercised by the sense organs. The origin and nature of the kinæsthetic sensations, as well as their general relations to speech, are discussed in Chapters IV and VI, and there is little to be added in this connection. Unquestionably the part they play in speech is the greatest in early childhood, when one is learning to speak. By the time the first words are uttered, the kinæsthetic sensations have already been sufficiently developed by the practices of cooing, screaming, etc., and the imitation of sounds made by others, to serve already as controls (though not yet very accurate) over the movements constituting true words. In the course of a few years the habits of movement become so firmly established that the initial impulse to a given movement is doubtless accurate enough to carry the movement through to its intended goal with as high a degree of precision as physiological conditions admit. After this time they doubtless provide frequent control sensations stimulated by movements that for one reason or another rather widely diverge from the normal. The senses of movement and position in the tongue are said to be very inexact, giving rise to gross errors as regards extent and direction of motion in making speech sounds.

*The Sense of Touch.*—In connection with the kinæsthetic sensations, mention should be made of the sense of touch in controlling speech. This control is due to the organs of touch found very unevenly distributed over the surfaces of the pharynx, palate, gums, lips, tongue and cheeks. Observations on one lady of keen mental faculties showed that she distinguished two points 1.5 millimeters (about $\frac{1}{17}$ inch) apart on the tongue tip and along the edge of the tongue to a distance of about 1 centimeter from the central point of the tip. Back of this for a distance of about 1 centimeter along the edge, she was able to distinguish points 2 millimeters apart, while still farther back they had to be placed about 3 millimeters apart to be distinguished as two separate points. Over the central area of the upper surface of the tongue, points about 3 millimeters apart were distinguished. Farther back there was greater sensitiveness. On the lower gum, points 1.5 millimeters apart could be distinguished over an arc 2 centimeters in length to the right and the same distance to the left of the center. Along the upper gum, points 1.5 millimeters apart could be invariably distinguished as far back as the center of the canine tooth on the right side and as far as the first bicuspid on the left side. They could be less accurately distinguished for the most part farther back even to the last tooth. Points this distance apart were for the most part correctly recognized as two along the central line of the hard palate clear back to the beginning of the soft palate. Experiments with artificial palates on a class of ten students at the University of Michigan pronouncing the sounds *t* and *k* showed an average of variation somewhat larger than the figures just cited.

The control by touch, like that of the kinæsthetic sensations, is probably more important during the process of learning to speak than it is later on. This control is, for the most part, unconsciously exercised and becomes conscious only when gross errors occur.

*Auditory Sensations.*—This last statement holds true also even of auditory control, as has been pointed out in Chapter VI. The inefficiency of conscious control by the ear is materially increased by two factors: (1) In ordinary conversation one gives little attention to the sounds of one's words, one's attention being wholly engaged with the thought which one is expressing; and when one listens to the speech of others, one likewise gives but little detailed attention to the sounds of the speaker, since here too one is primarily interested in the thought. (2) The sound images which are aroused in one's mind do not correspond exactly to the air vibrations that impinge upon the ear, but owing to the peculiar character of the mental processes, one gets either typical sound images (types) or images so divergent from the usual forms as to cause misunderstandings. Indeed, these subjective elements are a fertile source of error. Their general character is discussed in Chapter VIII. Their constant presence and magnitude can be appreciated, if when listening to an address or conversation, one should be so rude as to disregard for

## SOUND CHANGES IN LANGUAGE 239

a time the thought and note attentively the exact character of the sounds. Marked variations in the pronunciation even of the same word in different connections will not fail to appear. Some little practice may be needed to enable one not trained in phonetics to hear accurately and to keep the attention fixed on the sounds instead of the meaning. The writer recalls an instance in which he heard seven distinctly different pronunciations of the word *door* in as many minutes uttered by the same person (a university professor) as he was reading a learned paper. These illusions in hearing make the control of the ear over the voice much less effective than it otherwise would be. Finally, it cannot be overlooked that the auditory sensations cannot usually operate to alter the particular movement that produces them, since that movement is completed before the sound could operate to correct it. It operates, therefore, only to prevent the recurrence of errors.

*Visual Sensations.*—The exercise of control over speech movements by the visual sensations can, of course, occur only among people who read extensively. Abundant evidence for the existence of such an influence is found in *spelling pronunciations.* These arise when, from one cause or another, the written form of the word contains letters that are not pronounced, so-called silent letters. Such silent letters may creep gradually into the pronunciation. This appears to be most common in the case of borrowed words. Many instances can be cited of such alteration of French words introduced into Middle English. The military term *corps,* often pronounced like the English word *corpse* instead of like English *core,* is an example. Children are frequently observed to pronounce words according to their spelling—naturally only those words which they have not learned "by ear." It can hardly be assumed that this process has a very steadily operating and extensive influence in English, since in addition to the limitations just mentioned, which confine its operation to words more familiar to the eye than to the tongue, the nonphonetic character of English orthography and the habit of seeing masses of letters instead of individual letters operate to restrict the association of individual sounds with corresponding auditory and motor sensations.

The visual sensations, like the auditory, are subject to many illusions,[10] a circumstance which decreases the efficiency of their control over muscular movement. In general, the closeness of the lines of connection running from visual word images to motor impulse is made evident by the fact that when reading aloud one's mind may wander from the thought expressed and one may become absorbed in absolutely different ideas, and still one may continue for several minutes to pronounce the words so clearly and with so much expression that the listeners will be wholly unaware of one's abstraction.

The rapidity of visual control over the movements of the fingers in typewriting is illustrated by the following examples: In sixteen cases the error was recognized before the next following letter was written. In one case a letter was added completing the word. In one case the word *another* was begun, and after writing *an* the *t* key was pressed; but the error was discovered before it had been pressed down far enough to release the hammer (Hammond typewriter) and the proper correction was then made.

### BASES OF PHONETIC LAWS

Attempts to formulate phonetic laws have not in the past been based upon neuromuscular investigations. Most

---

[10] See Chapter VIII.

## SOUND CHANGES IN LANGUAGE 241

of the so-called phonetic laws, such as, for example, Grimm's law, are merely statements to the effect that in a given community at a given time a given group of movements has been changed into this or that other group of movements. While the promulgators of these laws have doubtless thought of the changes in terms of movement, they have seldom or never laid emphasis on that fact, and as a consequence their readers have commonly thought of them as changes simply of sounds or even of letters. Such statements as "Indo-European *b* becomes *p* in primitive Germanic" can base their claim to be called laws solely, as Oertel has justly observed, upon the relative universality (within the limits set) of the change. The validity of this criticism is not shaken by the fact that occasionally mention is made, as in the case of Verner's law, of one or more of the conditions under which the phonetic change takes place.

The student must guard against the acceptance of the universality of a change as an explanation of that change, nor should the linguist rest satisfied until every means has been exhausted of discovering the social, psychological, and physiological explanations. It is only on such a basis that a phonetic law can firmly rest. To discover the determining conditions of historical changes seems at present impossible, for the reason that, as the changes occurred in the more or less remote past, tradition has preserved only indirect and inconclusive evidence as to the nature of the conditions sought, and in most cases precise information is lacking as to the nature of the change itself. We must never forget how crude an indication of speech movements conventional alphabetic signs are, even in languages which are written "phonetically." The line of work which holds promise of throwing more light on the problems of sound changes consists in a combination of accurate research in

## 242   THE PSYCHOLOGY OF LANGUAGE

experimental phonetics with more complete knowledge of the nature of the biological processes.

### CLASSIFICATION OF CHANGES IN SPEECH MOVEMENTS

A classification of changes in speech movements on the basis of their causes is at present impossible. It remains only to group them according to the nature of the change in the movement itself.[11]

1. *Variations in the Rate and Duration of Movement.*— This heading refers to the speed and duration not of the discourse as a whole, but only of minor groups of movements. Examples are very common. In nearly all parts of the territory occupied by the Indo-European languages, the long diphthongs *ai, ei, ou, au, eu, ou* undergo a shortening into *ai, ei, oi, au, eu, ou*. Similarly, vowels are shortened before a nasal or a liquid followed by a consonant. In Modern English the vowel in unaccented syllables, especially in the syllable following the accent, has been shortened and in some cases entirely lost, as in *hope*. In words like *over, open* (often pronounced *opm,* particularly before an initial bilabial), *oval* and *oven* (often pronounced *ovm*), the final vowel is in some pronunciations reduced to a very brief obscure vowel and in others entirely omitted. Incidentally, this results in a greater prominence of the final liquid or nasal, which, after the loss of the preceding vowel, itself becomes a vowel. The same phenomenon is observed in Russian. However, whereas both in English and Russian the vowel following the accented vowel is shortened, the two languages differ in the fact that in English the first vowel before the accent is affected in a less degree, while in Russian it is the second vowel before the accent that is thus affected. This difference taken in connection

---

[11] This classification is merely illustrative and therefore incomplete.

with the difference in the order of sequence of the degrees of accentuation

| English: | weak   | weaker | strong [12] | weakest |
| Russian: | weaker | weak   | strong [12] | weakest |

is striking evidence that this weakening and shortening of vowels is bound up with the accent. The psychophysical reasons for this effect of the accent have not as yet been pointed out. Other reasons than accent must have brought about the change in Latin from *vēntus* to *vĕntus*.

The variations in speed and duration are closely related to variations in energy. It is a law of muscular action that movements of large extent can be made with greater speed than lesser movements. Greater extent of movement means greater output of energy.

2. *Variations in the Energy of Utterance.*—In languages which, like English, possess a strong expiratory or stress accent, this type of variation is very widespread. The articles, pronouns, and particles appear to be especially variable in this respect. A great variety of pronunciations of the definite and indefinite articles appears. In fact, the definite article is but a weak demonstrative pronoun. In at least one conspicuous case, variation in energy of utterance has given rise to differentiation between words, *off* and *of* being variants of the same word.

Greater expenditure of energy in the case of the contraction of certain muscles of the larynx produces greater tension of the vocal lips. Owing to the fact that the vocal lips not only produce the musical tones called voice but are also an important factor in the control of the outflow of breath and hence of the pressure of the air in the mouth cavity, there is necessarily some coördination of the movement of the muscles of breathing with those of the larynx.

---

[12] This is the accented syllable of the four-syllable word.

This brings the tension of the vocal lips into the problem of stress accent.[13] The relation of pitch to stress in English, Dutch, etc., has been investigated by John H. Muyskens and important conclusions have been reached.

Shifting of accent from syllable to syllable in various forms of the same word is another example of this type of variation. In many English words the location of the accent varies with individuals, the words having two recognized accents. Occasionally a shift of accent is bound up with a shift of meaning. An admirable illustration of this is found in a whole series of prepositional phrases, such as Russian *pó poliu* and *po póliu*, in which the difference in accent is correlated with slight differences in meaning. Such phrases have in a number of cases become stereotyped into adverbs, for example, *vóvse, záto,* etc.

Variation in the distribution of energy is the chief factor in the variations in the pronunciations *supperize* and *suprize* often given to *surprise*.

3. *Variations in the Extent of Movement.*—This type of variation is much less in evidence in the speech changes than are the preceding two. There are, however, many examples of its occurrence.

The change from stop to corresponding fricative is marked by a variation in the rate of movement. An emphatically pronounced explosive may differ from a weaker one in this respect. Palatograms show that the palate or gums sometimes come into contact over a larger area than usual.

4. *Anticipation or Delay of Specific Movements Which Form a part of a group.*—These are largely due to the instability of coördination. The following are illustrations:

(*a*) Relation of vocal lip vibrations to tongue movement. Under this head fall the voiceless consonants, for example, the change of a single Indo-European intervocalic *s* into *r* in

---

[13] It is, of course, the chief factor in pitch accent.

Latin (compare *quæsso* with *quæro* from earlier *quæso*). Records taken at the University of Michigan show very clearly that two members of the faculty in pronouncing the detached word *hissing* began the vibration of their vocal cords near the very beginning of the hiss of the *s*. This variation appears to be like that which produced in late Latin an *i* (as in *machine*) and in French an *e* before *s* in many words. Similar in character is the development of parasitic vowels, such as a short *u* sound (like *u* in *but*), as in a common pronunciation of *athuletic* instead of *athletic*.

(*b*) Assimilation of consonants both ot the progressive and the regressive types, the former consisting in the delay and the latter in the anticipation of a movement. Compare *watchmaking* (*ach* pronounced like the name of the letter *h* for normal *watchmaking*); *gimmi* cited above for *give me*. This is one of the most extensively operating changes to be found in the Indo-European languages, and there has consequently been much discussion as to its cause or causes. The frequent occurrence and the regularity of these changes, combined with a feeling that such universality and regularity are characteristic rather of the physical and physiological processes of nature than of the psychical, led scholars at first to look upon these changes as due to physical rather than psychological laws. This one-sided attitude is now rarely, if ever, advocated, and it seems unquestionable that one of the psychophysical facts that has most to do with the occurrence of these changes is that the formation of word images and impulses to movement is much swifter than the muscular activities that they initiate.

(*c*) Relation of movements of the soft palate (producing nasalization) with those of the tongue and vocal lips. Examples of loss of nasalization are: Indo-European *om* or *on* became in Russian *u* (pronounced about like *oo* in *boot*), while *i* and *e* plus a nasal became *ia* (pronounced, when accented, like the first two letters in English *yacht*). These Indo-European combinations had become nasalized vowels in primitive Balto-Slavic, and these nasalizations have been retained in some of the modern Slavic languages descended from them. An example of nasalization is: Latin *bonum* became French *bon*. Nasalization occurs very extensively in American both dialectically and in individuals. One member of the faculty of the University of Michigan shows in the records of his speech very extensive nasalization of his vowels and consonants, although no especially noticeable auditory effects of the nasalization appear. In the records of another member one can see how the vibrations of the vocal lips in pronouncing the word *disgusting* continued after the nose and mouth cavities had been opened at the end of the word. This continuing of the cord movement beyond its usual limit produces a faint obscure vowel sounding like the *u* in *but,* and makes *disgusting* a word of four syllables.

(*d*) Relations between movements of different portions of the same organ are found in the overlapping of tongue movements, mentioned above. Palatalization is a phenomenon caused by a shift in the coördination of the movements of the back of the tongue with those of its front part. This in connection with shifting of the coördination of the movements of the vocal lips and the tongue resulted in transforming Latin *sperare* and *spatium* into late Latin *isperare* and *ispatium,* which in turn developed into French *espère* and *épée*.[14]

5. *Transposition of Movements.*—While metathesis is recognized as an unusually fertile source of mispronunciations, there appear to be few well attested examples of his-

---

[14] Compare p. 225.

# SOUND CHANGES IN LANGUAGE 247

torical changes of this type. Late Latin *ispe* for earlier *ipse* is cited by Brugmann. Examples are frequent in handwriting as well as in typewriting.

6. *Omission of Small Groups of Movements from a Series of Movements.*—This type of change may be either the extreme to which the diminution of duration, extent, and energy [15] lead or it may be due to conditions similar to those which transform *give me* into *gimmi*. To the latter class appear to belong, for example, the common pronunciation *pfesr* for *professor* and *suprintent* for *superintendent*. The speech records of the University of Michigan abound in silent letters of this sort. Most of them are found in records of only moderately rapid speech.

### REFERENCES

See references to Chapter I.

[15] See rubrics 1 to 3.

# CHAPTER XII

## SYNTAX

THE traditional grammar ordinarily contains chapters or sections on (1) *inflection* (declension and conjugation), (2) *etymology* (word formation), and (3) *syntax*. The lines between these three divisions are both arbitrarily drawn and often inconsistently observed. For example, the formation of verb "stems" is usually treated under etymology, but the formation of the "stems" of gerunds and infinitives, which are also substantives, is treated under inflections. Again, the genesis of the meaning of most noun and verb forms is unintelligible apart from the forms. This is due to the intimate relations existing between meanings and forms of expression (muscular movements and their consequences—air waves and sensations). Vice versa, the genesis of forms is unintelligible apart from their meanings. In fact, all the phenomena (forms and meanings) embraced under these three heads can be understood only when regarded as the functioning of the unified neuromuscular organism. It is characteristic of this functioning process that the form of the functioning of each portion of that mechanism is conditioned by the form of the functioning of each other part. In other words, there is a unified functioning as well as a unified structure. The traditional classification may appear sufficiently clear to the student of superficial descriptive grammar, but its inconsistencies, contradictions, and arbitrary character are immediately apparent to the mind that views language from the organic and dynamic point of view. Of course, it is quite possible to learn inflections as forms, merely, without reference to their functions in discourse; but such a procedure, when employed as a method of acquiring a foreign tongue, is pedagogically unsound; and as a method for investigating the nature of the mental processes that in part underlie and in part constitute language, it is open to all the objections that are raised against the methods of the behavioristic school of psychology, who violently isolate the elements of the mental processes and draw inferences concerning the characteristics of normally functioning nervous tissue from the manner in which the mind acts in artificial situations. For these reasons and others, no attempt is made to separate the phenomena here discussed into the three grammatical fields.

#### VARIATION AND STABILITY IN LANGUAGE FACTORS

As we pass in this chapter from the field of phonetics over to that which more directly involves the thought processes and the problems of meaning, we are brought face to face at the outset with the same two striking characteristics of muscular movement and thought, namely, their restless and unceasing changes and, in contrast with this, their relative stability. The first quality is due to the instability of protoplasm as a chemical compound, reacting to the continual changes in its environment in a manner determined by the forces within itself, and to our lack of exact control over the protoplasmic changes occurring in our bodies. The second is due, in terms of current psychological theory, to the relative permanence of the synaptical connections formed by the continual repetition of like processes in our nervous, muscular and glandular systems. As an illustration of the former characteristic, we may take a German plural form of the type *Männer* (plural of *Mann*). The plural of this group of words was originally characterized by the suffix *er* alone, containing the high vowel *e* (as in English *bet*). This high vowel had the effect by assimilation [1] of "raising" the vowel *a* so that it gained a pronunciation similar to *e* in -*er*. As this change was brought about, visual, auditory, and kinæsthetic word images, corresponding to the altered movements, became closely associated with the idea of plurality, so that the modified *ä* as well as the earlier ending -*er* became a symbol of the plural, although this change was brought about by purely phonetic conditions and was not directly determined by the meaning of the form. In English the -*er* has disappeared in these words as a sign of the plural, leaving only the heightened vowel as the sign of the plural (the two English words *man, men*). Yet throughout the course of these changes there was never a moment when there was any doubt in the mind of the speaker or listener as to the meaning or usage of this class of words, and the speakers of German and English were wholly unaware that any change was taking place. Like nearly all spontaneous and unintentional products of the human mind, the changes of language usually occur by slow degrees, just as an automobile is the result of a long series of gradual improvements in small details. There is a slight change in an alloy at one point, a little alteration in the shape of a casting at another. Each new model represents a slight advance over the preceding. Similarly, the first railway coaches resembled closely an old English stagecoach, and have only gradually assumed their present form, material, and structure.

Thus continual change takes place both in the muscular movements and in meaning. There is only one factor in language that remains quite stable over long periods of time—the spelling of words. Spelling is not language. It

---

[1] See Chapter IX.

is an appendage to language and stands to language in much the same relation as does an attachment for a vacuum cleaner to the cleaner itself. It extends the usefulness of language through destroying the time limitations imposed upon speech by the ephemeral character of its processes and the limitations of man's memory. It is in reality an arbitrarily established convention, the changes in which are, with few exceptions, brought about consciously and intentionally. Unintentional changes in spelling occurring as the result of normal mental processes are for the most part confined to the semi-literate, and are immediately detected, pronounced to be errors, and rejected in favor of the established convention. Contrary to the widely current conception, the defects of a system of spelling such as the English do not correct themselves in the course of time. It is only by the general adoption of the recommendations of individual reformers that improvements in spelling are brought about. Left to itself, spelling tends to become more and more inconsistent with pronunciation, since the pronunciation alters and the spelling does not. For this reason, the student of language should keep the problem of orthography distinctly apart from those arising in the other fields of language study, and should not attempt to explain the phenomena of spelling by the same laws and principles as the other problems of language. Of course, there are cases in which the spelling of words determines their pronunciation (so-called spelling pronunciations), as French *corps* pronounced like English *corpse* instead of *core*. There are still more numerous instances of misspellings occasioned by incorrectly following the model of certain classes of words, as when *lamb* is spelled *lam* on the analogy of *Sam, slam, jam,* etc. These errors, however, are usually eradicated by the force of convention, and thus prevent what normal developments might otherwise take place in spelling.

The stream of thought (the ideas and feelings that make up the meaning of our expressive movements, including those of speech) during our waking hours is ordinarily continuous and a unit from the time we awaken in the morning till we fall asleep at night. Each successive thought grows out of the preceding and develops into the following without sharp breaks or interruptions, except when, now and then, a sudden change in our environment, such as a violent explosion in our vicinity or the striking of a clock which reminds us of a duty, entails a sudden shift of interest and attention. Even in such cases, elements of the older state often continue on into the new, though they be more or less incongruous or incompatible. Indeed, the older elements are sometimes so persistent that for a moment we are confused in mind and dazed while we are gradually adjusting ourselves to the new conditions.

Along with this characteristic of continuity, the stream of consciousness is also marked by the trait of unity, due to the fact, as stated above, that the content of consciousness at any given moment contains elements carried over from the preceding part. The coherence thus imparted to the stream may be designated as unity. These two factors of continuity and unity must always be borne in mind when we are dealing with linguistic problems.[2]

Two further essential factors of consciousness are particularly emphasized by Wilhelm Wundt in his chapters on meaning:[3] the degree of (1.) clearness and (2) vividness with which specific parts of the stream are appreciated. This is due, according to Wundt, to the act of attention, by virtue of which certain portions of our stream of thought are more favorably perceived, being in themselves of more marked intensity (vividness) and being sharply marked

---

[2] Compare Chapter IX, p. 216.
[3] *Grundriss der Psychologie,* Pt. III, § 15, 5.

off from other parts (distinctness) simultaneously present.[4] Van Ginnekin, under the term *Beamen*, has discussed in some detail the part played by the less favorably apperceived factors.

Lastly we must emphasize the fact that in normal human experience, and perhaps also in that of the higher animals, we are not conscious of isolated individual sensations or feelings, but only of more or less complex mental states. Even under the most highly artificial conditions that may be set up in a psychological laboratory, it seems impossible to isolate a simple sensation, and it may be doubted if such a sensation has ever occurred in mental experience, unless it was upon the very threshold of dawning consciousness in the lower animals, and even this seems unlikely. This fact is particularly emphasized not only by the recent *Gestalt* or "configurational" school of psychology, but also by Wilhelm Wundt in his *Völkerpsychologie*, although, of course, the configurational school differs materially from Wundt on the question of the origin, structure, and function of such unified portions of the stream of thought.

The import of this point of view (the configuration) is far-reaching, since it is diametrically opposed to the basal assumption upon which practically the whole structure of linguistic theory and interpretation has been erected in Western Europe from the days of the Greek grammarians until very recent years. It therefore demands very serious consideration on the part of linguists, the more so because it is in accord with the main tendencies of modern scientific thought, which seeks to find relativity everywhere in nature, to obliterate all sharp lines of distinction, and to unite into a harmonious whole the psychological, physiological, and physical.

---

[4] The causes that underlie this phenomenon are still under controversy.

The ancients, for example, used the term syntax (Greek συν, 'together'; and τάξις 'arrangement') because they conceived of the sentence as made up by arranging originally isolated words successively in a certain definite order or pattern, as the soldiers of an army are arranged in lines, squares, etc. On the contrary, we are not here interested in syntax from the analytic point of view. We do not regard it as the science or art of putting words together, as though they were individual units, each distinct in itself, which could be accumulated into groups called sentences. Rather, we ask, in this connection, three main questions: (1) What are the qualities of the various elements of discourse and what are the relationships existing between them? (2) By what forms, that is, special muscular movements, are these qualities and relationships expressed? (3) What is the nature of the connection between these qualities and relationships on the one hand and the forms with which they are expressed on the other?

THE SENTENCE

The sentence, the so-called unit of discourse, has been the subject of almost as extensive and ingenious controversy as has art, and owing to the illusive and complicated nature, not only of the forms of expression, but also of the underlying meaning, the most widely divergent views have been held regarding both. Grammarians, philosophers, and psychologists for the past two thousand years have been unable to agree upon the definition of the sentence. The reason for this lies in part in the complexity and variability of the language processes. Just as protoplasm assumes innumerable forms and is continuously undergoing change as long as it is living, so those vital processes, which we call language, being the manifestations of that same protoplasm

# SYNTAX

and being equally protean in their transformation, defy the efforts of the philologist to reduce them to fixed and rigid formulas, and like protoplasm, they lose their identity when killed and sliced with the mental microtome. They are, then, like a microscopic preparation, stained beyond recognition by philological theories and methods. We must, then, reiterate at the risk of seeming prolix, that even the simplest example of the communicative process, such as "Please, pass the butter!" or *à la Anglaise,* "Reach me the butter, please!" or even the single word "Butter!" [5] are life processes, intelligible only as part and parcel of the particular situation within which they came into being and of which they are an essential and formative factor, both determined by that situation and, in turn, affecting it, growing out of the needs of the individual in his surroundings, employing those surroundings for his self-realization, and, in turn, modifying those surroundings by his action.

But the complexity and variety of speech are not the only factors that render linguistic study difficult. Just as important is the fact that our attention when speaking is rarely directed upon those processes. We are primarily interested in the effect we desire to produce upon the listener and so are usually not attentive to the processes by which we produce that effect. We are in this way often faced by the preposterous task of recalling that which was not in consciousness. Much linguistic theory is thus the product of the imagination.

The grammarian would unhesitatingly pronounce the first two quoted expressions to be sentences, chiefly because each contains a verb. Concerning the single word "Butter!"

---

[5] The reader must always bear in mind that, unless the contrary is stated or implied, it is always the neuromuscular processes of the speaker and the listener, with all their delicate nuances, and not the written word which is under discussion in this book.

he would probably be in perplexity. Yet the single word plays its part as effectively as the longer expressions. The person addressed understands just what is meant and reacts accordingly. The grammarian would probably call it a sentence fragment, because it seems to him to be only a portion of a complete "grammatical sentence." If, however, we look squarely at what is before us, we, like the listener, since language is expressive movement not only of the vocal organs but of any or all parts of the body, must regard this communicative process as consisting not only of the uttered word but also of all the other movements involved: for example, the directing of the eyes toward the butter and toward the person addressed, together with the movements of the facial muscles expressive of the mood of the speaker, a slight inclination of the head and a delicate manipulation of the larynx muscles which give an intonation of the voice expressive of the request (expressed in the fuller sentence by the words *pass* and *please* in addition to the appropriate intonation). From the point of view of the expressive movements involved, there is nothing fragmentary about the one-word sentence. All the movements essential to the expression of an idea in a given situation are executed, and neither type of expression performs its function either more or less completely than the other. The appearance of fragmentariness arises only when we first limit our conceptions of language to spoken or written symbols and then lay down arbitrary definitions and attempt to standardize life processes, which by their very nature make this impossible, except perhaps on the basis of physico-chemical forces at present unknown to us.

To the traditional grammarian the sentence expresses a complete thought. As a matter of fact, the only completeness in our psychical life is that of the entire stream of consciousness during our waking hours, and even here we must make the reservation that when we awaken we usually pick up the stream of thought at some point in our yesterday's experience and the new stream of thought obtains significance as much through these older, carried-over elements as through the new experiences. Indeed, we understand the new experience chiefly because it incorporates elements of our past experience and thus becomes an inseparable part of our life. So, strictly speaking, there is really only one large complete unity—from birth to death, leaving, of course, the questions of inheritance, immortality, and the transmigration of souls in abeyance.

This unity of the thought stream is clearly reflected in the creations of the human mind, for example, in works of art, in scientific treatises, and in inventions. Since the days of the ancient Greeks, unity in one form or another has been accepted by Western civilization as an essential characteristic of a work of art. Likewise, the parts of every invention are determined by the purpose it is designed to serve, and any part is immediately rejected if found to be superfluous. No scientist incorporates irrelevant material in a book.

A logically written book aptly illustrates the nature of the thought process. It is divided into parts or chapters, each one of which treats of some coherent phase of the entire subject. The chapters fall into sections and paragraphs each devoted to some smaller unity. The paragraphs fall into sentences, the sentences fall into clauses or phrases, and the phrases fall into words, the words into still smaller significant units—not, however, into syllables and "letters," which are the products of arbitrary analysis. The farther we go in the analysis, the closer the relationships become, so that when we finally reach the sentence, we have attained such a degree of closeness that only the most superficial or thoughtless person could call the sentence complete.

From here on, through clause, phrase, word, and word element, the closeness of the relationship becomes such that the arbitrariness of a separation is immediately apparent. Indeed, there is really no definite standard or criterion which we can universally apply to the demarcation of successive portions of discourse into sentences. For example, "The parson told the sexton and the sexton tolled the bell" is classed as a single compound sentence; but, disregarding the rhythm, it might be expressed without the *and*. In this case, the expression would be classed as two distinct sentences. In case there are three or more such successive units, the cumulative conjunction is seldom used except between the last two and, when thus used, does not necessarily express a closer relationship than that which exists between the earlier members of the series. In case such a series is written or printed, one author might use commas to separate them, another semicolons, while the third might choose periods and an initial capital. These variations in usage indicate that there is no definite standard applicable, either for the delimitation of the sentence or for measuring the degree of closeness of the relationship connoted by the various marks of punctuation and by words of relationship. "All is in a flux" and the judgment as to the degree of relationship, if a judgment is passed at all, is purely subjective.

The closeness of the bonds that unite successive portions of discourse is reflected in a nearly universal characteristic of discourse, namely, each successive sentence repeats either *in extenso,* as often in legal documents, or in epitome or by implication some part of the preceding sentence and adds to this a new element, so that each sentence is thus new-old and no gaps appear between the sentences even though conjunctions are completely absent. Each successive sentence thus picks up the thread of thought in the preceding sentence and carries it a short step forward. The repeated portion commonly, though not necessarily, forms the subject of the sentence or is incorporated in it, while the new added element usually finds expression in the predicate. Incidentally, it may be noticed that this habitual arrangement of the sentence material, involving a contrast between old and new, contributes to the joy of achievement, which, according to some judgments, is the keenest of all joys.

When we raise the question as to the length (extent) of the sentence, we find it necessary to distinguish between two types: (1) the sentence as spoken in daily life, and (2) the sentences of a literary work or scientific treatise. The former are as a rule brief, pithy, and concise, and very simple and direct in form. The latter may be of this same type but are commonly much longer and more involved. In both these cases, but more especially in the latter, there are wide differences between individuals, between different social groups, and perhaps also between races. A very illuminating illustration of what may be a racial difference is found by comparing Theodor Mommsen's *Geschichte des römischen Münzwesens* in the German text with le Duc de Blacas' French translation of it. The translator as a rule breaks up the long and involved German sentences into a succession of brief, pithy French sentences.

There are two natural limitations to the volume of the spoken sentence, that is, to the amount of mental activity involved in it. The first is the time that elapses from the beginning of the expiration of the breath to the point at which the increasing carbon dioxide content of the blood begins to cause discomfort. In reading or speaking long sentences previously prepared for delivery, one can transcend this limit by a quick inspiration entailing a brief pause between two adjacent units. This period is not far from three seconds. In the second place, the volume of the thought is limited to that which can be easily grasped at once, by the mind. This question is not exactly identical with the widely investigated problems of attention. The questions concerning attention heretofore chiefly examined are how many objects or ideas one can attend to simultaneously, and how long the attention may be kept fixed. Authorities are generally agreed that one can attend to only one object at once and that the duration of attention is less than one second. During the course of speech, the attention to particular objects and ideas is continually shifting. The sentence may express only one idea, grasped by one fixation of attention. On the other hand, it may be extremely long, especially in the case of written sentences, and involve a number of fixations of attention.

When we ask how large a volume or range of thought can be grasped at once, we must take into account the element of meaning as connected not only primarily with words but also with closely related mental states. Indeed, Pillsbury observes that the subject matter of a whole treatise may be in mind at one moment; but it is evident that what is then in mind is but a mere skeleton of the contents of the book as developed in detail, attended by a feeling of confidence that we can easily bring into consciousness most, or all, of the details if desired. Such a skeleton conception might be formulated into a sentence; or, on the other hand, one might, on a different occasion, have in mind some detailed facts stated in the book. This likewise might be expressed in a sentence. Either sentence might be very brief, of not more than a few seconds' duration, or it might be long, covering, if written, many lines. In the latter case, we should find that it could be broken up into smaller units each having a length of from one to twelve words and a duration if spoken with ordinary speed of between one (or even less) and three seconds.[6] These smaller units are what in the Indo-European languages correspond roughly to the grammatical divisions called clauses, introduced usually by relative pronouns or subordinate conjunctions or by *but* and *and*, though these last two and the relative pronoun often introduce larger units divisible in turn into smaller units of the type under discussion.

An examination of the smaller units shows that as a rule they possess the characteristics of the ordinary English sentence; for example, each has a subject and a predicate. They may, therefore, be regarded as brief sentences bearing a very close resemblance to ordinary sentences, but very closely bound up in logical relationships to each other, much as a stimulus containing several objects in some logical form of arrangement, as, for example, five dots arranged in a quincunx

. .
 .
. .

may be attended to as though they were one single object. From this point of view, the sentence may be regarded as a section of the stream of thought having such an extent and logical coherence of parts that it may be grasped as one unitary conception in much the same way as a quincunx or a triangle or a square of dots is grasped. It seems likely, however, as suggested above in Chapter X, that ordinarily the details of such an idea are not at all clear in mind, but that under the control of the general situation and the purpose of speaking these details arise successively in consciousness and are then

---

[6] Statistics covering a large number of instances show an average length of about three and a half words for conversation and six and a half words for written matter.

clearly perceived, either just before or during or after the corresponding words are spoken. Thus it would seem from the evidence of language that there are two grades of complexity of thought. The simpler form is represented by single words and by brief phrases and compound words that have passed into the fusion stage. These appear to be of about the volume that corresponds to a single fixation of attention. Then there is a somewhat larger mass, which, unlike the simple units, is not clearly grasped or seen in its complexity, but is represented in consciousness by a quasi-intuitive conviction that all the details are known and can be used whenever needed. As stated above, this larger mass finds expression in ordinary spontaneous speech in from one to nine or ten words, an average of about three and a half. This latter figure may be taken as representing approximately the average length of the spontaneous spoken sentence. The more elaborate sentences found in printed matter are merely accumulations of this simple one. To measure the volume of thought included in a sentence by the above method of counting the words is, of course, a crude and inexact procedure, since often two or more words are employed as symbols of a single unified idea, and, vice versa, two or more such ideas may be symbolized by only one word. We have an example of the former case when we speak of a "girl with a *noli me tangere frangere* air" or "a *never-to-be-forgotten* event" or "a coat *of many colors.*" A great many compound words and phrases, like "nevertheless," "to-day," and "in the first place," not only in English but also in all other languages, express a single relatively simple idea. There are many long phrases, clauses, or even sentences of this type, for example, "it is not at all unlikely that," which expresses no more than "very likely" or "probably" or "in all probability," although all these expressions differ slightly in meaning. On the other hand, we must

SYNTAX 263

bear in mind that in highly inflected languages many ideas are expressed by formative elements incorporated into the word. This fact would tend to bring the linguistic expression into closer accord with the thought processes. On the whole this method of measuring the thought content by the number of words or by the duration of muscular movement required to express it gives an exaggerated impression of its extent and complexity. The thought is more simple than the layman would be led to judge by the number of words employed to express it. The spoken sentence is, after all, quite a cumbrous affair.

The question of the nature of the mental processes involved in the organization and utterance of a sentence are discussed above in Chapter X.

THE GRAMMATICAL CATEGORIES

The grammatical categories—the parts of speech, tense, mood, voice, aspect, person, number, case, object, subject, etc.—as commonly defined are abstractions of the philosophers and grammarians. In the West as contrasted with the Orient (India and China) the philosophers, Plato and Aristotle, began their formulation, and later philosophers— notably the Stoics—and scholars supplemented and modified the beginnings made by their two great predecessors. These definitions and the rules of usage based upon them are not present in the consciousness of the naïve user of language while he is speaking. They are not a part of language, but are only statements *about* language.

We are not directly interested in these abstractions, but in the states of mind on the basis of which they were formulated. These states of mind are emotions and qualities and ideas of relationship which enter as organic factors into the complex mass of thought. The terms quality and relationship require some elucidation. It is necessary to distinguish between the popular (naïve) appreciation of these phenomena and the conception which modern science holds of them. Since the grammatical categories and most of the grammatical terms came into usage before the rise of modern science, they are based upon more or less popular notions. We call the color of an object one of its *qualities*, while we say that the temperature of an object is one of its *states*, but we regard the sound that an object emits as one of its *effects*. We also regard the pain caused by touching a hot stove as an effect produced by the state of the stove. The modern physicist regards all these qualities, relationships, and effects as varying forms of atomic, molecular, or mass movement, involving transformation of energy. The psychologist has traditionally regarded them as sensations, while the physiologist fixes his attention more upon the chemical changes in protoplasm that are attended by the mental processes. In the case of light, heat, and sound, the movement is translated through the material media surrounding us to the nonnervous structures of our body (for example, the structures of the middle and inner ear, the crystalline lens, and the vitreous humor of the eyes), and after undergoing alterations through these structures is brought to bear upon the nervous protoplasm in such a way as to inaugurate chemical changes in it. In other cases, as taste, smell, pain, and the organic sensations, the movements do not pass through the surrounding media. In both cases the chemical processes thus inaugurated are propagated along the afferent nerves to the nervous structures of the cortex before the characteristic sensations—light, heat, sound, etc.—arise. The sensations corresponding to different sense organs bear no resemblance to each other. For example, regarded as sensations, light bears no resemblance to heat, neither resembles sound in any way, and all of them differ entirely from taste or pain. The feelings, also, as pleasure, displeasure, depression, and elation, are completely unlike any sensations. Because of this disparateness of the sensations, we hold them distinctly apart in consciousness—the senses of taste and smell seem to be exceptions to the rule—nor can we measure any one of them by the standards of any other. Nor can we directly compare them. This disparateness of the sensations is a great aid to us in appreciating the differences in the states of matter in the outside world and preventing confusion. Although these states of mind bear no direct resemblance whatever to the objective forces and movements which cause them, such of them as produce a physiological effect upon our sense organs result in sensations which within certain limits vary regularly and consistently in quality with the variations in the movements in the outside world.

It is impossible for us to avoid the assumption that the objects in the outside world stand in certain spatial relationships to each other. Furthermore, owing to the laws of force and movement, these patterns assumed to be existent in the outside world are proportionately and symmetrically represented by the patterns they initiate in our senses organs, for example, in the distribution over the retina of light rays coming from various directions, in the variations in amplitude of air waves reaching the ear from various directions, in the differences in intensity of the heat waves reaching various parts of our body from the same source, and so on. Furthermore, we assign these states of mind to various different spatial positions from those that they really occupy. Sound and light are projected into the outside world in the direction from which the stimuli reach the sense organs, others are assigned to the periphery of our bodies, to those parts in which the respective sense organs are located.

We treat in the same way the grammatical categories as states of mind. Spatial conceptions, *into, out of, near, far, beside,* etc., are projected into the outside world. The naïve man thinks also of temporal relationships as having an objective existence. The same is true of causal relationships, of person, number, etc. As for the moods, he regards potentiality, probability, condition as inhering in the objective world, whereas desire (optative mood) is characteristic of the speaker's mind.

It is a matter of universal experience that individual sensations and feelings do not occur in isolation except perhaps under most artificial conditions. The groupings in which these sensations occur correspond quite closely to the interrelationships occurring in the outside world. Hence it is a natural assumption that the conditions determining their groupings are given largely in the outside world. The unified, organized mass of sensations and feelings constitutes the entire content of consciousness. Our conceptions of space, time, and causal relationships are constant elements of such structures (configurations) and inhere in them in the same sense that the grain of a piece of wood inheres in the wood. They are inseparable elements of such structures, as inseparable as the grain is from the wood, and their characteristics are determined by the other elements of the structure. Since the afferent, the central, and the efferent parts of our nervous system form one organic and functional whole, the muscular movements and glandular secretions which result from the nervous processes occurring in the afferent and central fields inevitably develop in men and animals in corresponding forms and thus become expressive of the outside patterns. It is thus very natural to conceive of the physical configurations of the outside world initiating corresponding functional configurations in the nervous system, attended by phenomenal configurations in consciousness, and initiating corresponding functional and physical configurations in our muscular and glandular systems. This point of view has four distinct advantages: (1) It is based upon the conception that man, as all other forms of life, is an inseparable element of the universe, and that he mutually determines and is determined by it. The dualism, animate and inanimate, is thus to some extent done away with. (2) It is in complete harmony with the most modern conceptions of biological sciences, which after centuries of extreme analysis are now coming to lay more and more stress upon the unity (structural and functional) of the organism. (3) As stated above, it offers an instructive parallel to the theory of relativity. (4) The observed phenomena of language, so far as studied from this point of view, appear to be in harmony with it.

Thus it becomes clear that, as indicated above, the grammatical categories are of two sorts: (1) On the one hand, they are just these qualities and relationships (local, temporal, and causal) which exist in the objective world (in the form of interplay of forces), in our nervous systems (as chemical and phenomenal configurations), and in our muscles and glands (as movement and secretion). (2) On the other hand, they are statements formulated by logicians or grammarians of these phenomenal forms after they have been torn from their settings and thus stripped, more or less, of their organic character.

One of the most widespread ideas of the modern grammarians is that a sentence cannot exist without a verb. It is true that comparatively few verbless sentences are to be found in the ancient or modern literatures of Western Europe. Doubtless this is due to the fact that these literatures have preserved for the most part only the more formal conventional literature. However, if we turn to the dramatic literature which approaches closely the language of daily life, and to certain contemporary authors who have broken sharply with the old traditions, we shall find the proportions of such sentences greatly increased. And if we turn aside from the field of literature and examine the sentences used in daily conversation in the West, we shall find the proportion still larger. Still more are added by the Russian vernacular and literature. Medieval Sanskrit, going still farther, uses comparatively few verbs, while some languages of less highly civilized peoples do not even possess words identical with our verbs. The real situation as regards the use of the verb will be cleared up, if we first look more closely at the nature of the parts of speech.

### THE PARTS OF SPEECH

Aristotle, whose ideas of language were apparently more sane than those of his successors among the ancients, defined four parts of speech and only four: substantive, adjective, verb, and particle. It is possible to define these four in a fairly satisfactory manner, on the basis of the nature of the thought content involved in each. If we use thought as a general term for all mental experiences, we may designate a coherent and unified group of sensations with their attendant feelings, as a substantive (usually called a *noun* in English grammars). If now we abstract an element or group of elements from this mass and still conceive of it as characteristic of the mass, we shall have a quality (simple or complex). Such a quality may be thought of as permanent, for example, the color of a man's face or of a leaf, or it may be a transitory quality, for example, a movement.[7]

---

[7] Of course, the distinction between transitory and permanent qualities is arbitrary. Permanence and change are relative terms. Here as in other linguistic problems we are concerned merely with what is in consciousness at a given moment. We think of all Caucasians as white, although we on occasion notice variations in shade. A leaf that is not

On the basis of sensations we conceive ideas of relationship. In general, permanent qualities are expressed by adjectives, transitory qualities by verbs, and relationships by particles (adverbs, conjunctions, prepositions, numerals, and some pronouns). These four types of ideas correspond to the four parts of speech as defined by Aristotle. The basis of definition is uniform and consistent. Later grammarians introduced other parts of speech, all of which, however, can be brought under one or more of these four Aristotelian categories and represent, accordingly, only subvarieties or combinations of the four fundamental types. As the fundamental types of mental activity which form the basis of Aristotle's groups are characteristic of all normal men, and perhaps of the higher mammals, they are of universal application.

In the last paragraph we have been discussing the case in which the quality after abstraction has been kept in mind along with the mass idea and thought of as a characteristic of the mass. If we carry the analysis still farther and mentally separate the quality quite completely from the substantive idea, thus dropping the idea of the mass wholly, or almost wholly, out of the mind, we will again have a substantive idea, for example, *goodness, walking*. On the contrary, we may hold the mass conception and the quality less widely apart, that is, leave them merged in a more complete unity, at the same time attaching greater importance to the semi-abstracted idea, and thus picture the object as bearing the activity, rather than regarding the activity as a quality of the object. This gives us the substantivized adjective ("The *good* die young") and certain compound or quasicompound words, for example, *King Agamemnon,* and a substantive-verbal idea occurring in

---

green is an abnormal leaf, as in autumn, or a freak as in albicatio, or a curiosity as the begonia.

Bantu but seemingly not occurring in English, unless it existed as an earlier stage of such English proper names as Rider and Walker. The speaker in Bantu appears to be picturing a man in the act of speaking and represents the unified conception or image by a word corresponding roughly to *man-speaker,* much as we speak of a *boy-scout.* He then employs this word as a sentence, whereas we would say: "The man is speaking." If, instead of following Aristotle's method, we attempt to distinguish the parts of speech on the basis of form, we meet immediately with serious difficulties. There are languages which show no distinction of form between substantives and verbs, or between substantives and adjectives. In English the distinction between verbal and noun forms is in some cases so far obliterated that only the context can determine which is which.

Just as the verbal idea is derived by abstraction from the substantive, so the idea of the modal adverb is the result of a second abstraction, this time from the already abstract verbal idea. It represents a quality, therefore, even more temporary than that of the verb. Its intimate relation, as an abstracted quality, to the adjective is reflected in a widespread and persistently recurring "error" of English, that is, the use of an adjective as an adverb, for example, "He walks *fast.*" Again the close relation between the verbal idea and the adjective is reflected in such parallel forms as the Russian *sneg beleet* and *sneg belyi,* the former having the verbal form, the latter adjectival, but both meaning "the snow is white" (the latter in a suitable context white snow). Exactly parallel are the two Latin expressions *nix albet* and *nix alba,* "the snow is white." A further indication of the similarity in origin of adjectival and verbal ideas is shown in the fact that in such languages as have systems of formal agreement between parts of speech both adjective and verb have usually some form of agreement with the substantive, of which they symbolize qualities. The absence of any other than arbitrary connections between meaning and form is further evidenced by the fact that some languages for example, Chinese, are almost wholly formless in the commonly accepted sense of the word.

### THE VERBLESS SENTENCE

To return to the problem of the verbless sentence, commonly two distinct ideas or groups of ideas form the thought content of the sentence. The speaker assumes one of these, the subject, to be known to the listener; the other, the predicate, to be unknown. The second is usually very distinctly realized and indeed is felt at the moment to be the more essential element.[8] Hence it receives the greater emphasis, usually corresponding in terms of sensation to greater vividness or intensity, and in terms of physiology to more extensive transformation of energy through chemical changes in nerve, muscle, and gland. In case the idea assumed to be known to the listener is very vaguely apperceived, the binary character of the sentence largely disappears. A variety of such simple sentences occur, among them the much discussed impersonal sentences, like "It is raining again." This may be equally well, on occasions indeed even more effectively expressed by the mere words "Rain again." What is meant is that in our environment there has come about a certain state different from what immediately preceded it and resembling a still earlier state. If our conception of the universe is of such a type that there is no definite thing, such as God, a cloud, the sky, to which we attribute the phenomenon, we either leave it indefinitely expressed, for example, by *it*, or only vaguely implied. It seems more than likely that among peoples with few panthe-

---

[8] See Walter B. Pillsbury, *Psychology of Reasoning* (New York, Appleton, 1910), pp. 134 *f.*

istic ideas, there is little more in consciousness represented by *it* than the picture of the word itself and a sense of normality due to the presence of something which does duty for the usual subject. However, we have here a complete assertion, which cannot even be called a sentence fragment, since a unified and relatively complete experience is adequately expressed. Often the vagueness of the subject is attended by a very strong emotional experience. In such a case the ideational elements of the subject may be still simpler and the ·attention centered almost wholly on the predicate. Accordingly such sentences consist often of a single word. This unified idea may in such a case be called in terms of the new psychology a configuration. In any concrete instance of its use, it certainly implies more than the bare occurrence of a new state of affairs, as asserted above; for all the complicated consequences of such a state are implied, as, for example, the joy of the farmer that the crops will now prosper or the disappointment of the builder that his work is interrupted, and so on, the implication in each particular instance varying with the personality and interests of the speaker and the listener. A more complex sentence may be conceived of as a more detailed exposition of such a configuration, ushering into consciousness a larger number of details. The grammarian says that a noun *names* and a verb *asserts*. Certainly the words "Rain again" assert. My own conviction is that all of the words in a sentence contribute to the act of assertion. As the predicate holds the lion's share of attention the grammarian conceives the act of assertion to be attached to it as a core.

In many languages two forms have developed for expressing the binary type of sentence: (1) the copulative sentence, (2) the usual verbal type. The latter requires little comment for the speakers of Indo-European languages.

The verbal form, for example, the verb *requires* in the preceding sentence, both expresses the idea of requiring and also helps to express the relationship between subject and predicate. The verb may and commonly does simultaneously express other relationships. Since the quality symbolized is a transitory one, it is usually important to locate it in time. Accordingly, tense signs frequently develop in connection with verbs, taking the form of auxiliary words, prefixes, suffixes, and other variations. Frequently the performance of an act has an important effect upon the person who performs it, and this calls for expression. So special means are developed for suggesting it (reflexive verbs). Or again the act may be one which consists of a process or group of processes taking place within the subject's body and resulting in an altered state of the subject. In these cases the attention centers upon the subject itself and not upon something outside of him. Such verbs are called *middle verbs*. The fact that they imply a change in the subject allies them closely with passive verbs. For example, the so-called deponent verbs in Latin are really middle verbs and their form is a middle form, while the so-called passive verbs, owing to the kinship in meaning with the middles, have taken on the middle endings. The Roman grammars are, therefore, wrong in stating that a deponent verb is one which is active in meaning but passive in form.

Again the attitude of mind of the speaker toward the action or toward the fact of its relationship toward the subject may be felt as needing expression. In general, when a community comes habitually to regard any particular relationship or attitude of mind as important for the understanding of any situation, a special form is almost certain to arise to express it. Different communities differ greatly in what they regard as important and therefore demanding expression. Biological needs are usually general, but the social needs of various communities are different, and on this basis different grammatical categories arise in different communities. In English, tense is not regarded as an essential mark of substantives, because of their relative permanence, yet we often have an occasion to indicate time in such connections. So we speak of "ex-presidents," "ci-devant blacksmiths," "has-beens," "the future world," and so on. But with us only a very meager mechanism has developed for such expressions. Being sporadic, they find no place in the ordinary grammars. Sometimes such phenomena assume forms which strike us at first glance as capricious, but which appear quite natural when better understood. To illustrate: the Inuit language has a system of tense signs for nouns. In speaking of the gunpowder one used yesterday the past tense of the noun would be used, to-day's gunpowder would be equipped with the present sign, while the future tense of gunpowder quite naturally means "smoke"! We do not commonly think of number as indicating one thing in the verb and another in the noun. As a matter of fact, the dual, triad, and plural of a noun indicate the twofold, threefold, or manifold existence of the thing, while the dual, etc., signs of a verb indicate not the duality, etc., of the verb but of the noun. The plural occurrence of the action, on the other hand, is indicated in various forms called *frequentatives*, for example, Latin *agito* from *ago* and *factito* from *facto*. In America, the comparative means that one object possesses a quality in a greater degree than some other definite object does, while some others use the comparative form to express a degree higher than the average or usual. This latter we express in American by *quite, rather, noticeably*. We do not think of nouns as having degrees of comparison, but the Hindu author of the *Nalopakyana* finds it perfectly natural to speak of one horse in a drove as being the *horsest* (Sanskrit superlative, *açvatata*), that is, possessing the qualities of horsehood in the highest degree. In the English language no special forms have developed in connection with the adjective and substantive for expressing the ideas commonly found in the Indo-European languages in connection with the verb. For this reason the idea of a verbless sentence seems odd to us, especially to those of us whose conceptions of language have been distorted by the study of grammar. Yet, if we but cast our grammatical prejudices aside and observe the language as it is spoken about us, we shall find plenty of verbless sentences, some even in literature.[9] There are great numbers of such sentences, in none of which is any verb, not even a copula.

Passing over to conversation, we find an almost unlimited source of material for illustration: "Man overboard!" "This way, sir!"; "A glass of water, please!"; "No money, no goods"; "The quicker, the better"; and innumerable other examples of similar and different types. By means of the verbal substantive it is possible to convert nearly all declarative and interrogative sentences into copulative sentences. In late scientific Sanskrit this type is extensively used where classical Sanskrit would use the verbal type. In Russian an interesting development has taken place: (1) The verb corresponding to English *am, art, is, are* is entirely omitted as an auxiliary with the past participle (active and passive,[10] both perfective and imperfective), (2) the present form never occurs in simple copulative sentences, and (3) its place is very frequently taken by other verbs having

---

[9] See Shakespeare, "Hamlet," Act I, Sc. 2, ll. 82 *f*, 253 *f*; Act I, Sc. 3, ll. 44, 115; Act I, Sc. 4, l. 139; Act II, Sc. 2, l. 95.

[10] Compare in Latin the frequent use of the perfect passive participle (*factus, dictus,* etc.) without the auxiliary *esse* in the indicative mood.

ordinarily concrete meanings, which, however, in this type of sentence, almost entirely disappears, leaving the abstract copulative relation as its main implication.[11]

Let us now take up directly the question of how far verbs are necessary to the sentence. It is certain that innumerable sentences occur, the thought expressed in which contains no idea of action or state, for example, Russian, *On general,* "He is a general"; Latin, *Omnia præclara rara,* "All fine things are rare." Others contain the idea of an action only partially abstracted from the object in which it inheres, as *man-walker* mentioned above. We certainly cannot call such a concept a verbal concept. There are others which contain the idea of action in the form of a substantive: "To see is to believe"; "Seeing is believing." Others contain the verbal idea in adjectival (participial) form: Russian, *On ubit,* "He [is] killed." It might seem like straining a point to say that the substantive and participial forms are not verbs; yet from the point of view of the formal grammarian only the finite verb "asserts" and is thus essential to the sentence. Examples might be cited in illustration of the fact that any of the parts of speech may be used as a predicate with or without the copulative verb, in which latter case the sentence would be verbless. The copulative relationship, or, to put it more widely, the group of ideas commonly held to be signified by the copulative verb, are, of course, present in all such sentences. It is only the verb itself which is absent. This absence of the verb, however, does not imply that the copulative ideas find no expression in words. They may be expressed (1) by a pronoun, for example, Russian *eto,* 'this' or 'these': *Negry—eto aboriginy Afriki,* 'The Negroes are aborigines of Africa.' The absence of the copulative verb in this case, as in others, is often, though not always,

---

[11] These verbs are discussed below.

indicated by the dash. But this is a mere convention of writing and printing and means nothing for the real or spoken language. This use of the pronoun occurs in Basque, several languages of northeast Africa, Mexican (Nahwatl), the language of Encounter Bay, Sanskrit, Telegu, Arabic, and Russian. (2) In French the old imperative phrases *voilá, voilá donc,* and *voici* and in Russian the corresponding forms *ved* and *vot* are used as copulas. All five of these words are interjections having usually deictic force. (3) Case and gender endings of the adjective do duty in Russian for the copulative verb. Russian has two parallel gender forms for the nominative case of the adjective:

| MASCULINE | FEMININE | NEUTER |
| --- | --- | --- |
| 1. khorosh | khorosha | khorosho |
| 2. khoroshij | khoroshaia | khoroshoie |

Illustrations are: *khleb khoroshij,* 'good bread'; *khleb khorosh,* 'the bread is good'; *koshka khorosha,* 'the cat is good'; *koshka khoroshia,* 'the good cat'; *pero khorosho,* 'the pen is good'; *pero khoroshoie,* 'the good pen.' (4) Very often the copulative relationship is expressed by a finite verb that has entirely or almost entirely lost its special meaning. A list has been compiled [12] in which there are cited 115 verbs having ordinarily concrete meanings, but which are also used as copulas. The most common meanings of these verbs are: *stand, consist, become, constitute, present, sit, lie, remain, go, walk, meet, travel, arrive, follow, fall, revolve, turn, live.* English *am, was* and *be* and probably all other copulative verbs were originally verbs or other words with concrete meaning.

Being a highly abstract concept, the copulative idea is comparatively late in finding specific linguistic form. Until

---

[12] *Transactions of the American Philology Association,* Vol. 43, p. 179.

that occurs the copulative ideas find expression or implication in various other ways.

The function of assertion, generally accepted as the function of the verb alone, may, as stated above, be expressed by any part of speech. For example: Russian, *On general,* 'He is a general' (noun); *Koshka khorosha,* 'The cat is fine' (adjective); *Eto ia,* 'It is I' (pronoun); *Ia zdes,* 'Here I am' (adverb); *My troe,* 'We are three' (numeral). None of these sentences contains a verb. As stated above, the writer holds that not only the parts of speech enumerated above and forming the predicates of the sentences assert, but their subjects as well.

As regards verbless sentences, we may then summarize as follows: If we mean by a verb a word, spoken or written, signifying an action, being, or state and equipped with suffixes or other auxiliary elements expressive of tense, mood, and so on, such as exist in most Indo-European languages, then certainly there are millions of sentences spoken in the world every day that contain no verb. If we mean by a verb a word that "asserts," then we must logically conclude that all words are verbs, because all the words in a sentence contribute some quotum to the element of assertion. If we include the copulative verb under the category of verbal ideas, then we must logically conclude that there are many verbless sentences, for there are countless sentences in which the copulative idea is not expressed in any particular word but is suggested or implied by other movements or by the context, and there are others in which a substantive or adjective or even an adverb contributes chiefly to its expression.

It is difficult for an English-speaking person to think in terms of a sentence in which there is neither a verbal nor a copulative idea. But this form of sentence is not uncommon among simple-minded peoples in whom the analytic processes are less developed, and may be roughly represented by the following narrative: "Stranger man arriving, giving home man food and beads. Home man liking stranger man, giving him animal skins. Stranger man later making home man far away, no staying here. Then home man killer of stranger man." Expressed in English this would mean: "The foreigner comes and presents the native with food and beads and in return the native gives him furs. But later, when the stranger tries to drive the native from his land, the latter kills him."

PRIORITY IN THE DEVELOPMENT OF SPECIALIZED FORMS

The fact that language study has been conducted largely on the basis of the written language has entailed another misconception, namely, that the affirmative, declarative sentence is a sort of standard, "regular," or normal type, on the basis of which the other types—interrogative, negative, etc.—should be judged.

On the contrary, it would seem that, since language has always been a means of securing the coöperation of other individuals of the same class towards one's self-realization, the sentences expressing a need or a desire felt or a command, being a form of speech most distinctly and immediately serving this end, should be regarded as equally fundamental and typical as, if not more so than, the declarative sentences. Since in the individual uttering such sentences the emotional state is especially strong and occupies the foreground of attention, the sensational content of the sentence is reduced to a minimum or, to put it from Wundt's point of view, the analytic and synthetic processes, that is, the organization, are less in evidence. Accordingly such sentences tend toward extreme simplicity, like the whine of a dog begging to be let in out of the cold, or the simple movements of an infant reaching out for a desired object. The important elements are (1) the need felt, (2) the object or end desired, (3) the (conjectural) attitude of the other party towards satisfying the need, and (4) the act of that party essential to the securing of the object or end. When the end desired is the activity to be performed, the second and fourth elements of course coalesce. As that party is almost invariably present and is directly addressed, there is no need of any special characterization of it, usually even of any specific mention of it, so that the subject of the imperative is usually omitted, and even in highly inflected languages the verbal form has often no special formative elements to suggest the subject. The prominence of the object or goal often so completely absorbs the attention that even the specific mention of the action required becomes superfluous and may be either vaguely in consciousness or not at all. Such appears to be the case in commands like "This way!" "Quick!" In other cases, when the activity itself is the end desired, we have such forms as "March!" If it be true that language, both gesture and spoken, developed out of originally direct life-serving activities, then sentences expressing a need should be regarded as the most primitive and the other more elaborate types as later refinements.

In respect to simplicity, exclamations are most closely akin to imperatives. Their simplicity is likewise conditioned by the dominance of the emotional experience and the consequent lack of prominence of the rationalistic (ideational) activities of the mind.

It is well known that the earliest words used by children learning to talk do not symbolize individual things. For example, as far as one can judge from the child's conduct, *mamma* does not mean simply *mother,* but is probably only the child's way of expressing a desire. Later it becomes an

## SYNTAX

imperative addressed to an individual. For a long time, one child used the word as a name for anything he liked. The child's first words are expressive of his attitude toward the situation as a whole. Only later are words employed to indicate portions of that situation. The one-word sentence is, at least in the case of the child, the earliest form of speech, and this appears to be true not only of a child's commands and expressions of his needs or sufferings (by crying, for example, or screaming), but also of his expression of wonder and surprise and of declarative statements, represented, for example, by the imperative form, "See, see!" which is commonly expressive not so much of a command, as of the child's desire to communicate the fact that his toy is broken or that he has himself achieved something.

The question of the priority of development of the noun and the verb has been long and perhaps somewhat fruitlessly discussed. Several different problems are involved in the matter and they have not always been carefully distinguished. (1) We may regard the differentiation of noun and verb from the point of view of meaning, assuming the verb to mean an activity or movement or a temporarily relatively unstable state of being, and a noun to mean an object. There can be no question that great numbers, perhaps all, of the land vertebrates appreciate movements. The carnivorous animals especially depend largely on appreciation of movement for the getting of food. Peoples that live in the wilds know full well that absolute motionlessness is an effective protection against attack by a bear. Dogs react specifically not only to the slightest movement of their master's hand but even to the special character of that movement. So there can be no doubt that primitive man, even before the genesis of speech, discriminated a moving object from the same object when stationary.

Herein lies a sufficient phenomenal basis for a differentiation of motor reaction giving origin to two different words: one for the object at rest, the other for the object when in motion. (2) Although primitive man even before the genesis of speech had observed a great variety of objects both at rest and in motion, it may be questioned whether he had analyzed his phenomenal patterns to such a degree as to form a conception of a specific movement as distinguished from a conception of the object in motion. This stage must have been reached before the third step could have been taken, namely, that of developing a special motor reaction to such idea of movement. It is a still further, and indeed a very long, step to the conception of movement *per se*, as distinguished from specific movements, and to corresponding motor responses.

As for priority, it seems superfluous to raise the question. Since the capacity to appreciate an object as moving and as at rest antedates the origin of speech, it follows that as soon as special motor reaction develops to designate one of them as distinguished from the other, *both noun and verb have originated simultaneously.*

The Sterns, arguing from the order of appearance of the different parts of speech in the child's vocabulary, affirm (and Koffka[13] agrees, with minor reservations) that the thing conception develops first, then comes the stage of action, "in which the activities of persons or things attract especial interest," and the third stage is that of relations and properties.[14] According to William and Clara Stern, the child first uses substantives.[15] However, these substantives do

---

[13] Kurt Koffka, *The Growth of the Mind* (London, Harcourt, Brace & Co., 1924), p. 300.

[14] Relations and properties are so different from each other that they should not be put into the same category.

[15] Wm. and C. Stern, *Die Kindersprache* (3d ed., Leipzig, Barth, 1922), *passim*.

the duty of whole sentences and are not substantives in the grammatical sense. They represent total patterns. Later, when special patterns have arisen, they represent these smaller patterns—actions, properties, or relationships against the background of thing or things. It does not seem reasonable to separate movement too widely from special properties and relationships. The experiments of Wertheimer[16] have shown that the interdependence of movements, space, and time is very close, while the appreciation of odors and flavors may have as great a biological value as the appreciation of movement.

The appreciation of relatively permanent qualities may conceivably have developed later than that of movement. And here again we must raise the question of what degree of importance such qualities possess in the life of the individual and race, because the needs of an individual and race largely determine its interests and perceptions. In this respect, we should expect to find great differences between the different types of sense perceptions. Odors, sounds, colors,[17] flavors—each type of sense perception has its special value to special individuals or communities.

The same reasoning applies to variations in the character of movements—swift, slow, jerky, irregular, etc. These characters are inseparable from the movements and are appreciated simultaneously with them.

Quite distinct from the origin of the ideas is the question of the development of the form or expression of those ideas. In the Indo-European languages, words expressing relationships and characteristics of the action are, as far as has

---

It must not be forgotten that the grown-ups suggest the child's first words to it.

[16] *Zeitschrift für Psychologie,* Vol. 61 ((1912), pp. 161 ff.

[17] Valentine found preference for colors in infants to be in the following succession: yellow (most preferred), white, pink, red, brown, black, blue, green, violet. *British Journal of Psychology,* Vol. 6 (1914), pp. 363 ff.

been proved, modifications of either substantives, adjectives, or verbs. Latin *vel,* 'or,' is an imperative form of *volo,* 'I wish.' From nouns are derived the following adverbs: Latin *prorsus,* 'furthermore,' a nominative case; Latin *furtim,* 'secretly,' an accusative form; Latin *dius,* 'by day,' a genitive form; Latin *foris,* 'out of doors,' ablative; Old Bulgarian *domovi,* 'homeward,' dative; Latin *domi,* 'at home,' locative; Latin *gratiis,* 'in vain,' instrumental; and hundreds of other case forms in various languages. The thousands of cases like the above would suggest that all words expressing adverbial relations are derived from nouns, adjectives, and verbs; yet there are very many others in the Indo-European languages, mostly monosyllables, the origin of which is entirely unknown. In these cases, philologists have not been able to prove whether or not they have originated as modifications of the other parts of speech. Yet it would be presumptuous to say that some of these words did not have as independent an origin as some of the nouns and verbs are supposed to have had. It is commonly stated that words of abstract meaning are later developments of words which had concrete meaning. All that we know of the origin of adverbs is in harmony with this view. It is also generally assumed that substantives denoting concrete objects are named for some of their dominating qualities. A quality is more abstract than an object, since it is the result of an analysis of a mass concept. Accordingly, the naming of the object, that is, the formation of nouns, was preceded by the development of an adjectival (quality) concept.

### THE DEVELOPMENT OF CASE

As a rule, that portion of the unit of communication which is carried over from the preceding thought, which is assumed to be known to the listener and of which something is predicated, ordinarily requires no special mark to distinguish it as such, though it often, and perhaps we may say commonly, receives one, even though the distinguishing mark consists merely of a lesser output of energy, resulting in fainter or lower-pitched sounds, than those with which the words representing the predicate are uttered. The listener may not appreciate it as subject the instant he hears it,[18] since some portions of the predicate may be needed to make that fact clear; but both of them simultaneously in the mind are sufficient to establish a unified thought structure, in which the mutual relationships of subject and predicate are clearly implied. Similarly, the idea of the object directly affected or result produced by the action of the verb often needs no special form of muscular movement to symbolize it, since the action and its result, for example, *build* and *house*, cannot be conceived as standing in any other relationship. In other cases, as, for example, "John hurt Willie," this relationship may be made clear only by the wider connections of thought. The relationship of the indirect object, that is, the person indirectly affected by the action of the verb, requires indication by no external sign representing variation in muscular movement. To be sure, the close associative connection existing between these two concepts and the verb ordinarily carries with it their successive adjacent presence in consciousness and consequently favors the successive execution of the muscular movements that symbolize them. Hence, word order often becomes an indication of the relationships between them.

Just as these three relationships expressed by the nominative, accusative, and dative cases are inherent in the thought complex involving substantive and verb, so often

---

[18] In languages which like the English have a fixed word order, the initial position of the subject is an indication of its character.

the genitive relationship is implicit in the substantive thought complex.

To these four cases should be added a vocative. The motive for the use of this case is usually the desire to attract the attention of the person addressed, commonly in order to direct his attention upon a situation which the speaker desires to have altered, or to enlist his sympathy or coöperation to some end. The speaker having in mind these ends, involving as they do the close personal relationship of speaker and person addressed, usually experiences at the moment pronounced emotions of one type or another, which are automatically translated into muscular movements of various forms [19] which constitute characteristic modes of this case. As a rule, the mere mention of the name under the given situation, along with the tone of voice, is adequate to convey the meaning.

These five relationships inhering intimately in the concepts themselves, or clearly implied in the general situation, may well be placed in groups by themselves and contrasted with those cases (mostly expressive of space and time relationships) which, being less intimately bound up with the concepts, require expression by various formative elements. There is a great variety of such relationships both literal and figurative. The number of these cases having specially developed case endings in the Indo-European languages is not large: locative, place in which; ablative, place from which; accusative of goal [20]; instrumental accusative; and perhaps associative forms implying accompaniment, con-

---

[19] A high-pitched recessive accent was for a time characteristic of vocatives in primitive Indo-European.

[20] There is a close kinship between the ideas of object produced ("He built a house"), result achieved ("This action brought about a marked change in the situation"), and goal attained ("He walked home") which accounts for the use of the accusative in Indo-European for example in all three senses. It would be idle to speculate as to which of those usages was prior in origin.

tiguity, and simultaneity. It would be a mistake, however, to suppose that these cases in any particular instance of their usage represent a single simple relationship. On the contrary, they occur usually in concrete and complex thought structures and are expressive of a variety of detailed relationships. When we consider that besides this each successive instance of the usage involves a new situation, we will appreciate the fact that the variation in meaning is practically infinite. As a result of their continual use in this way, the sphere of their application steadily broadens and they lose more and more their concrete connotations and cease to be adequate symbols of the ideas they earlier expressed. This makes it necessary for the users of the language either to employ with them accessory words of relationship or resort to entirely new words in order to convey the more concrete ideas requiring expression at the moment. So, for example, the case representing the goal of a motion, identical in form with the accusative in several Indo-European languages, came to be more and more frequently attended by prepositions and adverbs designating more precisely the form of arrival—whether arrival within a place, to a point near an object, etc. With the increased frequency of the occurrence of these particles, they, of course, became also significant of other related ideas including that (or those) expressed by the original ending, so that the ending became superfluous and, when the movements constituting it disappeared for psychophysical reasons, their loss was not felt and a new group of forms arose. In this way the Latin language was gradually transformed into Italian, Spanish, and other Romance languages. Through continuous usage, the movements constituting the series in which these particles found place may undergo extensive modifications, so that the movements (and consequently the sounds and kinæsthetic sensations) representing the relationships may fuse with those representing the more concrete ideas and thus give rise to new formative elements. An illustration of this seems to be provided in the Sanskrit language by the fusion of the post-positive particle *a* with the dative ending *āi*, yielding a new dative ending *āya*. Similar is a case in the modern Bavarian dialect of German: The expression *hast du*, 'have you,' was so transformed through assimilation of the *d* and *t* and the alteration in the length and specific quality of the vowel *u* (which thereby became ə), that all symbolic connection between the ə (the remnant of the original *du*) and the idea of the person addressed was lost. Accordingly a second *du* was added, and thus a new expression *hastə du* was brought into existence.

Inflectional forms may arise, however, quite otherwise than by fusion of originally more independent elements. For example, the primitive Indo-European, because it possessed both the dynamic and the musical accent, showed a great variation in both stress and pitch throughout the word. As the distribution in stress and pitch was different in different forms of the same word, it resulted that the same syllable in different forms of the word showed now a diphthong, now a simple vowel (sometimes long, sometimes short), now no vowel at all; or in the same syllable there appeared in one form an *e* vowel or again an *a* or an *o* vowel. This phenomenon is called *vowel gradation* (Ablaut). The differentiated forms necessarily became significant of categorical differences. These variations are still preserved in many English words, as *see, saw, seen;* and in such Greek forms as *leipo, leloipa, lipe; tithēmi, thĕtos,* and *tethmos.*

Languages differ greatly in the number of cases they have developed. Greek has five, Sanskrit eight, Finnish eighteen. Some languages are known to possess sixty or more.

## THE RELATION OF INFLECTION TO THE EXPRESSION OF IDEAS

It would, of course, be a mistake to suppose that those languages which have few special cases are inferior in respect to their possibilities of expression to those which have many. On the contrary, we often find a very elaborate group of case forms in the language of a people of lower intellectual level and a less fully developed one in the language of a more highly cultured people. The reason for this seems clear. A people which is making rapid intellectual progress is continually developing new ideas and new combinations of ideas. For their expression new groupings of the muscular movements are necessary, and hence many new words arise, not only new substantives and adjectives, but more particularly particles expressing relationships. The rapidity with which they arise exceeds the normal rate of fusion of concepts and movements and thus the old inflectional forms disappear and the analytic type of symbols comes to dominate. For example, the modern languages of Western Europe and also Russian [21] have become mainly analytic languages. In the same way the ancient Greeks inherited a very highly inflected tongue, but from the sixth to the first centuries B.C., a period in which the nation's most vigorous intellectual life was manifested, it underwent very extensive changes, marked by the breaking down of its inflectional forms. This is made evident by a comparison of the Hellenistic grammar with the classical Greek grammar and by the enormous wealth of

---

[21] Though Russian has retained in its system of writing and printing a considerable part of its older elaborate inflectional system, in the spoken language it is retained (incompletely) only in those forms in which the accent falls upon the endings. In other cases the inflectional system has either been extensively modified or has disappeared. It would last only a comparatively short time if an accentual system of the Polish type (accent on the penultimate syllable) should be established in Russian.

dialectical forms found in the Greek inscriptions of the pre-Christian era. On the other hand, if the intellectual life of the people stagnates, few new ideas are developed, little recourse is taken to new combinations of movements, the older groupings fuse into more rigid forms, and the motor habits become more fixed. This implies the growth of more numerous inflectional forms. To put it otherwise, a language always serves as a fairly adequate instrument for the expression of the ideas of the people who use it as a vernacular. The language is a mirror of their minds. If their ideas change rapidly, their language changes with them; if their ideas stagnate, their language stagnates also.

The student whose experience with languages has been limited to the modern languages of Western Europe is likely to form too narrow an idea of the range and variety of grammatical form. Aside from limiting the degrees of comparison to the adjective as mentioned above, he also is likely to assume that the number of the noun and verb is limited to two, singular and plural, whereas in reality many languages have dual forms, used especially, though not exclusively, for objects that go in pairs, as eyes, ears, oxen, etc. Some languages have a trial and even a quadrual form. Some also possess inclusive plural forms, for example, a form for *you and I,* another for *he and I,* etc.

The category of tense is one in regard to which many misconceptions exist in the average student's mind. Under the term are included several different classes of ideas: (1) the idea of time as measured from the standpoint of the speaker (present, past, and future) and as measured from the standpoint of the speaker and some action or event, the so-called present perfect, past perfect, and future perfect, and the so-called progressive, which indicates the simultaneity of two activities in the past or future: (2) the stage of the action; (*a*) inceptive (Russian *zaplakat'*, 'start crying,' from *plakat'*, 'to cry); (*b*) *progressive* (Russian *razskayvat'*, 'to be narrating'); (*c*) *perfective* (*razskazat'*, 'to have finished narrating'); (*d*) terminative; (*e*) desinitive; and (*f*) indefinite (aorist). Besides these there are various other verbal categories represented in many languages, such as (3) the number of the action: (*a*) simulfactive, corresponding to the singular of nouns (Russian *stuknut'*, 'to knock once'); (*b*) iterative, corresponding to the plural (*stukivat*, 'to knock repeatedly); (4) type of the action: (*a*) abstract (Russian *ptitsy litaiut*, 'birds fly'); (*b*) concrete (*ptitsy letiat*, 'the birds are flying,' that is, on some particular occasion, in some particular direction); and (5) degree of the action: (*a*) normal (Sanskrit *dipyate*, 'to shine'); (*b*) intensive (*dedipyate*, 'to shine brightly'); (*c*) diminutive (Russian *pogovorit*, 'to talk a bit,' from *govorit*, 'to talk').

Many other types of verbal forms may be found by consulting an Inuit grammar. There are found in various languages about as many mood forms as there are varieties and combinations of desire, will, effort, and impulse experienced by human beings.

It should not be assumed that each of the ideas of relationship expressed in such forms finds its complete expression in any given instance in simply that form. On the contrary, owing to the organic unity of the whole mass of thought expressed, the individual idea usually finds expression in two or more forms, and, vice versa, the same form usually expresses two or more such ideas. It is this multiplicity and crisscross of meaning and form which render the systems of diagraming sentences practiced in our public schools so arbitrary and inadequate as a means of representing grammatical relationships.

We may conclude this chapter with a reiteration of the principle on which should be based the study not only of syntax but of all language phenomena, namely, the analytic process should never be carried to the point at which it ceases to be also synthetic. We must not deal with the mood, tense, or aspect of a verb as anything which has an independent existence. In the verb itself it "lives and moves and has its being"; and not only that, an action is always an attribute of a thing, a part of its nature. We are accustomed to think of an action as something which a person does. In reality it is what a person *is*. It is a characteristic of the subject. Accordingly the characteristics of the verb are the characteristics of the subject. Of course, the same thing is true of the adjective because the sentence is a description of a thing or a situation. All is one.

## REFERENCES

BRÉAL, M.—*Semantics,* Trans. by Cust (London, Heinemann, 1900; original French ed. published by Hachette, Paris, 1897).

BRUGMANN, K.—*Vergleichende Grammatik* (See references to Chap. I), Vols. 3-5 (Syntax) by Bernard Delbrueck and Vol. 2 (etymology and inflections) by Brugmann.

DE LA GRASSERIE, RAOUL.—*Etudes de grammaire comparée* (Paris, Maisonneuve, 1887-1899).

JESPERSEN, OTTO.—*Language, Its Nature, Development and Origin* (New York, Holt, 1921).

KOFFKA, KURT.—*The Growth of the Mind.* Transl. by Ogden (New York, Harcourt, Brace, 1925).

SHEFFIELD, A. D.—*Grammar and Thinking* (New York, Putnam's, 1912).

STERN, C. and W.—*Die Kindersprache* (Leipzig, Barth, 1907).

VAN GENNEKEN, J.—*Principes de la liguistique physchologique* (Paris, Rivière, 1907).

# INDEX

Abstract ideas as types, 180
Abstract terms, nature of, 178
Abstract thought, 14
Accent, stress or dynamic, 52 f.
Accuracy of expression, 14
Ach, 161, 170 f.
Action, "abstract," 291
   "concrete," 291
   desinitive, 291
   imagery and, 170
   incentive to, 169
   inceptive, 291
   intensive, 291
   iterative, 291
   learning of, 169
   perfective, 291
   progressive, 291
   purpose determining, 170
   singular and plural, 291
   stage of, 291
   stimulus to, 169
   terminative, 291
Adam's apple, 47
Affricates, 59
Air, amount used in speech, 52
Air pressure, in lungs, 53
   regulation of, 53
Air vibrations, amplitude of, 68, 75
   frequency or rate of, 68
Air waves, 8, 12, 53, 68
   physical character of, 63, 68
Aktionsart, 290
Alphabetic signs, origin of, 9
Alveolars, 61

Analogical processes and the higher centers, 235
Anatomy, 16
Animal mind, theories of, 122
Animals, mental states of, 122
   speech of, 12 f., 119
Angular gyrus, 41
Apes, language of, 124
Aphasia, 34 f., 39
   recent views, 41
   schools of, 34
   types of, 40 ff.
Apperceptive sentences, 204 f.
Aqueous humor, 82
Areas, association, 32
   motor, 32
   sensory, 32-35
Aristotle, grammatical categories of, 263
Aristotle's four parts of speech, 268 f.
Articulate speech, development of, 127
Arytenoid cartilages, 45
Assimilation, progressive and regressive, 245, 231
Associates, choice of, 130
Association, indirect, 95
   laws of, 95 f.
Association areas, 34 f.
   controls over, 98
   development of, in children, 140
   memory processes and, 94 f.
   perception and, 130, 134 f.
Associative processes, 8

Associative sentences, 60, 304 *f.*
Attention, effect on repetition, 107
Audils, 139
Audition, 22, 67-79
   theories of, 72-75
Auditory area, 32 *f.*
Auditory imagery, 100
Automatic speech, 206 *f.*
Axones, 22 *f.*

Bagley, 145
Bair, 169
Bannister, 75
Bantu, parts of speech in, 270
Basilar membrane, 71
   rigidity of, 74
   size of, 72
Beaunis, 166
Berkeley, 171
Bethe, 66
von Bezold, 74
Bilabials, 60
Binet, 159, 162
Biolinguistics, vi, 18
Bloomfield, 19
Blurred vision, 88
Bopp, 210
Border sciences, influence of, on language study, 213
Bouton, 124
Brain, action of, in speech, 35 *f.*
Brauchmann, 150
Breal, 292
Breath sounds, 57, 59
Breathing, mechanism of, 51
   process, 50 *f.*
   rate of, 52
Broca speech center, 7, 37 *f.*, 41
   function of, 38
Bronchial tubes, 43
Bronchioli respiratorii, 44
Brugmann, 191, 212, 292

Bryan, 148
Buehler, 162, 193

Calcerine fissure, 33
Carbon dioxide, 50
Case, meanings of, 284, 287
Cases, number of, in Indo-European, 286
   types of, 285
Censoring speech, 196
Cattell, 131
Cerebellum, 29 *f.*
Cerebral localization, 28
Cerebrum, 23, 30 *ff.*
Chest, 45
   expansion of, 51
Chest register, 55
Chimpanzee, 124
Chinese and the parts of speech, 271
Choroid coat of the eye, 82
Ciliary muscle of the eye, 84
Clopatt, 227
Cochlea, 71, 73
   tone differentiation in, 74
Coleman, 227
Color, cause of, 71
Communication, circle of, 12, 147
   most primitive form of, 123
Comparative philology, 3
Complementary air, 53
Completeness of expression, 14
Concept, nature of, 154
   word and, 158 *f.*
Concepts and language development, 14
Concrete thought, 154
   in animals and children, 222
Cones, foveal, 85
   processes in, 85 *f.*
   retinal, 82

## INDEX

Configurationist school of psychology, 253
Conjunctiva, 80
Consciousness, content of, 158 f.
  of relationship, 163
  of rules, 163
  primitive, concrete, 122
    indefinite and general, 122
  qualities of, 252
Consonants, number of, 64
  voiced, 59
Context, expression determined by, 110
  mental, in reading, 140 ff.
  wider, in association, 97 f.
Control, lack of, in the deaf, 110
  of associations, 98
Coöperation, motive of language, 10
  language and, 119
Copulative verb and middle verbs, 273
Cornea, 82
Corpora quadrigemina, 29
Cortex of the brain, 30
Corti, rods of, 72
Creatin, 50
Cricoid cartilage, 45
Crystalline lens of the eye, 82

Deaf and dumb, motor sensations in, 151
  sign language of, 127
  teaching of, 150
Deafness, partial, 74
Dearborne, 134 f., 150
Delabarre, 135
Delacroix, 186
DeLaguna, 121
Delbrueck, 19
Dendrites, 21
Dentals, 60

Descartes, 162
Deterioration of nerves, 33
Dialectical variation in sound, 130
Diaphragm, 45
Dockeray, 137
Dodge, 134 f.

Ear, 67 f.
  action of, 69 f.
  auditory meatus of, 69
  external, 68
  inner, 70
  middle, 69
Efferent nerves, 11
Eidetic images, 103
Elasticity of the chest, 51
Electrical phenomena, 50
Emotional cries, 6 f.
Emotional expression and the origin of language, 113
Emotions, expression of, 116
Emphasis, connotations of, 120
Environment, affecting understanding, 17
  analyzed, 15, 16
  effect on speech, 14
Erdmann, 134, 157
Errors in reading, amount of, 131
  cause of, 131
Etymology, 248
Eustachian tube, 69
Evolution of the speech processes, 13
Ewald, 73 f.
Experimental phonetics, 213, 241
Expiration, forced, 51
  modified during speech, 52
  normal, quiet, 51
Explosives, 52, 59
Expression, character of, 109
  only two forms of, 11

296 INDEX

Expressive movements, develop from useful, 116
   survival value of, 118 *f*.
Eye, discriminatory powers of, 86 *f*.
   focusing of, 84
   movements of, 81
   accuracy of, 81
   in reading, 135, 138, 141
   optical system of, 82
   structure of, 80 *f*.
Eye muscles, 80
Eyeball, structure of, 81

Facial expression, little developed, 123
   significance of, 125
Facial movement, 121
Falsetto voice, 55
Family of languages, Indo-European, 210
Fick, 227
Forced inspiration, 51
Form and function in grammar, 248
Formative elements, 277 *f*.
Fovea, 33, 85
Franklin, 167
French Academy on the origin of language, 112
Frequency, association facilitated by, 121
Fricatives, 59
Frictional sounds, 59
Furness, 124

Galton, 100, 104
Ganglion, spinal, 25
Garner, 124
General ideas, 155
   development of, 122

General linguistics, a biological science, 18, 293
   defined, 2
   problems of, 14 *f*.
Gestalt school of psychology, 253
Gesture languages, 6, 125 *f*.
Gestures, 6, 8, 125
   plastic, 8
Giles, 19
Glands, vii, 11
Glottal stop, 58
Glottis, 52, 58 *f*.
Glycogen, 50
Goldscheider, 131
Grammar, dynamic view of, 248
   historical, 3
   systematic, 3
   traditional divisions of, 248
Grammatical categories, as configurations, 267
   as states of mind, 266
   sciences and, 265
   two sorts of, 267
Grammatical forms, origin of, 248
de la Grasserie, 292
Gravity, action on the chest, 66
Gray, H., 66
Gray, W. S., 157
Greek and Roman alphabets, origin of, 9
Griffiths, 101, 104
Grimm, 210
Grimm's law, 212
   neuromuscular activity and, 241

Habit formation, 171
Harter, 149
Hartridge, 75, 90
Head, H., 39-41
Helmholtz, 72 *f*., 90
Hearing, 67-79
   as a control, 67

# INDEX

Hearing (*Cont'd*)
  range of, 75
  speech and, 75
  theories of, criticized, 75
Heredity and infantile sounds, 106
Hermann, 66, 76, 79
Herrick, 42
Hisses, 59
Holt, 136
Howell, 50
Huey, 134 *f.*, 157
Humanistic sciences, 17
  language study and, 213
Hymans, 227
Hyoid bone, 48

Ideas, formulation of, in words, 179 *f.*
  of form, 179
  movement and, connection between, 105, 194 *f.*
  origination of, 92
  relations of, to words, 92
Ideographs, 8
Ideo-motor action, 105 *f.*
Illumination in reading, character of, 88
Image and thought, difference between, 153 *f.*
Imageless thought, 162 *f.*, 183
Imagery and meaning, 176
  mental, 100 *f.*
  nature of, 176
Images, 158
  *See also* Auditory.
Imagined thought, 99
Imitation, complexity of, 107
  control over, 107
  in naming, 113
  incentive to learn speech, 107
  no specific impulse to, 107
  not indiscriminate, 107

Incentives to speech, 106-109
Incus, 69
Indian languages, 126
Indo-European family of languages, 210
Inflection, 248
Inheritance and expressive movements, 116
Inhibition of speech movements, 108
Inner speech, 101 *f.*
Inspiration, 50
  forced, 57
Inspiratory sounds, 52
Instinctive calls of the first humans, 119
Instincts and the origin of language, 116 *f.*
Intensity of sound, 75
Intention, 163
  general, controlling speech, 98
Intercostal muscles, 51
Interdentals, 60
Interpretation, effect on perception, 130
Intonation, meaning of, 120
Inuit, 291
Iris, 82

Jaensch, 103
James, 96, 157, 161
Jespersen, 292
Judd, 157
Judgment and sentence, 197 *ff.*

Keith, 72
Kinesthetic imagery, 100
Kinesthetic sensations, 7 *f.*, 58
  in control of speech, 110
Kinesthetic sense organs, 89
  stimulus to, 89
Koehler, 77

## INDEX

Koffka, 282, 292
Kuelpe, 262

Labeo-dentals, 60
Labials, 60
Lactic acid, 50
Language, as behavior, 10
  as muscular movement, 256
  censoring of, 196
  changes in, 128
  complexity of, 1
  coöperation and, 119
  definition by description, 256
  definitions of, 4 *f.*, 7
  dynamic view of, 248
  factors of variation and stability in, 249
  influence on thought, 14
  kinds of, 4-6
  modified by mental type, 101
  movements, originally directly life serving, 13
  processes preceding, 7
  not an invention, 114
  of animals, 124
  organic view of, 248
  problems of the psychologist, 92
  processes, chart of, 15
  manner of action of, 91
  unity of, 291
  psychology and, relations of, 18
  receptors, 129 *ff.*
  responses, reasons for, 91
  science of, defined, 2
  spelling and, 257
  study, as a natural science, 18
    branches of, 1, 3
  telegraphic, learning, 148
  thought and, 4, 11, 14, 49

Language (*Cont'd*)
  written, development of, 8
  written page and, 250
Languages, artificial, 147 *ff.*, 150
  origin of, 112 *ff.*
Laryngeal muscles, synergic action of, 54
Larynx, 45
  action of, 53
  movement of, 58
  nerve supply of, 48 *f.*
Learning to speak, 105 *f.*
  incentives to, 106
  trial and error, 105
Letters, familiar and unfamiliar, 132
  legibility of, 86
Light waves, 8
  characteristics of, 79
Lighting of rooms, 88
Linguistic paleontology, 3
Linguistic theory, a product of the imagination, 255
  theory of relativity and, 252
Lip-reading, laws of, 150 *ff.*
Listening, 67
  association in, 146
  context in, 117
  errors overlooked in, 145
  interpretation in, 145 *f.*
  mental processes in, 146 *f.*
  supplementation in, 146 *f.*
  to foreign languages, 146
  types of, 146
Localization, cerebral, 32 *ff.*
  of brain function, 34
Loudness, estimation of, 57
  of speech, what determines, 110
  of voice, 57
Luciani, 66
Lung cavities, 45

## INDEX

Lungs, action of, 50 f.
  capacity of, 44
Luschke, 66
Malleus, 69
McMurrick, 66
Meader, 217
Meaning, action and, 168 ff.
  adequacy of, 199
  analysis of, undue, 257
  analytic process in, 167
  attachment to sounds, 121 ff.
  changes in, 174 f.
  concept and, 157 f., 165 ff.
  degrees of completeness of, 168
  development of, 173
  evolution of, 174 f.
  forms and, 291
  general and specific, 175
  imagery and, 176
  in reading, 138 ff.
  irradiating elements in, 177
  perception and, 171
  recognition and, 172
  relating process of, 167
  sentence and, 257
  specific and general, 175
  spread of, 128
  theories of, 165 f.
  time of fixation of, 128
  unit of thought, 256
  universality of, 166
Meatus, auditory, 69
Memory, origin of language and, 121
  physical basis of, 92 f.
  processes in language, 92 f.
Mental imagery, 100
  types (audiles, kinesthetics, mixed, visuals), 100
  proportional frequency of, 101
Messer, 171

Metabolism, in language, 11
  of muscles, 50
Meyer, 74
Miller, 77
Mishearing, 17
Misprints, character of, 133
  overlooked, 132
Misreadings, 17, 131
Misunderstandings, 17
Modality, 290
Morgagni, ventricles of, 47
Motives to utterance of thought, 108
Motor areas, 32
Motor impulses, 118
Motor nerves, terminations of, 49
Motor phenomena in speech, 105-111
Movement, conditions stimulating, 105
  control of, 110
  direct life-serving, 116
  expressive, 5 ff.
  complexes of, 117
  survival value of, 118 f.
  facial, 8
  ideas and, 105
  instinctive expressive, 117
  *See also* Muscular movement.
Movements of language, 12
Mouth, action of, 59
  sounds, 58 f.
Müller, G. E., 184
Müller, Max, 112 f., 116, 158
Müller and Goldscheider, 131
Münsterberg, 131, 134
Murmurs, 59
Muscles, contraction of, 50
  crico-thyroid, 54
  intercostal, 51
  laryngeal, action of, 54
  lateral and posterior crico-ary-

Muscles (*Cont'd*)
    tenoid, thyro-arytenoid, transverse arytenoidal, 53 *f.*
Muscular action, nature of, 49
Muscular activity, chemical changes in, 50
Muscular movement, 5, 16
    accuracy and rhythm of, 230
    speed and, 230
    active, 5
    apoplexy and, 229
    assimilation and, 231
    changes of, classified, 242
    not yet classified, 242
    complexity of, 220
    continuous, in speech, 221
    control, test of, 218
    coördination of, 16, 220
    drugs and, 228
    experimental phonetics and, 241
    fatigue and, 227
    glides, 223
    Grimm's law and, 241
    inaccuracy of control, 229
    law of accuracy, 228
    malnutrition and, 228
    omission of, elision and, 247
    overlapping of, 222
    overlapping and palatization, 224
    phonetic alphabet and, 241
    phonetic law and, 240
    physiological conditions in, 226
    "positions" or "regions" and, 223
    range of, 16
    sandhi and, 222
    speed of, 16
    syphilis and, 229
    transposition of, 246
    variations, causes of, 225
        climate and, 227

Muscular movement, variations (*Cont'd*)
    due to nervous activity, 234
    due to overlapping, 244
    higher nerve centers and, 233
    in duration, 242
    in energy, 243
    in extent, 244
    in rate, 242
    special cases of, 244-247
    temperature and, 227
    Verner's law and, 241
Musculi vocales, 47
Musical tones, 53
Muyskens, 244

Nagel, 50
Naming from imitation, 113
Nasalization, 245
Nerve, auditory, 71
Nerve cells of the retina, 82
Nerve currents, 105
Nerve impulse, 25
Nervi recurrentes, 49
Nervous system, 21 *ff.*
Neurones, 21
Nitrogenous waste products, 50
Noise, 68
Non-communicative language processes, 13
Number of substantive, 274

Oertel, 19
Ogden, 90
Optic nerve, 80
Organs of speech, 43
Origin of language, 14, 112 *ff.*
    Wundt's view of, 115
Oval window, 69
Overtones, 68
    in vowels, 76 *f.*

# INDEX

Owen, 201

Palatalization and coördination of movement, 246
Palatals, 62
Paleontology, linguistic, 3
Papillon, 227
Partial tones in speech, 68, 76
Paul, 19
Perception, memory and, 129
  nature of, 129
  reading and, 129
Pharyngeal sounds, 63
Pharynx, 48
Philology, 3
  classical, 3
  comparative, 3
Phonation and output of air, 52
Phonetic alphabet and muscular movement, 241
Phonetic law and muscular movement, 240
Phonetics, 3
Phonology, 3
Physiological processes in language, 11
Physiological psychology, 18
Physiology, 16
Picture writing, 8
Piéron, 39, 41
Piersol, 66
Pigment cells of the eye, 82
Pillsbury, 42, 90, 131 f., 134, 159
Pillsbury's theory of thought, 163 f.
Plato and the grammatical categories, 263
Postdentals, 61
Preparation for communicating, 11
Primitive expressions, indefinite, 119

Primitive imagery, vagueness of, 122 f.
Primitive speech sounds, acquisition of meaning of, 120
Printer's illusion, 131
Problems, of expression, 14 ff.
  of interpretation, 14
  of sensation, 17
  of understanding, 17
Proof reading, 138
Psychology, of language, 3
  of movement, 5
Pupil, eye, 82
  adjustment of, 88
Purpose, as control, 10
  associates determined by, 97
  content determined by, 110
  of language, 14

Quintilian, 139

Reading, 67, 129-145
  affected by mental content, 132
  associative factors in, 89
  attention in, 144
  by sentences, 141
  by words, not letters, 133
  context in, 140 f.
  control in, wider, 140 ff.
  errors in, 130 f.
  eye and, 86
  for sense, 139 ff.
  habits in school, 135
  hygiene, 135
  kinesthetic imagery in, 139, 143
  laws of, 138, 144 f.
  laws of perception in, 129
  of foreign languages, 143
  psychological factors in, 131, 134
  purpose in, 144
  rapid, 143

Reading (*Cont'd*)
  summary of processes, 137
  technical terms in, 142
  types of, 139 *ff*.
  unseen elements in, 136
  vision and, 86 *f*.
  words not noticed, 139
Recall, dependent upon associations, 95
  dependent upon wider connections, 96
  nature of, 95
  vehicles of, 101
Recognition and meaning, 172 *ff*.
Reil, island of, 32, 36
Relation, representation of, 156, 160
Reserve air, 44, 53
Resonance, chambers, 58
  theory of hearing, 75
Respiratory air, 44
Respiratory tract, 120
Response, automatic, 11
  development facilitated by, 121
  instinctive, to emotional cries, 121
Retina, 33
  action in reading, 136
  area used in reading, 136 *f*.
  sensitive area of, 137
  sensitivity of, 86
Rods, cones and, 82
  Corti's, 72, 86
  number of, 73
Rolando, fissure of, 32
Rounding, 60
Rousselot, l'Abbé, 19

Scala tympani, 71
Scala vestibuli, 71
Schenk, 227
Sclerotic coat, 81

Scott, 14
Scripture, 19
Secretion. *See* Glands.
Semantics, 3
Semasiology, 3
Semitic, system of writing in, 9
Sensations, as controls over movement, 16
  as controls over speech, 67
  auditory, 8, 12, 71
  ideas and, 17
  involved in speech, 67
  kinesthetic, 7 *f*., 89
  of movement, 7 *f*.
  of touch, 7 *f*., 17
  movement and, 105
  stimuli and, 17
  visual, 8, 12, 85
  in language, 17
Senses involved in speech, 67
Sensory content, vagueness of, 155
Sensory factors influencing reading, 89
Sensory nerve endings, in muscle, 89
  in tendons, 89
Sensory organs in speech, 67
Sentences, analytic development of, 188 *f*.
  associative and apperceptive, 190, 204
  binary type of, 272
  categories and science, 264
  context of, 191
  definition of, 188 *ff*., 254
    physically determined, 259
  fluctuation of attention and, 261
  grammatical analysis and, 258
  grammatical categories and, 271
  impersonal, 271
  inception of, 194
  judgment passed upon, 197 *ff*.

Sentences (*Cont'd*)
  length of, 52
  of children, 280
  part of stream of thought, 261
  preliminary idea of, 188 ff.
  thought and, 188 ff.
  unit of discourse, 254
  verbless, 267
Sheffield, 292
Shepard, speech record of, 216
Sibilants, 59
Sight as control over writing, 67
Silence, artificial condition, 108
  conditions imposing, 108
Simultaneous association, 94
Slang, chance development of, 127
  ding-dong theory and, 127
  why appropriate, 127
Sobotta and McMurrick, 66
Social approval, effect on child, 106
Sociological sciences, 17
Solecisms, 199
Sonants, 60
Sound, as control over speech, 110
  by-product of useful movements, 117
  *See also* Speech sounds.
Sound changes, causes of, 212
  laziness and carelessness, 214
  chronological, 210
  classification of, 210
  ease of pronunciation and, 214
  explained, 213
  historical, 209
  local, 210
  nature of, 209, 212
  pleasant and unpleasant, 214
  "tendencies" of, 213
Sound waves, 16
Sounds, explosive, 58
  infantile, character of, 106

Sounds (*Cont'd*)
  meaning and, analogies between, 128
  physical character of, 215
Speech, abbreviated forms of, 13
  action of cortex in, 102
  articulate, development of, 127
  control, 109 f., 190 f.
  definitions of, 7 f.
  incentives to, 108 f.
  larger units of, 200 ff.
  parts of, 268, 270
  preliminary intention in, 191
  primitive, 125
  verbal thought different from, 107 f.
Speech movements, abortive, 13
  automatic, 7
  controlled by auditory sensations, 238
  controlled by complex factors, 235
  controlled by kinesthesis, 236
  controlled by touch, 237
  controlled by appearance of spelling, 239
  how evoked, 92
  how related to thought, 205
  inhibition of, 108
  involuntary, 5 f.
  voluntary, 5
Speech organs, v f., 13, 43
Speech sounds, 6
  analysis of, 16
  apparent small number of, 64 f.
  characteristic of movements, 216
  described, 60-63
  how perceived, 130
  kymographic records of, 217, 218
  muscular movement and, 215
  naïve idea of, 65

Speech sounds (*Cont'd*)
　not normal when isolated, 221
　palatograms of, 218
　primitive, 293
　viewed psychologically, 215
Spelling, English, criticized, 9
　language and, 257
　stability of, 10
Spinal cord, 27 *f.*
Stapes, 69
Stern, W. and C., 282, 292
Stimulus, auditory, 67 *f.*
　error, 182
　perception and, 130-133
　response and, in communication, 10
Stoics and grammar, 263
Stop consonants. *See* explosives.
Stops, where produced, 59
Stout, 156, 162
Stream of thought, interruptions of, 95
Stroboscope, 56
Stumpf, 77 *ff.*
Subject and predicate in thought, 201
Successive association, 94
Supramarginal gyrus, 41
Surds, 59
Suspensory ligament, 84
Sylvian fissure, 31, 36, 41
Synapses, 25, 94
Syntax, 248 *ff.*
System of knowledge and thought, 181 *f.*

Talking to one's self, 13
Telegraphy, 148 *ff.*
　span of attention in, 149
Tense of the substantive, 274
Thalamus, 29 *f.*

Thinking, individual differences in, 100
Thorndyke, 101
Thought, anesthetics and, 155
　coherence of, 252
　continuity of, 252
　essence of, 183 *f.*
　imageless, 101 *f.*
　influence on language, 14
　language and, 4, 11, 14, 158 *ff.*
　　alternation of, 99
　　control over, 99
　　difference between, 99, 159, 162 *f.*
　　eclectic view of, 159, 163 *f.*
　　identity of, 158 *ff.*
　　relation of, 99
　　separate processes of, 99
　　sensationalistic theory of, 159-161
　linguistic problems of, 252
　meaning and, 157
　nature of, 158 *ff.*
　of infants, 155
　of savages, 155
　problems of, 177
　relation to language, 158 *f.*
　speech and, 194 *ff.*
　theories of, 182
　translated into words, 187
　without language, 4
Throat, 158
Thyroid cartilage, 47
Titchener, 86, 156, 160, 164
Timbre, 25 *f.*
Time, ideas of, 290
Tissue movement, passive, 5
Tones, characteristic of vowels, 75
Tongue-back sounds, 62
Tongue-blade sounds, 62
Tongue-tip sounds, 60
Trachea, 43

## INDEX

Trial and error in learning to speak, 105
Trills, 61, 63
Tucker, 19
Tympanic membrane, 69
Types and thought, 180
Use, effect of, 128
Useful movements become expressive, 116
Uvula, 48
Uvular sounds, 63

van Ginnekin, 253, 292
Velar sounds, 62
Velum palati, 48
Ventricles of Morgagni, 47
Verb and noun, genetic relations of, 283
Verb or noun, priority of, 281
Verbal imagery, 101 ff.
Verbal-visual associates, 33
Verbless sentences, copulative, 276
  in English, 275
  in Russian, 278
  summary, 278
Verbs, development of, in Indo-European, 283
  in Russian, 275
Verner, 212
Verner's law, 241
Villiger, 42
Vision, 79-81
  acuteness of, 87
  blurred, cause of, 88
  clearness of, in reading, 137
  effect of illumination on, 87
  nature of, 86
  inclusiveness of, 131
  range of, 131
  subjective element in, 1,'2
Visual area, 33
  purple, 86

Visuals, 139
Vitreous humor, 82
Vocal cords, false, 47
Vocal lips (cords, folds or ledges), 47
  action of, 64
  in whispering, 57
  bulging of, 57
  control over, 55
  finer structure of, 47
  mechanics of their vibration, 56
  variation in length, 54, 56
  variation in tension, 57
  vibrations of, 53, 59
  direction of, 56
  physics of, 56
  rates of, 54 f.
Vocal movements, control of, 105 f.
Vocal muscles, 47
Vocal sounds, interestingness of, 106
  motives to repetition of, 106
Vowel quality, 63, 76-79
Vowel sounds, number of, 65
Vowel table, 64
Vowels, differences between, 68
  open and close, 63 f.
  produced in mouth cavity, 79
  resonance theory of, 64

Watt, 96, 161
Wave form, 68
Weber's law, 87
Wernicke center, 7, 36, 40
Wertheimer, 283
Whispering, 53
Whitney, 112, 116
Woodworth, 159, 162, 168, 171, 192
Words, as imagery, 101
  choice of, 196 f.
  how developed, 123

Words (*Cont'd*)
  in contexts, 114 f.
  how present in consciousness, 92
  how related to ideas, 92
  replacing concrete imagery, 101
  replacing ideas, 14
  thought and, 92
  used in abstract thought, 99

Wundt, 19, 47, 115, 188-194, 252 f.
  sentence structure and, 188
Wundt's theory criticized, 203 f.

Yerkes, 127

Zeitler, 132